Social Change and Corporate Strategy: The Expanding Role of Public Affairs

Social Change and Corporate Strategy

The Expanding Role of Public Affairs

By

ANDREW B. GOLLNER

Stamford, Connecticut

Issue Action Publications
105 Old Long Ridge Road
Stamford, Connecticut 06903

Library of Congress Catalog Card Number: 83-081612

ISBN 0-913869-00-7

First printing: December, 1983

Printed in the United States of America

*For Linda
and my boys,
Adam, Miska and Julian*

Why do you look so sad and forsaken?
Don't you know—
When one door is closed,
Another is open.

—Bob Marley, the King of Reggae
in *Coming in From the Cold*

Table of Contents

Table of Figures

Table of Tables

Acknowledgements

Our leading institutions, be they government agencies, private corporations, labour unions or universities, have experienced with increasing intensity over the past few decades what I call "the crowding-in of external issues" upon their traditional domains. I have long wanted to examine the sources and dynamics of this transformation in organizational-societal relationships, for in my view, it carries the embryonic forms of a new political-economic system.

The opportunity to do this study presented itself in 1980 while I was serving as Vice-Principal of Concordia University's recently established School of Community and Public Affairs (S.C.P.A.). In drafting the proposal for this study, I benefitted immensely from consultations with some of the officers and external advisors of the School. Since I look upon members of this consultative network as "The Founding Fathers" of this book, I wish to acknowledge their contributions by name. The are: Michel Fournier, vice president, public affairs, Air Canada; David Grier, vice president and chief advisor, public affairs planning, The Royal Bank of Canada; Gerald Gummersell, former executive vice chairman of the S.C.P.A.'s Advisory Board (now corporate and government liaison advisor to the Rector of Concordia University); Robert E. Landry, vice president and manager, external affairs department, Imperial Oil Ltd.; and Blair Williams, the founding Principal of the School.

This initial consultative process was critically important. It ensured that the project would reach out beyond the academic community to encompass the ongoing real world problems of corporate leaders and public affairs practitioners. The two individuals who deserve the greatest credit for this are both former senior administrators of the School of Community and Public Affairs—namely, Blair Williams and Gerald Gummersell. Their commitment to socially attuned research, and their belief that academia's responsibility is to serve both the needs of its external community, as well as the standards of its internal constituents, set the stage for a splendidly gratifying level of cooperation between academicians and practitioners.

In preparing this study I consulted with a large number of people in Canada and the United States, both in face-to-face interviews and through extensive written survey questionnaires. Without their generous assistance, trust and confidence, without the painstaking efforts of so many senior corporate public affairs executives and deans of business schools in responding to my survey questionnaires, this project would not have achieved its goals.

Among all these individuals there are some whose assistance was especially important. In the United States, the late Walter Hamilton, vice president of The Conference Board; Raymond L. Hoewing, vice president of the Public Affairs Council; James Post, Boston University; Lee E. Preston, University of Maryland; and Joe Robertson, executive director of the National Association of Schools of Public Affairs and Administration were particularly helpful.

In Canada, I owe special gratitude to Ken Colby, vice president, corporate affairs, Norcen Energy Resources, Ltd.; James Gillies, director, Max Bell Program in Business-Government Studies at York University; Peter Broadmore, program manager, external programs, I.B.M. Canada, Ltd.; Peter Bartha, manager, strategic studies and corporate planning, Imperial Oil, Ltd.; Jon Johnson, senior manager, information and analysis, The Bank of Montreal; Michael Robinson, president, Public Affairs International, Ltd. and Rick Anderson, consultant with Public Affairs International, Ltd.; James Frank, vice president, The Conference Board of Canada, and Ken Hart, director of public affairs research and their very able staff. Allan Gregg, president of Decima Research, Ltd., greatly improved the corporate survey questionnaire. He tolerated, with unusual grace, my clumsy efforts at becoming a pollster. While the final responsibility for whatever flaws there may be in the questionnaire is mine alone, the instrument undoubtedly benefitted greatly from his experience.

A special advisory committee to Concordia University's Academic Vice Rector, Russell Breen, also played an important and useful role. Chaired by Dr. Breen, the committee consisted of Cynthia von Maerestetten, director, corporate affairs, Benson and Hedges (Canada) Ltd.; Norman A. Dann, vice president, public relations and communications, Imasco, Ltd. (now retired); V. H. Kirpalani, chairman, department of marketing, Concordia University; and David Grier, vice president and chief advisor, public affairs planning, The Royal Bank of Canada.

Two untiring and very able undergraduate students from Concordia, Michele Babin and Robert Cannon, provided assistance and critical advice at every stage of this study.

Ms. Maureen Habib had the unenviable task of keeping the books for my research account and helping me in administrative matters. Maureen is unequalled in efficiency, poise, understanding and just plain good cheer. I shall always be grateful to her for making this aspect of the project not only bearable but, indeed, enjoyable.

This original manuscript was typed by Faye Pennell, who in addition to her excellent work in this area, also helped in other project areas, providing inspired assistance and advice. I also thank Bridget C. Wells for the important role she had in preparing the final manuscript for publication.

Finally, I owe special gratitude to W. Howard Chase, president, Howard Chase Enterprises, Inc., for his skillful editing of the text in both form and substance, and to T. Yancey Crane, my publisher, for her support and encouragement.

Six companies contributed funds towards this study: Alcan Smelters and Chemicals, Ltd.; Canadian National; Air Canada; I.B.M. Canada, Ltd.; Imperial Oil, Ltd.; and The Royal Bank of Canada. The initial financial support of this project by these corporations will always be appreciated.

It is often difficult to identify the one person without whom a research project could not have gone forward. In this instance I have no such difficulties, and indeed, consider it imperative to emphasize the decisive influence of Concordia's Academic Vice Rector, Russell Breen, on the outcome of this venture. Dr. Breen's support of my work at critical junctures, his capacity to delegate responsibility rather than meddle in day-to-day operations, and most importantly his trust, provided the environment in which this book could be completed.

It should be noted in closing that the views expressed herein are not necessarily those of Dr. Breen's Advisory Committee, those of the School of Community and Public Affairs, nor of any other person or group whose cooperation has been so rewarding. Final responsibility for the contents of this work is entirely mine.

Foreword

A popular truism of the past two decades is that there are probably more decisions affecting business now made in Cabinet rooms than boardrooms. Simplistic as this statement may seem, it has the virtue of all truisms in that not only is it largely true, but it captures in succinct fashion one of the reasons why contemporary management practices are changing so rapidly.

Business cannot operate successfully without full understanding and comprehension of the social and political environment within which it is functioning. As this century began, there was a perceived natural harmony between the goals of business and the goals of society. People and governments wanted more goods and services at lower prices and the corporate form of business organization was the most effective way to get them. However, as basic needs began to be met, the goals of society changed. Conflict between business and society became not only a possibility but a reality. When everyone has a car, the production of more cars may not be as important a goal for a large number of people as clean air.

The extent of the change is perhaps best illustrated by the rise of various movements of the 1960s. Managers who had always believed that their central responsibility was to earn a maximum rate of return for their shareholders discovered that the likelihood of their doing so varied in direct proportion to their ability to understand, and adjust to, the new political and social conditions. As a consequence, they began to seek ways to regain harmony with their environment and the art and science of management was expanded to include consideration of environmental factors in the decision-making process.

As to be expected, capabilities of most executives in this area were not high. They had not been trained for it. The expertise of most corporate affairs staffs—when they existed—was often limited to simple lobbying or to the issuing of news releases concerning new projects and products. Such a situation had to change and has changed. Most leaders of modern corporations have come to recognize that assessment and reaction to the environment is a central requirement for successful corporate operations.

The changes in the values and demands of society in the 1960s also elicited a response from governments. It took the form of legislation and regulation—the consequences of which have been to move governments into the heart of business decision-making.

Some may argue that the need for understanding the social, political and economic environment is declining because the relationship between business, the public it serves and government appears to be becoming somewhat less adversarial. Such an interpretation of the need for constantly evaluating the environment and reacting to it is not only short-sighted but also incorrect. The nature of some of the problems has changed but not the need to understand the new issues that are emerging. For example, the executive who does not have in place a capability to assess world economic development, and the implications of the changes which are taking place for business in North America and Europe—the implications of what is commonly referred to as de-industrialization—is in for great surprises and consequent economic difficulties.

Knowing the needs does not, however, guarantee solutions. Modern chief executive officers are often neither equipped to deal with the environment nor do they know how to create within their organizations effective departments to help them with this vital management activity. Moreover, the schools of management, frequently held responsible for the preparation of managers in our society, have not been overwhelmingly innovative in teaching, indeed even in recognizing, the significance to management of the corporate affairs function. Because there has been so little general emphasis on this aspect of management, there has been a limited amount of research and very little organized writing about the issues.

Now this gap has been closed. In this book, Professor Gollner lucidly and comprehensively analyzes the responsibilities of corporate affairs departments in the context of the economic, social and political framework within which modern corporations operate. Moreover, he demonstrates the linkage between corporate profitability and effective management of environmental problems, and shows how corporate affairs activities are most effectively brought into the management decision-making process. Chief executive officers of the modern industrial age, corporate affairs managers, operating managers and students will find the work invaluable. Anyone interested in the modern corporate affairs function—and this must include anyone interested in modern management—will find this book indispensable.

James Gillies
Director
The Max Bell Business–Government
   Studies Program
Faculty of Administrative Studies
York University, Toronto

June 1983

Social Change and Corporate Strategy: The Expanding Role of Public Affairs

1
Underlying Concepts and Premises

Men whose research is based on shared paradigms are commit-
ted to the same rules and standards for scientific practice. That
commitment and the apparent consensus it produces are
prerequisites for normal science...Normal science does not aim
at novelties of fact or theory, and when succesful, finds none...
But when paradigms change, the world itself changed with
them.

—Thomas S. Kuhn

There can be no view except from a viewpoint.

—Gunnar Myrdal

STRATEGIC OVERVIEW

This book examines a rising tide of societal forces that are changing the
way in which corporations select and pursue their objectives in capitalist
mixed economies. It argues that our public and private institutions are
undergoing an irreversible transformation at the hands of a powerful new
set of technological, economic, social and political variables.[1]

The imperative of change has many sources. Two of the most important
are the growth of institutional *interdependence* and *paralysis*. During the
past twenty years, interactions among government, business, labour and
other sectors have become increasingly frequent and close range. But,
rather than enhancing our capacity to act, growing interdependence has
produced greater adversity and frequent paralysis in our key institutions.
The Achilles' heel of our current political–economic system is the inability
to manage the dynamics of interdependence.

Not surprisingly, the public credibility of our leading institutions has
plummeted as the figures in Table I.1 show. Rightly or wrongly, substantial
majorities of the public in both Canada and the United States believe that
many of the policies and actions of these key institutions neglect the
broader interests of society.[2]

1

Table 1.1 Confidence of the American Public in Major Social Institutions (percentage reporting a "great deal of confidence")

	Percent				
	1966	1972	1973	1974	1975
Medicine	72	48	57	50	43
Higher Education	61	33	44	40	36
U.S. Supreme Court	51	28	33	40	28
The Military	62	35	40	33	24
Organized religion	41	30	36	32	32
Televised news	25	17	41	31	35
Executive branch, U.S. Government	41	27	19	28	13
Press	29	18	30	25	26
Major companies	55	27	29	21	19
Congress	42	21	29	18	13
Organized labor	22	15	20	18	14

Source: L. Harris, "Record Lows in Public Confidence," *The Harris Survey*, October 6, 1975.

The collapse of public confidence in our major institutions is matched by a sense of growing frustration and concern on the part of the leaders of these institutions. They recognize that they are less the masters of their organizations' destinies and more the prisoners of diverse and often conflicting external influences. Powerful new public issues are struggling to co-pilot our major institutions. They inhibit traditional leaders from charting independent courses of action and from pursuing policies that brought earlier successes. In the words of one observer, government, business and labour appear to be "locked in each other's grip, counterpoised and immovable without the action of some outside agent."[3]

As the immobilization or paralysis of our institutions spreads, their credibility erodes, opening the door to other rounds of external interventions. These new external pressures—often motivated by public demands for greater institutional social responsibility—overload already crowded decision-making circuits and emerge as one of the most serious challenges of industrial societies. The nature of our response to this challenge will determine whether our socio-economic systems flourish or decay in the years ahead.[4]

For corporations, the growth of non-market influences upon their operations is the most visible sign of these trends (e.g. governmental intervention, changing social values, consumer and public interest group activism, demands from interest groups for increased participation in corporate decision-making, concentrated media scrutiny, pressures for increased public accountability or social responsibility). External demands are increasingly in conflict with traditional corporate structures and practices. The growing disharmony between corporations and their environment during the 1960s and 1970s (or for that matter between most other major institutions and *their* environments), and the adversarial relationships that flow from these contradictions are major impediments to our economic revival.

Finding the way to cope with the "crowding-in" of external issues and with the general crisis of authority emanating from this is no simple exercise. Many commentators in the United States and Canada have diagnosed this malaise as a degeneration of social values. The decline of institutional authority and "excessive" societal demands are seen as a cultural crisis precipitated by the misguided influences of a "new class," "new ideology" or "adversary culture."[5] Standing at the centre of this new ideology, and the main source of our problem, we are told, is an unsatiable egalitarianism[6] which, if left unchecked, will completely destroy the social and economic fabric of our society.

We are told that only by shifting the adversarial values and attitudes of opinion leaders and the public, can we regain our social, institutional and economic dynamism. The suggested cure for the problem of institutional paralysis, in short, is lowered public expectations, and a thorough overhaul of the "cultural" *environment* of our institutions.

The above diagnosis interprets the expansion of non-market forces as a deeply threatening phenomenon. It argues that, by and large, traditional managerial structures and decision-making systems can be maintained, provided that we communicate business interests more effectively, and fight to roll back the expanded non-market environment to its *status-quo-ante* position.[7]

The above prescription for reform relates to Bertolt Brecht's celebrated comment: "The people lost confidence in the government so the government dismissed the people and elected a new one."

This book offers an alternate diagnosis of our malaise, and proposes different remedies. It views the "crowding-in" of external issues on organizational decision-making as an irreversible phenomenon. This phenomenon will not be resolved by a defensive and one-sided strategy aimed at shifting public opinion towards a more pro-business stance. Behind the shifting beliefs, opinions, values and attitudes that contemporary voices label the motors of change, lies an equally important force-field of political, social, economic and technological variables. These variables are interdependent with each other and with the "world" of ideas. They act interchangeably as both causes and effects of change.

All this is part of the age old debate: is societal change the product of the movement of ideas or of matter in time and space? My answer is negative in both instances. Societal change is the exclusive child neither of ideas nor of material forces. It is rather, the product of an irregular and freely changing genetic blend of ideas and material forces. The approach to the management of environmental change which bases itself exclusively on attitudinal engineering has about as much potential for development as an unfertilized egg. The strategy of change must be holistic. It must take into account the symbiotic linkages between a wide range of environmental conditions.

My own conclusion is that the problem of demand overload and institutional paralysis is unsolveable by environmental engineering alone. *The road to our societies' rejuvenation begins within the walls of our institutions.* Transformations in the technological, economic, social and political realms demand no less than a "new bottom line" in the management of government, business and labour. Without new institutional priorities, roles, structures and values, the "crowding-in" of external issues will increasingly inhibit us from selecting and pursuing policies that will take us through the challenging decades ahead.

The strategy of change that I propose recognizes that the expanded non-market environment, while highly objectionable or misguided in some of its forms, is here to stay. To use the words of Thornton Bradshaw, chief executive officer of RCA, "the growth of government regulation is as certain as death and taxes."[8]

Lest it be misinterpreted, it is important to underline that the strategy proposed here is not at all receptive to the call for bigger governments. It does not preach tolerance of bureaucratic waste and the growth of public spending. It does not suggest that we should happily swallow every new regulatory pill doled out by the state. It does not advise that business leaders should simply *kow-tow* before an increasingly critical or probing media, or that they should say "Yes Sir" to every new demand raised by an army of "public interest" pressure groups; nor does it suggest that corporations should discard the profit motive in favour of a new, collectivist "bottom line" or some other ill-defined concept of "social responsibility."

What is being suggested, rather, is that through a new management strategy, through the adoption of a new vision and leadership, private enterprise can significantly reduce the constricting effects of external intrusions into its traditional domains.

The new management, based on pragmatism, recognizes that there is no return to the past. The survival of private enterprise, and indeed, our entire socio-economic system, depends on substantive reforms in the management of relations between organizations and their environments. The challenge to business leaders is *not* the obliteration of non-market forces. The challenge, rather, is to be able to *anticipate* and *harness* environmental change, and to *participate* creatively in the shaping of those forces that will affect the future of private enterprise. The "bottom line" of the new corporate strategy this book will emphasize is stated simply but forcefully by William Gruber and Raymond Hoewing: "Business sales and profits in the 1980s may depend more on successful public affairs functions than on any other aspect of corporate practice."[9]

Reginald Jones, formerly chairman, president and chief executive officer of General Electric, reinforces this concept: "Public policy and social issues are not peripheral to business planning and management; today they are in the mainstream of it.... Those who aspire to top management positions must learn to swim as comfortably in societal and political waters as their predecessors swam in the waters of technology and finance."[10]

New approaches to the management of interdependence, and a closer synthesis of societal–institutional change could significantly improve our fortunes and decrease adversarial tensions and their negative economic effects. This book is addressed both to the converts to this option and to their more traditional colleagues. My hope is that it will help to focus the debate over public and private choice, that it will guide us in the search for more effective mechanisms to manage organizational–environmental change, and that it will provide a more solid foundation for public affairs education.

THE CONCEPT OF CORPORATE STRATEGY

During the past three decades, voluminous literature has grown up around the concept of corporate strategy.[11]

Peter Drucker made an early serious effort to understand and define the significance of strategy to management.[12] Strategy for Drucker was a process by which management determined the basic purpose or mission of the corporation. Subsequent writers have stressed that strategy encompasses not only the basic objectives of the firm but also the means by which those objectives are to be attained.[13] More recent discussion tends to be divided; one school of writers emphasizes the "means"[14] as the essence of strategy, while the other feels that the "objectives" themselves constitute strategy's essence.[15]

This book is not aimed at resolving the debate between the "broad" and "narrow" usage of the term. It concerns itself rather with the well demonstrated rise to prominence of strategic management and focuses attention on why and how strategic management is increasingly involved with sociopolitical forces.

Studies during the past fifteen years have shown that successful corporate performance is increasingly related to formalized strategy formulation.[16] But the nature of the "strategic problem" itself has undergone and is undergoing a massive transformation towards "the emerging importance of psychological-sociological-political variables...aspects of which by the mid-1980s bid fair to become the dominant aspect of the strategic problem for the firm, both internally and externally. The fundamental cause of this is the 'crisis of identity' caused by loss of the social centrality historically enjoyed by the firm. As a result, new patterns of power and influence are emerging within the firm, basic norms and values are being challenged, the image of the firm as an instrument of national economic progress is no longer clear, and ultimately the basic concept of the firm's legitimacy and social utility will have to be redefined."[17]

The concept of corporate strategy used in this book is flexible. While analytical separations of "broad" and "narrow" components are possible and indeed desirable, *in practice one should not separate the question of what a business should be from how it should get there.*

While the need to distinguish between "strategy" and "planning" is a proper one, this book does *not* look upon these two activities as mutually exclusive. Indeed, this book implicitly advocates the *congruence* rather than *exclusivity* of strategic and planning processes.

The usage of the term "strategic planning" in this text is therefore a broad one in that it endorses the above noted congruence, and is similar to the complex strategic matrix developed by such writers as Igor Ansoff. My usage of the term "corporate strategy" is equally broad—i.e., it is not used in the context of the hierarchy of corporate, business and functional strategies, but encompasses all of those levels.

Given these caveats, this book sees strategy as "the match an organization makes between its internal resources and skills (sometimes collectively called competencies) and the opportunities and risks created by its external environment."[18] To help achieve this "match" between internal competencies and external environments of the firm is today's challenge to public affairs management.

THE DEFINITION OF PUBLIC AFFAIRS

The term "public affairs" invites many interpretations. To eliminate confusion, it is important to define the usage applied in this study.

The Everyday Usage

"Public affairs" has been part of our language for a long time. In everyday parlance, it refers to issues that are perceived to be significant to the well-being of a community. Thus, for example, television networks will identify their public affairs programmes as those in which issues of public concern are presented and discussed. The range of issues covered by such programmes is unlimited, including such varied topics as: the hunt for baby seals off the coast of Newfoundland, the sale of weapons to South Africa, juvenile crime, the financial viability of registered pension funds or the depletion of our forest resources, to name just a few. In short, the commonsense use of the term "public affairs" is recognized by the man in the street as just another name for issues perceived to be currently important.

The Traditional Social Science-Based Academic Definition

In academia, this popular interpretation has been carved up into many smaller turfs, each of which is given a generic "public affairs" designation. Thus, for example, the National Association of Schools of Public Affairs and Administration (NASPAA), which lists over 215 academic institutions in its membership in the United States and Canada, considers that the essence of public affairs is public policy and public sector management.[19] To quote from NASPAA's 1979 guidelines, "...the term 'public affairs' is defined within the scope of public policy and management of public organizations."[20] Thus defined, public affairs can be taught either as a subfield of political science (and many political science departments are clinging tooth-and-nail to this approach) or as an interdisciplinary program linking relevant elements of the social sciences into a focused public management or public policy course of studies.[21]

In other academic areas, public affairs is conceived of as urban affairs, as community affairs or as public relations. In short, for social scientists, public affairs can mean many different things. Because the conventional social science-based academic approach is so eclectic, there is no common denominator for talking of "trends" or "state of the art" in this field. While some subsections of this usage do have an identifiable focus and core— e.g., public administration—the overall approach is vague and indeterminate. On an individual basis, there are excellent researchers working on a wide range of important policy or management issues, but the traditional *programme* approach—especially its interdisciplinary variant—is by and large *the creature of personalities, academic politics and chance.* Public affairs as defined above has no theoretical base, conceptual framework or focus around which to organize its followers.

The Institutional Approach

In large scale non-academic organizations, we find an entirely different, yet virtually unanimous, definition of public affairs, and one that is central to this study. Ninety-four percent of the respondents from a sample of Canada's top corporate public affairs executives agreed with the following definition that I proposed in a recent survey:

> Public affairs is a process by which a corporation anticipates, monitors
> and manages its relations with those social and political environmental
> forces that shape the company's operations and environment. Broadly
> similar to corporate external relations, the public affairs function
> includes, among others, such activities as: government relations, commun-
> ity relations, media relations, environmental monitoring and issues man-
> agement.
>
> The public affairs function involves a two-way exchange of signals
> between the corporation and its environment, based on the concept of
> mutual benefit. Thus, while on the one hand the function is designed to
> increase the adaptability of corporations to environmental change, it is
> increasingly active in shaping the direction of future environmental-
> change.[22]

Another recent survey of American corporate public affairs behaviour
identifies the activity in similar terms as "...a *window out* of the corporation through which management can monitor and understand external
change, and simultaneously, a *window in* through which society can affect
corporate policy and practice. Public affairs is, then, *a boundary-spanning
function,* with one foot firmly planted in the organization, the other in the
social and political environment."[23]

A closely related definition of the term, which applies not only to corporations but to all institutions, is that of the National Association of Manufacturers:

> Public affairs involves relationships between institutions—between a
> city government and the state government, between a university and the
> local city council, between a citizen's committee for better schools and
> the school board, and between a consumers' group and a corporation....
> Public affairs is the interaction of one institution or organization in
> society with another.[24]

Public affairs then, as described here, is the mechanism through which
the increasingly frequent and complex interactions of government, business and labour, and other organizations are mediated. It is through public
affairs that corporations seek to understand and manage those increasingly
vociferous non-market forces that are banging on the corporation's front
door.[25] This conceptualization of public affairs is clearly focused. Its analytical boundaries and substance are defined by the nature and dynamics of
the interaction between organizations and their environment.

This "macro" definition of public affairs has been almost unanimously
accepted by the practitioners of this management function. Nevertheless,
"micro" elements of the activity are important and controversial, thereby
requiring clarifications. Further sections of this book will provide them.

THE FOCUS OF THIS BOOK

The first objective of this study is to describe the interplay of technological, economic, social and political forces that compel corporations to develop new priorities and new decision-making systems for the management of changing corporate-environmental relations.

Despite voluminous literature on the relationship between corporations and their environment,[26] I have found few practical guidelines on how to anticipate, understand and manage the "crowding-in" of external issues upon the corporate agenda.

Treatment of the *symptoms* of environmental change as though they were *causal* factors is a major problem in this field.[27] False diagnosis of issues and consequently misdirected management actions are prevalent. In the quest for a quick fix and effective action, causal analysis is therefore given short shrift by organizations. This is the route by which the proverbial short term gain becomes the long term pain. This book attempts to redress this shortcoming in causal analysis.

This second important objective of the study is to examine the corporate public affairs function, a particularly significant institutional innovation, precipitated by the changing environment. This rapidly evolving management function can, if properly organized, be used and integrated at highest levels with profit center management, serve as a key to the successful conduct of changing organizational-environmental relations.

Public affairs is a frequently misused instrument, and confusions about what it can or cannot contribute to the corporation are widespread. Some view it as simply a less "offensive" label than public relations. The question is not infrequently asked—is this function simply a mechanism by which prosperous organizations can enhance their societal "sex appeal," a status symbol usually reserved for the financially well-endowed megacorporation, or is it an essential item in the survival kit of all organizations?

There are other confusions. Is public affairs a line function or a staff function? What should be the relationship between strategic planning and public affairs? How can public affairs serve corporate planners, senior management and operating units in an era of rapid and complex environmental change? Is public affairs a tool reserved for the management of important but nevertheless secondary organizational objectives? Or is it central to the pursuit of the "bottom line"? If public affairs is the management of an organization's relations with its environment, precisely what sectors of the environment are germane to the function? These questions deserve serious answers.

While vast amounts of money are being spent each year by North American corporations on institutional public affairs, there is a very shallow basis of understanding at all levels of the corporation about these questions. Are the financial outlays in these realms an essential or efficient use of scarce corporate resources?

The "theoretical poverty" of this function is illustrated by the fact that the nature and extent of an organization's commitment to public affairs is often dependent on the personal predisposition of its chief executive officer. If the "chief likes this stuff," then the function is vigorously pursued. If he or she has little use for or understanding of this tool, the function will play a precarious and peripheral role in the decision-making processes of the organization.

Corporate public affairs practitioners frequently complain that their superiors and colleagues perceive them as purveyors of luxury goods— affordable when profits are up but easily disposed of in lean times. Many of the professionals working in this field are convinced that their skills could significantly enhance the pursuit of their organization's *primary* mission. Yet, in practice they find that their capacities are underutilized or are directed at targets that are of secondary importance to institutional survival.

External comment on this function also frequently compounds the problem. Public affairs is often depicted by academic and professional commentary simply as societal "do-gooding"—an effort to convince citizens that corporations have a "soul" or that they are good corporate citizens. This inevitably creates the impression that this management activity is designed primarily to minimize certain public expectations, and that its relationship to the pursuit of corporate profitability is only of secondary or indirect importance.

An understandable, yet largely inefficient application of public affairs emerges from such attitudes. Many practitioners spend much of their time promoting their craft rather than doing their work. This rather lop-sided missionary emphasis is a negative phenomenon. It underutilizes scarce resources, including time and energy, on primary public affairs missions and overutilizes resources on internal politics.

Once again the problem is one of misplaced emphasis. Public affairs officers are agents of change—both externally and within an organization. Increased emphasis on maximizing the congruence between institutional and environmental change, and a corresponding de-emphasis on role legitimization, will certainly increase managerial effectiveness. Thus, this study hopes to clear up lingering doubts and conceptual confusions surrounding public affairs so that its practitioners can better shift from proselytizing to performance in their executive conduct.

The stage is set for an integration of trends in this field. Analytical and conceptual order is essential to develop a sharper focus for public affairs. There is a need to evaluate experiences of the past, measure strengths and weaknesses, and provide directives for the future. Wider knowledge in this area will not only promote improved performance, but will also improve career futures, research and education. Key questions examined in this context include the following:

- What are the general and specific environmental forces propelling public affairs towards the centre of corporate decision-making?
- How should a corporation determine its appropriate public affairs needs and levels of social involvement?
- How can we improve anticipation, prioritization and management of public issues?
- Why and how should strategic planning and public affairs be connected?
- How can senior corporate management *participate* in public policy formation, rather than merely reacting to policies made by others?
- Should public affairs capabilities be diffused throughout an organization? How can public affairs skills of operating managers be improved?
- Why is government intervention growing? Will it continue? What can be done about it?
- How can academic institutions support and stimulate the development of public affairs as a vital management function?

The overriding message of this study of corporate public affairs is simply this: once it becomes clear that public affairs management *can* contribute significantly to a corporation's profit, operational effectiveness and viability, *nothing will be gained, and much will be lost, by holding this function and its practitioners at arms-length from central decision-making processes.* Indeed, the greater the extent of an organization's sensitivity to environmental change, the greater the need to integrate this function into decision-making processes *throughout* the organization as a whole.

This book is directed towards a diverse audience. However, one segment is of supreme importance: the corporate chief executive officer. Until or unless the senior executive decision-maker takes the responsibility to reorganize the old forms of management, and to integrate public affairs management into both near and long term operating strategy, as demanded by evidence presented here, "new management" is flesh without bones.

THE IDEOLOGICAL AND METHODOLOGICAL UNDERPINNINGS

The reader will find no claims that this is a value-free study. Gunnar Myrdal's observation in this regard is relevant:

> Valuations are always with us. Disinterested research there has never been and can never be.... Our valuations determine our approaches to a problem, the definition of our concepts, the choice of models, the selection of our observations, the presentation of our conclusions—in fact the whole pursuit of a study from beginning to end. If we remain unaware of the valuational basis to our research, this implies that we proceed to reason with one premise missing, which implies an indeterminateness that opens the door for biases.[28]

The value premises that infuse this study have been identified earlier in this chapter. To be more explicit, the paradigm of organizational–environmental interaction and societal progress that underlies this study, is in sharp contrast to Marx's dialectical materialism, Darwin's theory of evolution and Adam Smith's laissez-faire model of capitalism. Human or social behaviour over certain time-spans has certainly reflected images of change developed by these giants of the 18th and 19th centuries. In my opinion, however, the present and future are so hopelessly out of phase with their sweeping prognostications about human behaviour and social change that even the retrospective accuracies of these three philosophies are now suspect.

For a whole series of complex reasons to be developed in subsequent chapters of this book, the future survival of today's institutions will depend less and less upon adversarial capabilities and more and more upon cooperative capacities. The fittest to survive the future will not be the ones with the capacity to devour the weak. The "weak" have power structures of their own and now fight back. The future belongs to those with the ability to harmonize interests with large and small competitors concerning the management of increasingly limited environmental resources (technological, economic, social and political).[29]

The concept of progress based on cooperation rather than conflict, which underlies this study, has had a profound effect on both the direction and content of my work. Thomas Kuhn's dictum, "When paradigms change, the whole world changes with them" is nowhere more appropriate than here. Clearly, those who choose conflict over cooperative networking will find much to oppose in this work. Neo-Marxists will most likely dismiss this study as a rescue effort on behalf of capitalism, or as a manifesto for corporatism. Free-marketeers will no doubt take the opposite course and see in this work yet another "liberal" effort at binding those miraculous "unseen hands" of the market that have provided our earlier economic, social and technological achievements. Alas, I can only hope that those who work at the centre of the storm bequeathed by the collapse of Marxism, Smithian, and Keynesian theory will find some intellectual nourishment.

The analytical approach used in this study is that of Institutionalism. This analytical approach is lucidly defined by Lee Preston as follows:

> The distinguishing characteristic of the Institutionals is their attempt to deal with society and social processes on an aggregative or holistic basis and in terms of major historical and institutional categories, among which the corporate sector is an important, but not the single, object of interest. To repeat, the Institutionals begin at the *society* end of the corporation–society spectrum.... The Organizationals begin at the *corporation* end of the spectrum. Their principal focus is on how individual organizations *do* in fact behave, not how they are *caused* to behave by the processes of social change.[30]

The Institutional approach used here is part of an intellectual tradition that emerged sometime in the 18th century. It went underground, especially in economics, around the end of World War II, only to resurface recently with renewed vigour.[31] This approach freely admits the role human valuations play in research; indeed, it considers them to be essential in any scholarly undertaking. It is an approach that requires an interdisciplinary focus, rather than narrow academic specialization. It analyses problems in terms of all relevant or irrelevant "economic," "social" or "political" conditions.

The Institutional approach is certainly *not* a one-sidedly deterministic model of societal change. It does not single out economics, for example, as the basic determinant of everything else. Rather, it takes a holistic approach to causation, emphasizing the circularity of cause and effect relationships.

Gunnar Myrdal again excellently summarizes the essence of this analytical approach:

> The most fundamental thought that holds institutional economists together is our recognition that even if we focus attention on specific problems, our study must take into account the entire social system, including everything else of importance for what comes to happen in the economic field.... The dynamics of this social system are determined by the fact that among all the endogenous conditions there is circular causation, implying that, if there is change in one condition, others will change in response.... There is no one basic factor; everything causes everything else. This implies inter-dependence within the whole social process. And there is generally no equilibrium in sight.[32]

The final fundamental premise of the contemporary Institutional approach, and one of the values underlying this book, is that the generation of wealth and the distribution of goods and services in industrially advanced societies appears to be less and less the *exclusive* responsibility of economic market forces. Rather, it is increasingly conditioned by newly emerging complex relationships between such key institutions as government, business, organized labour and other pressure groups.

As far as the theoretical underpinnings of this study are concerned, I did not set out to test a general theory of corporate affairs, for there was no such theory to be found.[33] The subject of this work is in a pre-theoretical state, by which we mean a "systematically related set of statements, including some lawlike generalizations, that are empirically testable."[34]

The absence of a general theory of corporate public affairs presents a number of interesting choices, such as the selection of dependent and independent variables. This book designates environmental change as the independent variable and corporate public affairs as the dependent variable. In other words, the development of the corporate public affairs function is explained in terms of demands (or pressures) generated by changing institutional environments.

This choice, once again, is the product of the author's values. It is, however, consistent with the main thrust of modern social science since the late 18th century (conservative, liberal and socialist). The comments of John Kautsky will serve here since they express the analytical rationale behind this choice:

> One must explain some phenomena in terms of others; one must choose one's dependent and independent variables.... The question is not what determines what, but, rather, what is to be analysed in terms of what.... It need hardly be pointed out that to designate something as a dependent variable is not to denigrate it, but on the contrary, to focus on it in order to explain it.[35]

These efforts to illuminate the corporate public affairs function from the shifting platform of environmental change do not imply that corporations play or ought to play merely a reactive role in the societal change process. Indeed, the *model* of the relationship between corporations and their environments used here is the so-called "Interpenetrating Systems Model" developed by Talcott Parsons, and adapted by Lee Preston, James Post and others.[36] The essential features of this model are best described by Preston and Post as follows:

> We assume that the larger society exists as a macro-system, but that the individual (and particularly *large*) micro-organizations also constitute separable systems within themselves, neither completely controlling nor controlled by the social environment. It is the ability of one system to change the *structure* of the other, and not simply to alter the volume or character of inputs and outputs, that distinguishes the interpenetrating systems

model from simpler collateral or suprasystems conceptions.... Thus society may take into account and seek to influence the goals of managerial units; and they, in turn, may take into account and seek to influence those of society at large. Neither are the two systems completely separate and independent nor does either control the other; their relationship is better described in terms of interpenetration.[37]

The data applied to the above outlined approach and model of the new dynamics of public affairs management were generated through a variety of techniques. They include: face-to-face interviews with specialists in the field, written survey questionnaires, primary and secondary publications, manuscripts and position-papers.

If this exercise stimulates academicians, corporate executives and students to understand the confluence of forces propelling corporate public affairs towards increasing decision-making prominence, and to organize themselves and their institutions accordingly, its basic purpose will have been achieved.

Notes

1. There is a large number of works available on the topic of the changing values and roles of institutions in advanced industrial societies. Some rejoice in the change; others lament it, and all are shaded by various degrees of ideological bias. There is no consensus at all in this literature about either the causes or the future direction of change. The following works provide a good introductory snapshot of the ideological spectrum, going from Right to Left as follows: R. Nisbet, *The Twilight of Authority* (Oxford University Press, 1975); G. Gilder, *Wealth and Poverty* (Basic Books, 1981); J. Schumpeter, *Capitalism, Socialism and Democracy* (Harper and Row, 1969); D. Bell, *The Coming of Post-Industrial Society* (Basic Books, 1973); G.C. Lodge, *The New American Ideology* (A.A. Knopf, 1976); M. Crozier, S. Huntington and J. Watanuki, *The Crisis of Democracy* (New York University Press, 1975); J.D. Rockefeller III, *The Second American Revolution* (Harper and Row, 1973); R. Heilbroner, *An Inquiry into the Human Prospect* (W.W. Norton, 1974); J.K. Galbraith, *The New Industrial State* (Penguin Books, 1980); A. Hacker, *The End of the American Era* (Atheneum, 1970); C. Reich, *The Greening of America* (Bantam Books, 1970); and J. O'Connor, *The Fiscal Crisis of the State* (St. Martin's Press, 1973).

A large number of works deals exclusively with the shifting priorities of business in an era of rapid change. C. Brown, in a recent study entitled *Beyond the Bottom Line* (Macmillan, 1979), examines changes in social values and their impact upon the corporation. His thesis is that the movement of "quality of life" considerations to the centre stage of public attention is compelling corporations to shift from a single purpose consciousness (profits) to a multipurpose consciousness (economic, social, psychological, educational, environmental and even political).

J. Hargreaves and J. Dauman, in an excellent study entitled, *Business Survival and Social Change* (John Wiley and Sons, 1975) stress not only the changing climate of opinion but the general external environment of business as forces of change. They argue for a new social and political role for business not on the basis of a sudden change in business *values* but rather, as they put it, "because traditional objectives, indeed survival itself, are threatened." Between these two positions lie a number of useful works concerning changing corporate priorities and their "raison d'être." See for example, T. Levitt, "Management and Post-Industrial Society," *The Public Interest,* No. 44, Summer, 1976; D. Linowes, *Strategies for Survival* (AMACOM), American Management Associations, 1973); V. Day, "Business Priorities in a Changing Environment," *Journal of General Management,* Vol. 1, No. 1, 1973; W. Halal, "Beyond the Profit Motive: The Post Industrial Corporation," *Technological Forecasting and Social Change,* Vol. 12, No. 1, 1978; L. Preston and J. Post, "The Third Managerial Revolution," *Academy of Management Journal,* Vol. 17, No. 3, 1974; F. Steckmest, *Corporate Performance: The Key to Public Trust* (McGraw-Hill, 1982); C. Spitzer, *Raising the Bottom Line* (Longman, 1982) and G. Steiner, *The New CEO* (Free Press, 1983).

2. For some additional, and highly revealing insights into this question of declining public confidence in our institutions see also the following: W. Hamilton, "On the Credibility of Institutions," *The Conference Board Record,* March, 1973; G. Gallup, "Public Opinion and Social Crisis in the 80s," *Public Relations Journal,* Vol. 35, January, 1979; K. Graham, "If Business Credibility Means Anything," *Conference Board Record,* March, 1976; S. Lipset and W. Schneider, *The Confidence Gap: How Americans View Their Institutions* (Macmillan, 1981), as well as their shorter piece entitled "How's Business? What the Public Thinks," *Public Opinion,* July-August, 1978; D. Ross, "Business Confronts Itself at the Credibility Gap," *The Conference Board Record,* July, 1973; D. Yankelovich, *Corporate Priorities: A Continuing Study of New Demands on Business* (New York, 1972); R. Coulson, "Corporate Credibility: What's It All About?" *Business Quarterly,* Vol. 45, Spring, 1980; A. White and M. Hochstein, "The Climate for Business in the 1980s: New Challenges, New Opportunities," *Business and Society: Strategies for the 1980s* (Report of the Task Force on Corporate Social Performance, U.S. Department of Commerce, December, 1980).

3. J. O'Toole, *The Immobilized State: An Assay on the Future of Government/ Corporate Relations* (Summary Report of the Third Twenty-Year Forecast Project, Center for Futures Research, Graduate School of Business Administration, University of Southern California, July, 1978, p. 15).

4. "Demand overload" is a frequent term associated with this phenomenon. Within the political realm, I would suggest reading *The American Commonwealth, 1976,* which was a special 10th Anniversary issue of the journal *The Public Interest.* The chapters by P. Huntington, A. Wildavsky and J.Q. Wilson are particularly revealing. The central theme of all these writers is that our political systems are being short-circuited by the unrestrained and excessive political pressures of citizens and special interest groups. The ungovernability of American democracy is attributed by and large to the excesses of that democracy. A similar theme runs through a special

report commissioned by the Trilateral Commission, and prepared by M.J. Crozier *et al., op. cit.* On the corporate side of the equation, the writings of J. Brown at The Conference Board in New York are particularly useful. See for example, *This Business of Issues: Coping with the Company's Environments* (Conference Board, 1979) or *Guidelines for Managing Corporate Issues Programs* (Conference Board, 1981). Also recommended are: S. Morris, Jr., "Managing Corporate External Affairs," *Management Review*, March, 1980; L.E. This, "Critical Issues Confronting Managers in the '80s," *Training and Development Journal,* January, 1980; R. Amara, *The Future of Management: Ten Shapers of Management in the '80s,* (Institute for the Future, February, 1980); P. McGrath, *Managing Corporate External Relations* (The Conference Board, 1976); R. Moore, "Planning for Emerging Issues," *Public Relations Journal,* November, 1979; *Chemical Week,* "Issues Management: Preparing for Social Change," October 28, 1981; D.B. Thompson, "Issue Management: New Key to Corporate Survival," *Industry Week,* February 23, 1981; "Issue Management," *Dun's Business Month,* December, 1981.

5. This is, by and large, the conclusion of the above mentioned Trilateral Commission study, and that of a wide spectrum of authors including A. Wildavsky, I. Kristol, M. Novak, G. Gilder and J.Q. Wilson, to name just a few. For an excellent review of the ideas of these writers, and of the orientation that seeks to explain our current malaise in terms of a degeneration in client values, I strongly recommend P. Steinfels, *The Neoconservatives: The Men Who are Changing America's Politics* (Simon and Schuster, 1979).

6. See for example, I. Kristol, "About Equality," *Commentary,* Vol. 54, November, 1972; D. Bell, "The Revolution of Rising Entitlements," *Fortune,* April, 1975; *Business Week,* "Egalitarianism: Threat to a Free Market," December 1, 1975; N. Chamberlain, *Remaking American Values: Challenge to Business and Society* (Basic Books, 1977); H. Williams, "Egalitarianism and the Market System," *The Columbia Journal of World Business,* Winter, 1978. The one academician whose ideas on equality are seen to be particularly "disruptive," and who is seen as the intellectual father of this new, yet "harmful" egalitarianism that stresses not simply "equality of opportunity" but also "equality of results," is J. Rawls. See his *A Theory of Justice* (Harvard University Press, 1971).

7. This is, by and large, the option propagated, for example, by M. Friedman in his celebrated article entitled "The Social Responsibility of Business is to Increase its Profits," in *The New York Times Magazine,* September 13, 1970 or in "The Line We Dare Not Cross" in *Encounter,* November, 1976.

8. T. Bradshaw, "Business and Society: Decade of Decision," *Business and Society: Strategies for the 1980s* (Report of the Task Force on Corporate Social Performance, U.S. Department of Commerce, 1980), p. 93.

9. W.H. Gruber and R.L. Hoewing, "The New Management in Corporate Public Affairs," *Public Affairs Review,* No. 1, 1980, p. 13.

10. R. Jones, "The Mainstream of Business Responsibility," *Business and Society: Strategies for the 1980s, op. cit.,* p. 66.

11. For detailed analysis, see I. Ansoff, *Corporate Strategy* (Penguin Books, 1968);

R. Rumelt, *Strategy, Structure and Economic Performance* (Harvard University Press, 1974); C.W. Hofer and D. Schendel, *Strategy Formulation: Analytical Concepts* (West Publishing Company, 1978); B.B. Tregoe and J.W. Zimmerman, *Top Management Strategy* (Simon and Schuster, 1980).

12. P. Drucker, *The Practice of Management* (Harper and Row, 1954).

13. K. Andrews, *et. al., Business Policy: Text and Cases* (Richard D. Irwin, 1965) and K. Andrews, *The Concept of Corporate Strategy* (Dow-Jones-Irwin, 1971).

14. Scholars such as J.T. Cannon and T.J. McNichols fall into this category.

15. A. Chandler, R.L. Katz or G.A. Steiner belong to this "school." For a good discussion of the "broad" vs. "narrow" usage, see C.W. Hofer and D. Schendel, *op. cit.,* pp. 16-20.

16. See, for example, D.W. Karger and F.A. Malik, "Long Range Planning and Organizational Performance," *Long Range Planning,* December, 1975; D.M. Herold, "Long Range Planning and Organizational Performance: A Cross Validation Study," *Academy of Management Journal,* March, 1972. Also useful is B.B. Tregoe and J.W. Zimmerman, *Top Management Strategy, op. cit.*

17. I. Ansoff, R.P. Declerc and R.L. Hayes (eds.), *From Strategic Planning to Strategic Management* (John Wiley and Sons, 1976), p. 3.

18. C.W. Hofer and D. Schendel, *op. cit.,* p. 12. These writers move on from a general level to a narrower usage by defining the "match" as "a statement of the fundamental means" towards achieving corporate objectives, *ibid.,* pp. 23-24.

19. National Association of Schools of Public Affairs and Administration (NASPAA), *1980 Directory,* (A Survey Report of the Member Institutions of NASPAA, Washington, D.C.).

20. *Guidelines for Community and Junior College Students Who Intend to Transfer to Baccalaureate Degree Programs in Public Affairs/Public Administration* (NASPAA, February 6, 1979), p. 1. R.T. Golembiewski, in a paper presented at an international conference on the future of public administration organized by the Ecole Nationale d'Administration Publique in Quebec City, in May 1979, also defined "public affairs" in the same vein: "Public affairs. . . refers to broad training for elites prepared to serve in politics/administrative roles, as diplomats or ambassadors, as high-level aides at various levels of government, etc." in *The Near-Future of Graduate Public Adminstration Programs in the U.S.* (Manuscript, 29 May, 1979), p. 19. For a similar usage, see A.P. Pross and V.S. Wilson, "Graduate Education in Canadian Public Administration: Antecedents, Present Trends and Portents," *Canadian Public Administration,* 20th Anniversary Issue, 1979, pp. 139-153.

21. NASPAA, *1980 Directory, op. cit.,* p. iii.

22. The survey was conducted in the middle of 1982 to generate data for this book. A selected sample of 384 corporations from the 1981 Canadian "Financial Post 500" list were invited to participate. The overall response rate was 37 percent, while for the top 100 corporations, the response rate was close to 60 percent. Selected tables from the results of this survey are contained in this study.

23. Public Affairs Research Group, *Public Affairs Offices and Their Functions: Summary of Survey Responses* (School of Management, Boston University, 1981).

24. National Association of Manufacturers, *The Public Affairs Manual* (NAM, 1978), p. 1.

25. And indeed, many are already inside. See for example, J. Cameron, "Nader's Invaders are Inside the Gate," *Fortune,* October, 1977; A. Reilly, "Assault on Corporate America," *Dun's Business Review,* Vol. 115, April, 1980; and D. Vogel, "Ralph Naders all Over the Place," *Across the Board,* Vol. 16, April, 1979.

26. For an excellent review of this literature, see: L. Preston, "Corporation and Society: The Search for a Paradigm," *Journal of Economic Literature,* Vol. 13, No. 2, June, 1975. Preston distinguishes between three broad schools of thought—the institutionals, the organizationals and the philosophicals. The institutionals include such writers as A. Shonfield, R.T. Averitt, E. Furubotn, S. Pejovich, J.K. Galbraith, R.A. Solo, P.A. Baran and P.M. Sweezy, going from right to left along the ideological spectrum. The institutional approach to the corporate-society relationship is via the society end of the spectrum. The organizationals, in distinction, begin their analysis at the corporation end of the spectrum. As Preston points out, the institutional approach is related to organizational analysis as macro-economics is related to micro. Prominent organizationals are K.J. Cohen, R.M. Cyert, H. Simon, R. Bauer and R.J. Roeber, to name just a few. The philosophicals include such a diverse group of writers as K.J. Arrow, M. Friedman, N. Chamberlain, P. Drucker, J. Cohn and C.H. Madden. The distinguishing feature of the last approach, according to Preston, is that "they deal in terms of 'ought' and 'should' rather than 'is' and 'do.'" Preston's conclusion is that while this three-pronged literature lacks both a central theoretical conception and a common methodological base, it serves a useful purpose in softening up the shell of public and academic ignorance that surrounds this subject matter. As he puts it "some future J.B. Clark Medalists and Nobel Laureates will simply convert the basic goal structures of both the corporation and society to a single set of comparable concepts and categories; insert the relevant data for technical tradeoffs, preference orderings and social choice mechanisms; and the new model of corporation-society interaction will be ready to run." Using Preston's categories, this study falls into the institutional school.

27. The two most frequently recurring cases of cause and effect confusion are in the area of changing social values and the growth of government. There are numerous analyses in print, and an even more widely spread professional consensus, that these are the two principal causes of the increasingly complex external challenges faced by institutions. On changing societal values, see for example, the following works, each of which stresses more or less the same theme with varying degrees of optimism or pessimism: G.F. Cavanagh, *American Business Values in Transition* (Prentice-Hall, 1976); G.C. Lodge, *The New American Ideology* (A.A. Knopf, 1975); R.H. Bock, "Modern Values and Corporate Social Responsibility," *Michigan State University Business Topics,* Spring, 1980; C.H. Madden, *The Clash of Culture: Management in an Age of Changing Values* (National Planning Association, 1972); N. Chamberlain, *Remaking American Values: Challenge to a Business Society* (Basic Books, 1977); A.H. Reiss, *Culture and Company* (Twayne, 1972); K.M. Dolbeare

and P. Dolbeare, *American Ideologies, the Competing Beliefs of the 1970s* (Markham, 1971); J. Kuhn and I. Berg, *Values in a Business Society* (Harcourt, Brace, Jovanovich, 1968). The problem with these analyses is not that they are inaccurate in describing the dimensions of the "new American ideology." Lodge's book, for example, is a brilliant description of the workings and profile of new social values. The problem lies, rather, with silence on the one hand and superficiality on the other, concerning the *sources* of these values themselves. Far too often, the operating assumption is that the new social values are simply reflections of subjective values held by other influential opinion leaders in society. Thus an operational strategy emerges, in which future attitudinal or value change is perceived essentially in manipulative communications terms—in terms of transforming opinion-leading elites and so on. As suggested in the text, such strategies of change will never bear the fruit expected of them because of their false diagnosis of the origins of changing values.

The problem of governmental growth is similarly mishandled. Here again, while there are some exaggerated statements, both ways, about the *enormous increase in governmental interventions,* by and large, analyses are relatively accurate in demonstrating some of the *constraints* that such interventionism imposes upon institutions. See, for example, G.W. Nutter, *The Growth of Government in the West* (American Enterprise Institute for Public Policy Research, 1978); A. Andersen and Company, *The Cost of Government Regulation* (Business Roundtable, March 1979); M.L. Weidenbaum and R. DeFina, *The Cost of Government Regulation of Economic Activity* (American Enterprise Institute, 1978); M. Weidenbaum, *Business, Government and the Public* (Prentice-Hall, 1977). As in the case of the "value" factor, however, the sources of governmental growth once again are given extremely short and inaccurate shrift. The causes of governmental growth are quickly reduced to any of the following: changing values, a new and destructive egalitarianism, the influence of a liberal establishment, bungling politicians or excessively influential and self-serving special group interests. Again, the strategic response is given a manipulative orientation by this diagnosis—i.e. change the values, clean out the harmful ideas, the bungling politicians, the liberal "do-gooders," the public interest groups, etc., learn to communicate business interests more effectively—and government will be rolled back to its proper place. This strategy, like the one described earlier, has limited prospect of succeeding even on the short term. On the long term, it is most certainly unworkable. A brief, clearly articulated and sympathetic summary of the above strategies vis-à-vis changing values and governmental growth is found in D. Vogel, "Business's 'New Class' Struggle," *The Nation,* December 15, 1979. By 1981, Vogel has proclaimed that business has indeed come out victorious in this struggle to reverse "the momentum toward increased government regulation and in transforming the political agenda." See his "Business, in Victory," *The New York Times,* February 21, 1981. Such rejoicing, in my view, is both misplaced and premature. Vogel may be correct in saying that, "A number of neo-conservative intellectuals have helped convince many corporate executives that the future of American capitalism is dependent on the attitudes and beliefs of a 'new class' of upper-middle class professionals. As a result, corporate executives are now engaged in an unprecedented effort to influence the social values of the nation's highly educated citizenry." He is, however, creating false hopes among businessmen by suggesting that such a strategy will significantly reduce the external challenges that business has come to experience over the past decade-and-a-half.

28. G. Myrdal, "Institutional Economics," *Journal of Economic Issues,* Vol. XIII, No. 4, December, 1978, pp. 778-9.

29. The paradigm is not one of a risk free, centrally planned society. While Marxist readers of this work will recognize quite early on that this is no Marxist or socialist treatise, I feel that my neo-conservative colleagues should be explicitly told this, lest they begin to jump to false conclusions. While my vision of the future is in many respects diametrically opposed to that presented by G. Gilder's *Wealth and Poverty* (Basic Books, 1981), I agree with him that *"Heroism, willingness to plunge into the unknown, in the hope that others will follow,* is indispensible to all great human achievement. . . . Natural history is a saga not of balance but of convulsive changes, wiping out whole species left and right, transforming continents, evulsing mountains, and flooding vast plains and valleys. There is no such thing as equilibrium, in ecology any more than in economics. Any static state is doomed to disaster" (pp. 253-257). My desire in this book is not to advocate a risk-free society or to diminish the need for individual creativity, heroism and struggle. My point, rather, is that the convulsive changes that lie ahead, the inevitable challenges and need to transform "mountains, plains and valleys" cannot be achieved by the same mechanisms that we have used in the past. Indeed, the paradigm static analysis is that which argues that while everything else around us must change, the structures and *mechanisms* of change themselves should remain unchanged. I'm afraid that this rigidity is in effect the central flaw of the whole so-called neo-conservative school of thought currently stalking America.

30. L.E. Preston, "Corporation and Society: The Search for a Paradigm," *Journal of Economic Literature,* Vol. 13, No. 2, June, 1975, pp. 438-41.

31. For some cogent statements on this approach, see: P.A. Klein, "American Institutionalism: Premature Death, Permanent Resurrection," *Journal of Economic Issues,* June, 1978; A.A. Eichner, "Post-Keynesian Theory: An Introduction," *Challenge,* May-June, 1978; A.G. Gruchy, "Institutional Economics: Its Influence and Prospects," *American Journal of Economics and Sociology,* July, 1978; W.C. Peterson, "Institutionalism, Keynes and the Real World," *Challenge,* May-June, 1977; and finally, G. Myrdal, "Institutional Economics," *op. cit.*

32. G. Myrdal, *ibid.,* pp. 773-4.

33. This is the conclusion of L. Preston, *op. cit.,* p. 447, as well as R.A. Buchholz, *Business Environment/Public Policy: A Study of Teaching and Research in Schools of Business and Management* (American Assembly of Collegiate Schools of Business, February, 1979), p. 111.

34. R.S. Rudner, *Philosophy of Social Science* (Prentice-Hall, 1966), p. 10.

35. J.H. Kautsky, *The Political Consequences of Modernization* (John Wiley and Sons, 1972), p. 8-9.

36. See L.E. Preston and J.E. Post, *Private Management and Public Policy* (Prentice-Hall, 1975); or K.C. Cohen and R.M. Cyert, "Strategy: Formulation, Implementation and Monitoring," *Journal of Business,* Vol. 46, No. 3, 1973.

37. L.E. Preston and J.E. Post, *op. cit.,* pp. 25-27.

2

The Societal Forces Transforming the Corporate Agenda

We are in the opening phases of a revolution that will, if it runs its apparent course, radically change the character and performance of business institutions in our society. . . . The significant question facing managers is not how to prevent the change (because this will be self destructive and impossible), but rather how to understand it, accommodate to it and bring constructive influences to bear upon it.

—Melvin Anshen
Paul Garrett Professor of Public
Policy and Business Responsibility
Graduate School of Business
Columbia University

In this chapter, the dynamics of the societal forces pushing public affairs towards corporate strategy centres are examined in detail. The objective is to illuminate the growing dependence of corporate performance on public affairs know-how. Increased reliance on public affairs management, as we shall see, is not a passing phenomenon. Rather, this management function is fast becoming an integral element of corporate strategy because of the impact of irreversible societal changes.

Many recent works on corporate public affairs create the impression that this management function has just been invented, in response to the last twenty years of socio-political turmoil. This interpretation is misleading. While it is true that public affairs management has gained prominence during these years (see Table 2.1), its origins are far deeper. Corporate concern with social responsibility, for example, is not a new phenomenon. It emerged as soon as the state issued its first corporate charter requiring the corporation to be accountable to the state for meeting the conditions laid down in its charter. To suggest that this accountability, inherent in the granting of the corporate charter, was ignored in the past and that it is only *now* that corporations have found it necessary to account to society for their actions, is sheer nonsense. Corporations always have been and always

Table 2.1 The Origins of Corporate Public Affairs Departments in Canada

Date of Establishment	% Respondents	
Before 1950	11.6 ⎞	
Between 1951-1960	15.8 ⎬	44.2
Between 1961-1970	16.8 ⎠	
Between 1971-1975	17.9 ⎞	55.8
Since 1976	37.9 ⎠	

will be accountable to society. What *has* changed and will change further are the limits of this accountability and the management forms through which this accountability is expressed and executed.

We witness today, then, not the birth of a new management function but a revolutionary transformation in traditional forms of management. This transformation is due largely to the expansion of economic intervention by governments, the increasing socio-political complexity of the business environment and the impact of external issues on corporate profits (see Tables 2.2 and 2.3).

In the following pages and subsequent chapters, the dynamics of governmental growth and environmental complexity are closely examined. If management is to come to grips with these forces and with the "crowding-in" of external issues, it must fully understand the precise causes, forms and managerial implications of these and other emerging environmental changes. The absence of such a precise or detailed understanding will forever hinder corporate leaders from developing genuinely effective strategies of their own.

As a final preface to this section, many of the environmental forces presented below have been known for a long time. But as in linguistics, where a new language can be created out of existing letters, so it is with environmental change: *a new combination* of traditional as well as emerging societal forces is transmitting a whole new set of messages to management. It is these new "messages" that are changing the managerial agenda. As a consequence, the need for public affairs managerial capabilities will intensify— though by no means uniformly for all corporations.

What then are these new societal forces, or this new constellation of environmental demands, that are propelling public affairs management towards the centres of corporate decision-making?

THE GROWTH OF INSTITUTIONAL INTERDEPENDENCE

A universally accepted by-product of the process of industrialization which continues on even in the so-called post-industrial era, is the growth of insti-

Table 2.2 Perceived Causes of the Establishment of Corporate Public Affairs Departments in Canada

	% Respondents Considering This to Be				
	Highly Significant		Moderately Significant		Insignificant
Factors	**1**	**2**	**3**	**4**	**5**
The increasing assertiveness of consumer advocacy groups	9.5	12.6	33.7	20.0	24.2
The increasing power of organized labor	2.1	6.3	18.9	34.7	37.9
Demonstration effect from U.S. corporations	1.1	7.4	37.2	31.9	22.3
Increasing socio-political complexity of business environment	36.8	43.2	14.7	3.2	2.1
Personal interest of CEO	17.9	38.9	30.5	7.4	5.3
Decline of business credibility	8.5	33.0	38.3	16.0	4.3
Growth of government intervention	44.7	29.8	18.1	5.3	2.1
Growing awareness of social-ethical responsibilities	9.5	36.8	38.9	12.6	2.1
The impact of external issues on profits	26.3	37.9	21.1	12.6	2.1
The growth of media scrutiny	16.8	30.5	31.6	15.8	5.3
A particularly significant single event (e.g. the National Energy Program)	15.5	9.9	8.5	15.5	50.7

tutional interdependence.[1] In less technical terms, the industrialization process has sharply reduced the capacity of organizations to remain islands unto themselves. This is not a hypothesized developmental pattern but a demonstrable one—a pattern that is both apparent and theoretically unassailable.

The impact of this societal by-product of the industrialization process is readily felt by management. It has created a situation in which the decisional out-puts of one organization increasingly serve as the decisional inputs for another (and vice-versa) so that corporate, or any other organizational decision-making, is more and more *externally driven.* Whether a government is trying to reduce inflation, or a corporation is trying to enter new markets or to increase its profits, external hands weigh increasingly heavily upon the steering mechanisms of all our major institutions.

Table 2.3 The Ranking of Forces Responsible for the Creation of Public Affairs Departments in Canada
(Scale: 1 = Highly significant; 5 = Insignificant

Forces	Mean Score
1. Growth of government intervention	1.904
2. The increasing socio-political complexity of the business environment	1.905
3. The impact of external issues on profits	2.263
4. Personal interest of the CEO	2.432
5. Growing awareness of social-ethical responsibilities	2.611
6. The growth of media scrutiny	2.621
7. The decline of business credibility	2.745
8. The increasing assertiveness of consumer advocacy groups	3.368
9. Demonstration effect from U.S. corporations	3.670
10. A particularly significant event	3.761
11. The increasing power of organized labour	4.000

John Hargreaves and Jan Dauman have provided a useful explanation of the above process by reference to a stone-in-the-pond analogy[2] (see Figure 2.1). They suggest that organizations make waves in their environment much the same way as stones make waves when they are dropped into a pond. The various rings of the waves produced by such an immersion are seen as various reaches of institutional responsibility, which over time, and especially if many stones have been dropped into the pond, begin to overlap. Adapting this analogy helps us to recognize that the industrialization process of the 19th and 20th centuries left in its wake an expanding area of overlapping responsibilities (my concept of the"crowding-in" of external issues) which demands focused attention.

The growth of institutional interdependence may also be examined in terms of the growth of externalities. In economic terms, "externalities," or "external economies," refers to the unintended or unanticipated consequences (costs or benefits) accruing to society from various private technical-economic activities (e.g. the cost to society of cleaning up the environment after it has been polluted by a chemical plant). One consequence of the growth of externalities is that it accelerates external *and* internal interventions into traditional management domains. As Roy Amara remarks in this connection, "The primary impact on management of the increasing importance of externalities is that power and decision-making will need to be shared with a great many groups, both inside and outside the corpora-

Figure 2.1 The Overlap of All Interests

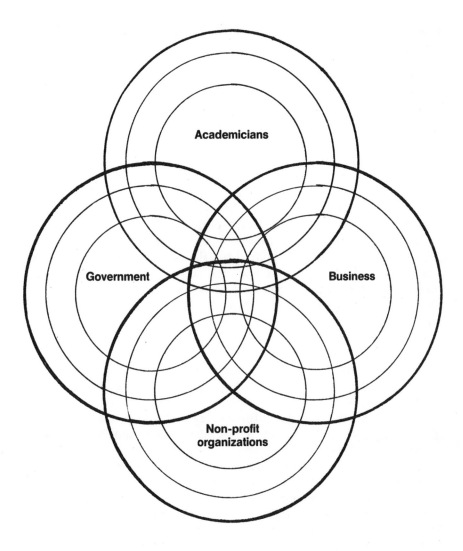

Source: J. Hargreaves and J. Dauman, *Business Survival and Social Change* (John Wiley and Sons, 1975), p. 26.

tion: employees, consumer groups, environmentalists, and regulatory agencies, for example."[3]

The above can be briefly illustrated by the decision to provide public financial aid to the troubled Chrysler Corporation. The United States as well as Canadian governments lent support not because of favouritism towards large business. The injection of substantial amounts of taxpayer funds into this company was perceived to be necessary by the state on *both* capital and social accumulation grounds. (The neo-Marxist thesis of the relatively autonomous state playing trade-offs between these two forms of accumulation in order to legitimize itself cannot be applied, because here, as in many other cases, the trade-off is not discernible.)[4] Financial assistance to Chrysler from the state, and even from its own union members, came because most everyone involved recognized that Chrysler's collapse would set off a massive negative ripple effect on other corporations *and* upon hundreds of thousands of other workers who had nothing whatsoever to do with the possible failure of that company.

One can argue, as many do, that a market economy's demands for on-going structural rejuvenation require that a floundering corporation, regardless of size, should be allowed to sink and to pull down in its wake hundreds of thousands of innocent passengers. One cannot, however, dispute the fact that the sinking of a giant corporate ship would have a considerably greater cross-societal impact today than decades ago. The negative cross-cultural impacts in the Chrysler bail-out case, and of others related to it, cut both ways. Whether Chrysler is to sink or is to be rescued by the state, citizens (i.e. taxpayers) with no equity in Chrysler are paying a large part of the bill. But as the saying goes, he who pays the piper calls the tune, and with the rescue of Chrysler comes a heightened degree of external intervention into the affairs of that corporation. Chrysler is only one dramatic example of the "crowding-in" of external issues upon corporate decision-making.

The growth of institutional interdependence has historically expressed itself primarily within the territorial confines of national regions or nation-states. During recent decades, however, it has taken on, and will take on especially in the future, increasingly powerful *international* dimensions. The internationalization of institutional interdependence—of which the global impact of OPEC has been perhaps the most convenient illustration— will have a second wave effect on the growth of interdependence, accelerating *it* and the general demands for new managerial responsibilities.

Because organizations and their leaders are less the masters of their own destinies, because they are increasingly buffeted by the decisional waves of other organizations, they have no choice *but* to become more knowledgeable about decision-making processes of those organizations that affect their operations and environment. To reduce the levels of planning uncertainty, to reduce the chances of costly surprises, to provide a more stable foundation for corporate decision-making, managements are called upon to *interpenetrate* the decision-making systems of particularly those organizations and pressure groups that are making the largest "waves" upon them. These comments about the growth of institutional interdependence, and its suction effect whereby management is called on to participate in the shaping of its environment, are conveniently summed up by Edward B. Harvey:

> As societies become more functionally complex, so do the patterns of interdependency. What happens in one segment of a social system can have complex implications for another segment of the system.... Because of high levels of complexity and functional interdependence, any action is likely to have unanticipated consequences and feedback effects. The goal of effective planning is to try to anticipate and control as many of these consequences as possible.[5]

The point to bear in mind, as far as public affairs management is concerned, is this: The growth of interdependence, say strictly of an economic or technological nature, produces wide ranging *societal* and *political* effects. Economic interdependence *activates or energizes* a new set of social and political players, who then try to become active participants in the very technological-economic processes that are of crucial importance to the firm. Corporate leaders thus can no longer interact only with one set of players (i.e. with economic and technological forces) but must contend with a range of socio-political forces that have been sucked into their decision-making arena by the complexities of technological-economic interdependence.

Both common sense and survival dictate that management become, through the sound conduct of public affairs, a *proactive* or *interactive* rather than a *reactive* participant in the shaping of those critical decisions that will affect the evolution of its life support system. The organization that can optimize the utilization of these new interactive mechanisms with *its* own changing environment, will have a competitive edge over the organization that insists on playing by traditional rules while the world changes around it. This is particularly true of large corporations, which by virtue of their size alone "make bigger waves" in their environment, and in return are touched by more "waves" emanating from their milieu.[6] As Table 2.4 shows, larger corporations will experience the need to establish management capabilities in these areas earlier than medium sized or smaller firms.

Table 2.4 The Origins of Corporate Public Affairs Departments in Canada: The Top 100 Corporations

Date of Establishment	% Respondents	
Before 1950	22 ⎫	
Between 1951-1960	20 ⎬	57
Between 1961-1970	15 ⎭	
Between 1971-1975	15 ⎫	43
Since 1976	28 ⎭	

THE TECHNOLOGICAL REVOLUTION

Recent technological changes have many implications for management. The focus here is only on those technological changes that are propelling public affairs management closer to the centres of corporate decision-making. In order to demonstrate this, it is necessary first of all to sketch the salient features of the new technological revolution.

a. The most noticeable feature of recent technological change is its *speed.* Many studies have documented the quantum leaps that have taken place recently in both the rate of invention and diffusion of new technologies. It has been said, for example, that "...of all the scientists of whom civilization has any knowledge, 90 percent are alive today. And industrial technology—the practical handmaiden of science—is equally new. Half of all the research and development expenditures in the history of the United States have been made in the last ten years."[7] With respect to the rate of technological diffusion—i.e. the time it takes for a new invention to be generally applied throughout society—we have also witnessed a drastic acceleration in rates as the figures in Table 2.5 clearly indicate.

By now, as Donald Schon argues, "the time required for the diffusion of major technological innovations would appear to be approaching zero as a limit."[8]

Table 2.5 Changing Rates of Technological Diffusion

Invention	Time Required for Diffusion in Years
Steam engine	150-200
Automobile	40-50
Vacuum tube	25-30
Transistor	about 15

Source: D.A. Schon, *Beyond the Stable State* (W.W. Norton and Co., 1971), p. 24.

b. The second important feature of modern technology is its relative *complexity.* Owing to the rapidity of the creation of new technologies, and accelerating obsolescence of existing ones, humanity's capacity to understand *and* control the inventions of its era has been significantly reduced. It is not an exaggeration to say that human beings today are more remote from their technological environment, more ignorant of their technological inheritance and of the changes that engulf them, than ever before.[9]

Another source of this increasing complexity is that the technology of innovation itself has been revolutionized. Whereas in the past, new technologies were produced by *human* thought alone, today vastly increased leaps of technological design are possible through the link-up of creative minds with the computer. Indeed, the next wave of innovative technology facing us will be designed not by human beings but by machines.

c. The third significant aspect of our current technological revolution is that it has become increasingly *pervasive.* New technology is capable of producing (at greater speeds) far deeper and wider societal effects than previous technological revolutions. The impact of the automobile, for example, was not restricted to one industry, or to industry alone. It has had a profound effect upon the whole profile of business, upon geography, upon land use, upon urban planning, housing, social relations, consumer behaviour, entertainment and even the relationship between generations. Even more far reaching effects will flow from the diffusion of the new communications and transportation technologies, and from such products and processes as the home computer, the word processor, the "office of the future," robotics, etc.

d. The fourth significant aspect of recent technological change resides in its *content.* The main line of the new technological revolution is almost exclusively infrastructural, and is designed to transport facts, ideas, messages, goods, money and people with increasing speed and sophistication. In other words, the substantive novelty of the new technological revolution is its high concentration in the areas of *communications* and *transportation.*

e. The fifth significance of modern technology is its increasing *centrality to future economic growth* and development. In a classic study, Edward F. Denison demonstrated (and this was subsequently confirmed by other studies)[10] that whereas prior to the twentieth century, labour and capital were the two most significant sources of economic growth, during the last few decades, these two factors have given way to education and technological innovation.

f. The sixth and final feature of modern technology is its sharply *escalating cost.* The American space programme, which is, perhaps, the best illustration of the unique blending of communications, information and transportation technologies, was clearly outside the reach of a single or even a consortium of private investors. Even most of the subcomponents of the complex technological mix that brought man to the moon for the first time, were themselves attainable only with the help of massive state subsidies. This is not to suggest that state financing should become the sole foundation for future technological revolutions. Indeed, there are many examples where such involvement can produce exactly the opposite effect from that which was intended.[11] Rather, the major point here is simply that relatively larger in-puts of capital are needed to generate high technology today than was the case in the past. The source of this capital is problematical.

How then do these six features of modern technology affect the managerial agenda? In what ways do these technological revolutions intensify the need to bring public affairs management closer to the centres of corporate decision-making?

First of all, these six technological factors together have massively accelerated, and will continue to *accelerate the need for corporate strategic planning.* In the minds of some people, the word planning is akin to socialism or to rigid state control, and conjures up the political-economic problems of Poland, the U.S.S.R. and of other planned economies. In *practice,* however, more and more Western corporations are finding that only by planning are they able to adapt to and survive in this new technological age. Putting rhetoric aside, most, if not all, of the major corporations in the United States and Canada have introduced some type of strategic planning model into their decision-making systems during the last decade. While this technological induction of strategic planning has been identified by a number of writers and in several surveys of corporate behaviour in the United States and Canada,[12] no one has formulated the inseparable linkage between technology and planning more clearly than that often criticized commentator on the new industrial state, John Kenneth Galbraith:

> We thus come to... the conclusion which is that the enemy of the market is not ideology but the engineer. The enemies of the market are thus to be seen, although rarely in social matters has there been such a case of mistaken identity. It is not socialists. It is advanced technology and the specialization of men and process that this requires and the resulting commitment of time and capital.[13]

Thus, the first impact of technology on management is that it forces the utilization of planning mechanisms into the management process. (This is not to suggest that planning and the market are antithetical forces, or that the advance of corporate planning fosters the demise of the market economy.)

A second impact of the new technology stems from its forms. Because it is primarily infrastructural, new technology has *contributed to the expansion of adversarial relationships.* As Donald Schon remarks, "The new electronic technologies of communications have, in particular, evolved as though they were going to produce... instantaneous confrontations of every part of our society with every other part. As a result, social inequities leap to universal attention.... Conflicts long suppressed by separation and isolation escape the bounds that had confined them, and as new societies come into contact, new conflicts emerge."[14] Modern communications technologies, in short, energize current and latent special interest groups and provide them with the tools and the information to challenge the managerial prerogatives of the modern corporation.[15]

Due to their rapid rate of change, new technologies reduce our capacity to understand their mysteries. Thus a growing number of citizens and organized pressure groups have reacted with various strategies aimed at *reducing the speed of innovation*—if only to make the products of innovation more comprehensible. The pervasiveness of new technology has ignited a whole series of suspicious and hostile reactions from citizens and their political representatives. Employees are fearful that they can be displaced from their jobs anytime by a machine. Consumers are distrustful that in the pursuit of rapid technological innovation, corporations are less careful about the physical or ecological side effects of their inventions. In short, the rapid fire penetration of technology into daily lives has precipitated a reaction which intends to *limit* the technological prerogatives of management. This tendency has activated political parties, pressure groups, the media and other "non-market" players to intervene in precisely that process (i.e. technological innovation) which is the chief source of our continued economic growth (see factor "e" above). This sociopolitical feedback effect, which reaches into the very centre of traditional corporate prerogatives, presents an extremely serious challenge to management. Selecting the appropriate response, in this instance, will be critical for long term business survival.

In the face of this new reality, in which socio-political forces are attempting to dictate the terms of technological innovation, management has only one realistic choice. If the modern corporation is to maintain the momentum of technological innovation needed for its economic survival, it must *fuse into its planning system those emergent socio-political forces that are set off by its technological plenum.*

A manipulative approach in this area will react against the corporation. What needs first and foremost to be recognized is that technology and societal values are inseparably connected. One cannot be changed without changing the other.[16] George Lodge's argument that "we have tended to be unmindful of our ideology and we have allowed it to degenerate"[17] is only partially correct. We could better restate this as follows: Managements have been unmindful of the socio-political impacts of their technological inventions and this has contributed to the degeneration of our ideology. The recognition by management of this linkage between ideology, public opinion and technology can result in substantially enhanced corporate performance.

The only management option in this area that promises to bear long term fruit as far as regaining corporate credibility and authority is concerned is that which (1) takes into close consideration the possible socio-political consequences of technological innovations *prior* to their implementation, and which, (2) actively *solicits* and uses the in-puts of external stakeholders during the planning of future technological investments and diffusion strategies. This responsibility is one of the central tenets of the new managerial revolution.

The interconnection between socio-political forces and innovation, and the ensuing implications of this for management have been illustrated in a recent study by James O'Toole. While O'Toole is careful to point out that "the process of innovation has no single well-spring (or, obversely, no single impediment)" his conclusion is the following: "It would seem that the underlying inhibitor of innovation is the *goal structure* of large American corporations. . . . The challenge then, is to find ways to free older, larger corporations from the constraints their past successes place on their ability to innovate. This requires more than changing an assumption here or there. Since assumptions all come together to form a consistent world view, *change often requires altering the entire culture of the firm. To do this— indeed, to institutionalize the process of doing this—the corporation must learn to read changes in the environment.* Then, it must provide incentives to managers to continually change their behaviour as the environment changes"[18] (emphasis added).

THE CHANGING STRUCTURES AND RULES OF THE MARKET ECONOMY

The third set of forces accelerating demands for a new managerial agenda is bound up with the changing rules and structures of the capitalist mixed economy. The most relevant economic variables here are: the emergence of the megacorporation and economic concentration, the expansion of the service sector and the decline of productivity growth rates.

a. One of the striking phenomena of this century, especially in the United States, has been the gradual emergence of the megacorporation together with the increasing control of larger and larger market shares by fewer and fewer economic players.

This structural transformation of the capitalist market economy did not happen overnight and is most certainly not the product of a "bankers' conspiracy." The giant, more often than not multinational, and concentrated capitalist firm is largely the product of the communications, transportation and overall technological revolutions of the recent decades. The demands of economic growth and scale, the exhaustion or saturation of domestic markets, the new linkages to international communications-transportation opportunities are major forces that have made the giant corporation both possible and inevitable.

There are a number of consequences of this transformation. One is that the workings of the "unseen hand of the market," which has brought us many economic benefits (and economic rules), has been fundamentally altered. Indeed, the rise of the megacorporation and oligopolistic markets has created a deep contradiction within the mechanisms of the market system. In a competitive setting, a fall in consumer demand tends to lower prices and spur producers towards increasing efficiency, cost consciousness, product innovation and productivity. In an oligopolistic or concentrated setting, the corporation can, and often does, take the route of least resistance. Rather than utilizing its earlier sources of profitability, the oligopolistic firm may simply increase its prices, reduce its out-put and thus maintain a stable profit margin even during a cyclical downturn.[19] In short, many allege that the price mechanism and all of the vital responses of the firm to market signals are switched into reverse and work in a contradictory fashion once a certain level of oligopolistic production has been reached. [20] The pricing behaviour of firms in concentrated market sectors in the United States and Canada during the late 1960s and 1970s tends to support this statement (especially in the case of the automobile industry). In the United States, for example, the 1969-70 recession produced an aggregate price *increase* of 5.9 percent in the concentrated sectors of the economy. Only the competitive sector reacted according to the laws of the market, by reducing its prices by 6.1 percent. Similarly, during the 1973-74 inflationary spiral, while the competitive sector only increased its prices by 2 percent, the non-competitive sector registered an across the board price increase of 22 percent.[21] Once again, one conclusion is pervasive. While government is most certainly one of the significant originators of non-market rules in the capitalist economy, parts of the private sector are also powerful agents of the growth of non-market forces.

The above conclusion leaves us in a classic double bind situation. On the one hand, the growth of concentration and megacorporations appears to be necessitated by the demands of *global* competition. On the other hand, the same corporations appear to be in profound contradiction to the domestic rules of the market economy. These developments have been a long time coming, and efforts at legislatively altering them can and do create economic havoc.[22] In other words, breaking up the giant corporations, and legislatively lowering the limits of concentration could, so as to derive the benefits of competition, invite drastically *increased* governmental intervention as the consequences of such a restructuring wind through the economy. For such an exercise to be successful, patterns of consumption must be drastically altered. Strict tariff and trade controls intended to protect the small economies-of-scale producers against their larger external competitors would also be inevitable.

There is no doubt that the competitive market model is a highly ingenious and efficient allocative mechanism. The hitch is that the real world of economics today bears decreasing resemblance to this model. The leading edge of the corporate community, on its own, simply will not take (and indeed will fight) the massive structural steps needed to translate this "competitive" model into reality.[23] In fact, contrary to the rhetoric, "big business" is deeply opposed to any efforts aimed at dismantling large corporations and at reducing the size of the concentrated market sector.[24]

In conclusion, while efforts no doubt will be made from time to time in both Canada and the United States to strengthen anti-combines (anti-trust) legislation and to restrict—even roll back—the forces of non-competitive markets, substantial reforms in these areas are remote. Small may well be beautiful; it is, however, not feasible.

The implications of the above for public affairs management can now be enumerated. The freely competitive market system needs comparatively less public affairs involvement from its corporate constituents (though even here other factors, such as technology, will raise the ante). The concentrated economic sector requires a substantial degree of public affairs capacity from its corporate members. While the competitive sector is the obedient servant of market forces and requires managerial expertise almost exclusively within market domains (all things remaining equal), the concentrated sector—no longer the exclusive plaything of market forces— requires "market-plus" managerial knowhow. I find myself in *some* agreement this time with the dynamics laid out by George Cabot Lodge of Harvard University:

> In the face of the serious pressures from Japanese and European business organizations, which emanate from ideological settings quite different from our own, there will be more and more reason to set aside the old idea of domestic competition in order to organize U.S. business effectively to meet world competition [sic]. Managers will probably welcome if not urge such a step; they may, however, be less willing to accept the necessary concomitant: If in the name of efficiency, of economies of scale, and of the demands of world markets, we allow restraints on the free play of domestic market forces, then other forces will have to be

used to define and preserve the public interest. These 'other forces' will amount to greater regulation by the political order, in some form or other.[25]

My agreement with Lodge is qualified for the following reason: Greater regulation by the political order is only *one* logical consequence of the refusal to dismantle the megacorporation and the non-competitive domestic economic sector. *The accelerating regulatory consequence can be pre-empted by the new managerial revolution. The institutionalization of public affairs capabilities by the megacorporation can substantially moderate the external intrusion of the state and of public interest groups into the corporate decision-making arena, and stabilize relationships between them.* As in the case of increasing technological innovation, so it is in the case of economic concentration, that public affairs as a management discipline is the missing link that could be vitally beneficial not only to the corporation but to society as a whole.

Even if the megacorporation decides not to develop pro-active or interactive socio-political capabilities, it will find itself drawn into the socio-political arena by the forces to which Lodge has alluded. In this case, public affairs will be introduced to management through the "back door," as it were. Instead of participating in the management of environmental change, and thereby being in "tune" with its environment, the corporation will find itself strictly in a "fire-fighting" situation as unforeseen events continuously overtake it.

b. Additional economic causes of the rise of public affairs can be discussed in considerably less detail. The second of the relevant economic changes is the *expansion of the service sector* in industrially advanced Western economies (e.g. trade, government services, transportation and other utilities, finance, insurance, real estate, nursing, teaching). Whether the service sector produces lesser or greater degrees of productivity growth than the manufacturing sector is not the issue here.[26] What is of significance is that service occupations tend to be (with exceptions) rather loosely structured as far as work patterns and social relationships are concerned (e.g. the job of the cab driver). This looser structuring and less stable social relationship system creates an occupational culture that may produce increased militancy and distrust of management among its rank and file members. (The rise of service sector unions and their growing militancy is not coincidental.) While productivity gains in the service sector during the initial phases of this economic restructuring have often been lower than in the other sectors, recent developments (automation of the office, etc.) indicate that a major "catching up in productivity" is under way. But while productivity appears to be heading for a substantial increase in the service sector, the technological sources of that productivity will increase the already widespread militancy and distrust of the rank and file service sector employee (e.g. witness labour's reaction to the introduction of automation in the Post Office or to the diffusion of video display terminals).

In short, the source of the future disruptive power of labour, or of worsening labour relations lies not so much, as Marx suggested, with the rise of the industrial proletariat, but with the growth of the service sector. This new trend, once again, will limit the workings of the market, and as such will demand, new "non-market" managerial capabilities, especially in the employee communications and human relations areas of public affairs. The comments of Robert Heilbroner are relevant to this discussion:

> The shift of society's activities in the direction of services lessens that margin of safety. Unlike goods, there is no way of stockpiling services.... The shift to services, like the rise of affluence, adds to the 'disruptive' power of labour, thereby further undermining the efficacy of the market mechanism.[27]

c. The *decline of productivity growth rates* since the end of World War II in both the United States and Canada (and in all of the other OECD countries) is well known. There is no consensus on the causes of this productivity decline. Some blame governments, some the unions, some the rise of the service sector, but none of these supposed causes can stand up to the test of statistical analysis.[28]

The sharp decline in productivity growth rates has ensured that this issue will become, if it isn't so already, one of the main targets of managerial and, indeed, governmental attention in the 1980s.[29] While there is no agreement on the remedy, one thing is becoming apparent—namely, that productivity can be influenced by a whole range of non-economic, non-market tools. The studies of William Ouchi and Harvey Leibenstein during the past few years are in a way footnotes to the "Human Relations" school of motivation going back to the 1930s. They nevertheless reinforce the thesis that productivity gains in the future will be more a function of a new managerial culture, a new managerial revolution, than anything else. Earlier references to the work of James O'Toole on innovation are equally supportive of this thesis.

THE SOCIAL CAUSES OF CHANGE

In addition to these technologically and economically induced societal changes, we need to look at three further social variables that are particularly germane to the emergence of improved corporate public affairs managements—namely, the growth of egalitarianism, participation and education (keeping in mind that none of these social factors is independent of technological-economic factors).

a. As indicated earlier, *the spreading of egalitarian values* during the past few decades has frequently been singled out as the main source of governmental growth and of the "crowding-in" of external issues upon corporations. The manner in which egalitarianism increases demands for new managerial forms has been amply reviewed by others. Suffice to say that this "value" factor has substantially altered the weights on the scale by which the market mechanism balances its allocation of goods and services to a community. Whereas in the past the allocation and investment decisions of management were based largely on financial signals sent out by the market, today management finds itself responding to a range of non-financial signals dictated by this value factor. While individual management leaders may not like this new value shift, they cannot hide from it. When the alternative is to fight or to harness egalitarianism, modern management has little choice but to develop capacities that will include the force of this new environmental value category into its decision-making centres.

b. The second significant social force which makes increasing public affairs capabilities mandatory, is the expanded demand for *participation* in corporate decision-making. Sources of this demand are both inside and outside the corporation.

As far as external policy participation demands are concerned, their existence is amply illustrated in Tables 2.6, 2.7 and 2.8. There are also numerous studies documenting the escalation of internal participatory demands. These pose an additional challenge to management. The extent of this internal participatory urge is clearly summed up by a Task Force Study conducted in the United States during the early 1970s:

> What workers want most, according to more than 100 studies made in the past 20 years, is to become masters of their immediate environments and to feel that their work and they themselves are important—the twin ingredients of self-esteem.[30]

Even from the compressed evidence presented here, the implications of these participatory forces are unmistakable. Obviously, management cannot abrogate its final decision-making responsibilities, but neither can it perpetuate out-worn practices by holding an impenetrable fortress around itself. Management's future performance will depend very much on its ability to develop anticipatory knowledge, integrative and gate-keeping capabilities vis-à-vis these external-internal demands. It must, in short, develop new systems to coordinate the sharply increasing "two-way traffic" of horizontal (external) and vertical (internal) communications with its constituents. This is but one important responsibility of the overall public affairs function.

c. The third and final social force pertaining to this discussion is the *growth of education.* While expanding education is responsible for many good things, and is an essential prerequisite of economic-technological development, it is an equally powerful source of the *fragmentation* of

Table 2.6 Judgments as to Whether Outsiders are Trying to Have an Increasing Influence on or Involvement in Company Decision-Making (as a percentage of executive responses)

	All Executives*	U.S.	Europe	Developing Nations
Yes	93	96	98	84
No	7	4	2	16

*Includes executives from all parts of the world as well as those from the United States, Europe and the Developing Nations.

Source: A.R. Janger and R.E. Berenbeim, *External Challenge to Management Decisions* (The Conference Board, 1981), p. 3.

Table 2.7 Kinds of Decisions in Which Outsiders Try to Participate (as a percentage of executive responses)

In What Kinds of Decisions Did They Try to Participate?	Worldwide*	U.S.	Europe	Developing Nations
Location of facilities	15	14	16	14
Financial and investment policies	11	10	20	8
Expansion and reduction of facilities	11	10	10	8
Pay and social welfare practices	11	7	14	15
Hiring practices	9	14	8	6
Advertising and pricing	8	6	12	8
Layoff and redundancy	8	4	8	6
Product design, function, use	8	6	8	6
Purchasing processes	6	7	2	6
Production processes	4	1	4	6
New production research	2	3	2	3

*Includes companies from all parts of the world as well as those from the United States, Europe and the Developing Nations.

Source: *Ibid,* p. 4.

Table 2.8 Outsiders Attempting to Participate in Company Decision-Making (as a percentage of executive responses)

What Groups Have Attempted to Participate in Your Company's Decision-Making?	Worldwide*	U.S.	Europe	Developing Nations
Unions	71	56	82	65
Environmental groups	56	68	54	35
Political parties	47	26	62	46
Consumer groups	43	46	44	32
Business and industry associations	40	32	40	48
Minority and ethnic groups	35	68	16	12
Religious groups	35	61	24	15
Community groups	32	50	24	18
Women's and feminist groups	22	40	12	8
Handicapped individuals	15	22	10	6
Others	19	13	24	· 23

*Includes companies from all parts of the world as well as those from the United States, Europe and the Developing Nations.

Source: *Ibid.*, p. 5.

societal consensus and of the growth of countervailing external demands upon our institutions. Education has fuelled the divergence of public opinion and attitudes, making it more difficult for management to discern clearly defined signals of change emanating from its environment. This skewering or fracturing of public opinion and of social consensus requires a systematic and thorough environmental assessment capacity from management in order to reduce the dangers of "false" or misguided response. Expansion of education, in short, and its impact upon social values, create demands for increased managerial capacity in the disciplines and systems of environmental scanning and issues management.

THE IMPACT OF PUBLIC POLICY AND GOVERNMENTAL GROWTH

For many corporate leaders, the single most important political force demanding a new managerial approach has been the growth of government intervention. A quick scan of the *dimensions* of this expanding state intervention is now in order.

Prior to the turn of the century, government expenditures in Canada, for example, comprised approximately five percent of the GNP. Today this figure is over 40 percent. In Canada, as in all other countries in the West, the public sector is the largest single employer—providing direct employment to at least 23 percent of the employed labour force.[21] (This figure does not include part-time contractual services, but does include teachers, hospital workers, and employees of crown corporations.) Canadians and Americans spend a far higher proportion of their personal income on government than on any other single supplier of goods and services, and, as Grant Reuber adds, "... with little apparent choice about what they get"[32] in return.

But public expenditures and employment figures are not the only indicators of expanding government. Equally relevant and far more rapidly expanding, has been the growth of regulation—"the hidden half of government."[33]

A recent study by the Economic Council of Canada has shown that Canadian regulatory activity rapidly accelerated during the 1970s. More regulatory statutes were authorized by Ottawa between 1970-1978 than in the preceding three decades[34] (see Figure 2.2).

The final, although sometimes disguised, aspect of governmental growth is *tax expenditure*. Tax expenditure refers to foregone government revenue or, to use Maslove's words, "special provisions in the tax laws providing for preferential treatment and consequently resulting in revenue losses."[35]

Tax expenditures are often seen as mere "loopholes" in the government tax structure. This interpretation, however, ignores a very important point: These gaps are in fact consciously designed instruments of public policy (e.g. to facilitate the creation of jobs by corporations or public institutions, to increase the availability of investment capital, to increase or decrease personal savings as a means of affecting inflation, etc.). In fact, tax expenditures have become extremely important government instruments by which governments pursue leading political-economic objectives, such as employment and price stability.

As with regulation, this fourth dimension of governmental involvement has also witnessed a significant rate of growth during the previous decade or so. "Between 1971 and 1976 total tax expenditures in Canada grew at an average annual rate of about 32 percent, substantially faster than either budgetary revenues or expenditures. As a consequence, tax expenditures as a portion of federal revenues grew from six percent to 15 percent, and as a portion of direct expenditures, from six percent to over 14 percent."[36] (Note: this is only personal income tax expenditure.)

Taken together, public policy and state intervention in both Canada and the United States have reached deep into the internal workings of corpora-

Figure 2.2 Number of Federal and Provincial Regulatory Statutes by Decade of Enactment or Enactment of Their Predecessor

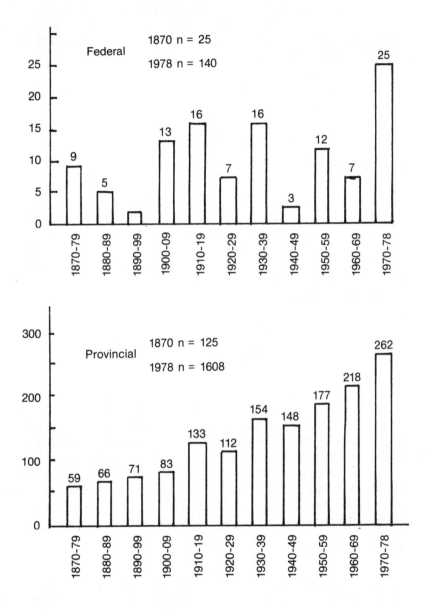

Source: The Economic Council of Canada, *Responsible Regulation* (Ottawa, 1979), p. 15.

tions. They exercise a powerful influence upon corporate strategic decision-making. For this reason alone, a growing number of corporations
has recognized that relationships with governments, and with public policy require a new and more intensive managerial responsiveness and
reaffirmation of the "right" to participate in policy decisions that affect
them. This responsiveness is a bread-and-butter issue for many corporations, and is eliciting a feverish search for mechanisms by which it may be
better managed.[37] The ability to anticipate, monitor, and if possible manage changes in public policy, or at least to contribute to them, has thus
reached high premium. It is thereby propelling the public affairs function
closer into the heart of corporate strategic planning.

CONCLUSIONS

In this chapter, we saw the complex interplay of technological, economic,
social and political forces, which together have made corporate profitability and survival increasingly dependent on public affairs management
skills. The environmental changes referred to are in all cases irreversible.
In most cases each will intensify in the future thereby advancing the need
for corporate public affairs capabilities. Management sensitivity to these
changes will indeed become an essential condition of corporate survival.
There is no running away from the "law of large numbers" described in
this chapter. Or, as one prominent study showed, while 15 years ago "...80
percent of planning was concerned with what management wanted, 20
percent with how the world affected the company; now the figures are
reversed—or at least ought to be."[38]

The evidence presented above is intended to help boards, senior managements, profit centre leaders and staffs to understand the sources of this
change, its enduring characteristics, and some areas of inevitable corporate
involvement. Declining corporate credibility with all its attendant dangers
and liabilities is indeed one important symptom of management inatten-
tion to the forces and issues outlined above. Not only corporate credibility,
but the very survival of private enterprise requires that management
confront its responsibilities in these issue areas with renewed vigour and
vision. How to do this effectively is the substance of this book.

Notes

1. See for example, R. Aron, *18 Lectures on Industrial Society* (Weindenfeld and
Nicholson, 1967); or W.E. Moore, *The Impact of Industry* (Prentice-Hall, 1965).

2. J. Hargreaves and J. Dauman, *Business Survival and Social Change* (John Wiley
and Sons, 1975), p. 17.

3. R. Amara, *Five Emergent Features of U.S. Society and Their Impact on Management in the Next Decade* (Institute for the Future, December, 1975), p. 2.

4. Ralph Miliband utilized the idea of "ransom" to rationalize the capitalist state's occasionally unfavourable behaviour towards the bourgeoisie. These measures, argues Miliband, are undertaken simply to appease the proletariat, and thereby maintain *on the long run* the supremacy of the capitalist class. In other words, short term "ransoms," such as welfare payments, are the necessary costs associated with the perpetuation of capitalist exploitation. See his, *The State in Capitalist Society: An Analysis of the Western System of Power* (Quartet Books, 1973), especially pp. 72-73. While this thesis may indeed offer a way out for Marxist *theory* from some of the contradictions which contemporary Western political behaviour presents it with, its explanatory power is unconvincing. It is difficult to accept the Marxist assertion that bailing out Chrysler Corporation and saving, in the process, hundreds of thousands of workers from the misery of unemployment, is ultimately more in the interest of the employer than that of the employee. Indeed, there are capitalist theorists who could just as easily argue the reverse, that by such an intervention the bourgeois state is steadily undermining the effectiveness of the market mechanism, and thus, is steadily eroding the foundations of the private enterprise system. While for neo-Marxists such rescue efforts are seen as attempts to enhance the durability of the capitalist economy, equally, such actions could be described as the slamming of the final nails into the coffin of capitalism.

5. E.B. Harvey, *Industrial Society: Structures, Roles and Relations* (The Dorsey Press, 1975), p. 357.

6. Both the Public Affairs Council's Survey of the Fortune top 500 industrial corporations and that by the Public Affairs Research Group of Boston University, of the top 1,000 U.S. corporations, indicate that "the larger firms have taken the lead in the utilization of new management practices." See, W.H. Gruber and R.L. Hoewing, "The New Management in Corporate Public Affairs," *Public Affairs Review*, Vol. I, 1980, p. 19; and Public Affairs Research Group, School of Management, Boston University, *Public Affairs Offices and Their Functions* (Boston University, 1981).

7. R. Heilbroner, "The Impact of Technology: The Historic Debate" in J.T. Dunlop (ed.), *Automation and Technological Change* (Prentice-Hall, 1962), p. 8. See also, C.R. Walker, *Technology, Industry and Man* (McGraw-Hill, 1968), and E. Mesthene, *Technological Change* (Harvard University Press, 1970).

8. D.A. Schon, *Beyond the Stable State* (W.W. Norton and Company, 1971), p. 24.

9. On these points see C. Reich, *The Greening of America* (Random House, 1970), and A. Toffler, *Future Shock* (Random House, 1970).

10. E. Denison, *The Sources of Economic Growth in the United States* (Committee for Economic Development, 1962).

11. One of the most thorough analyses of state-led technological innovation is the study carried out under the auspices of the Center for Policy Alternatives at the Massachusetts Institute of Technology during the early 1970s. This study examined

the financial sources of successful and unsuccessful innovations in Germany, Japan, France, the Netherlands and the United Kingdom, and concluded that governmental supports did not effect in any statistically discernible fashion the outcome of the projects under analysis. The study was written by N.A. Ashford, as *National Support for Science and Technology: An Examination of Foreign Experience* (Massachusetts Institute of Technology, 1976). See also, K. S. Palda, *The Science Council's Weakest Link: A Critique of the Science Council's Technocratic Industrial Strategy for Canada* (The Fraser Institute, 1979).

12. See for example, N.A. Hall, "Impact of Technology on Organizations and Individuals," *The Business Quarterly,* Winter, 1966.

13. J.K. Galbraith, *The New Industrial State* (Signet Books, 1967), p. 44.

14. D. Schon, *op. cit.,* p. 26.

15. The phenomenon of special interest group networking through the facilities of modern communications technology has already arrived. Public interest groups in various parts of the world are increasingly pooling information and tactical responses and are thus becoming even more effective in penetrating corporate barriers. On this, see R. Drobnick, *Emerging Issues: Concepts, Methods, and Forecasts* (Center for Futures Research, Graduate School of Business Administration, University of Southern California, December, 1980), p. 27; or A.R. Janger and R.E. Berenbeim, *External Challenges to Management Decision* (Research Report No. 808, The Conference Board, 1981), p. 5.

16. D. Schon, *op. cit.,* p. 36

17. G.C. Lodge, "Top Priority: Renovating Our Ideology" in H. J. Leonard, J.C. Davis and G. Binder (eds.), *Business and Environment* (The Conservation Foundation, 1977), p. 13.

18. J. O'Toole, *Declining Innovation: The Failure of Success* (Center for Futures Research, Graduate School of Business Administration, University of Southern California, January, 1982), pp. 13-14.

19. See P.J. Wiles, "Cost Inflation and the State of Economic Theory," *The Economic Journal,* Vol. 83, June, 1973, especially pp. 383-384. Also useful in this connection are the following works: H.M. Wachtel and P.D. Adelsheim, "How Recession Feeds Inflation: Price Markups in a Concentrated Economy," *Challenge,* September/October, 1977; H. Sherman, "Monopoly Power and Stagflation," *Journal of Economic Issues,* June, 1977; A.E. Kahn, "Market Power Inflation: A Conceptual Overview" in G. Means and J.M. Blair (eds.), *The Roots of Inflation* (Burt Franklin, 1975); W.G. Shepherd, *Market Power and Economic Welfare* (Random House, 1970); and J.M. Blair, *Economic Concentration: Structure, Behaviour and Public Policy* (Harcourt, Brace, Jovanovich, 1972).

20. There are a number of ways to measure the level of concentration. One is to look at the share of the GNP produced by the 100 largest firms, or the share of the work force employed by the 100 largest companies. Another approach is to examine the share of the market that is controlled by the top four corporations in a particular

market sector (e.g. banking, automobile manufacturing, chemicals, etc.). According to conventional definition, a *tight oligopoly* exists when more than 40 percent of the market is controlled by the four largest firms, a *loose oligopoly* constitutes 20-40 percent market share and *effective competition* exists when the four largest sellers together earn less than 20 percent of total sales within their sector of the market. By these definitions, Canada today is one of the most highly concentrated economies in the Western world, because close to 50 percent of its goods and services are the products of the above defined tightly oligopolistic market situation. On this, see, for example, the Royal Commission on Corporate Concentration (Ottawa, Minister of Supply and Services, Canada, 1978). In his otherwise excellent study of Canadian government-business relations,— *Where Business Fails* (The Institute for Research on Public Policy, 1981), p. 16—J. Gillies comments that "there appears to have been relatively little change in corporate concentration over the years.... Concentration was approximately the same in 1950 and early 1960" as it is today. His statement is not convincing. While I know of no detailed public analysis of the shifts in concentration in the Canadian setting, one study by W.N. Leonard—"Mergers, Industrial Concentration, and Antitrust Policy," *Journal of Economic Issues,* June, 1976, pp. 355-364—shows that concentration ratios in the United States have not at all been constant during the past three decades. Leonard's findings show that whereas in 1955, the top 200 American firms controlled 49 percent of manufacturing sales, 53 percent of assets and employed 40 percent of the labour force, by 1974, these figures had increased to 63 percent, 67 percent and 61 percent respectively. Canadian corporate behaviour does not suggest a divergent pattern from that in the United States, especially in light of Canada's milder antitrust laws.

21. On this, see, G. Means and J.M. Blair (eds.), *The Roots of Inflation, op. cit.*

22. I am aware of studies that argue with great conviction that the megacorporation, and the demands of international trade are not connected in a one-to-one fashion, or which suggest, again with substantive forcefulness, that the demands of international competition need not produce domestic concentration. One of the best of these analyses is by R.E. Caves, M.E. Porter, A.M. Spence (*et. al.*), *Competition in the Open Economy: A Model Applied to Canada* (Harvard University Press, 1980). I am not suggesting that such an arrangement is theoretically impossible, or that it would, if implemented, not provide us with the best possible world. My point, simply, is this—the forces of *real politics and real economics* make it virtually impossible to engineer, especially in the Canadian context, such a refusion (all other things remaining equal).

23. Business Council on National Issues, *A Report of the Task Force on Competition Policy* (B.C.N.I., 1981). For a critique of the B.C.N.I. position, see W.T. Stanbury, "The B.C.N.I. Study on Competition Policy: A Review," *Canadian Competition Policy Record,* September, 1981, pp. 15-28.

24. For an analysis of this opposition in the Canadian context, see I. Brecher's recent study, *Canada's Competition Policy Revisited: Some New Thoughts on an Old Story* (The Institute for Research on Public Policy, 1981). Advocating a major reform

of Canadian competition laws, Brecher identifies the corporate community as one of the mainline opponents of such reforms. Or as he puts it, "I found, like others before me, that Canada's big business community bitterly opposed competition reform because it perceived a change in the status quo to be in sharp conflict with its own private interest. . . . Such pressure goes a long way to explain the ultimate negative outcome. . . . But misunderstanding and ignorance. . . . also provide an important part of the total explanation for failure. . . . Some responsibility for the 'knowledge gap' rests, no doubt, with business people who know better but were enormously reluctant to enlighten their colleagues. . . . There was more, however—a highly critical and incredibly undereducated daily and financial press; an only marginally helpful Canadian academic community;. . . and perhaps most vital, a succession of federal Cabinets and top ranking public servants that suffered from, and contributed to, the intellectual fog surrounding competition reform" (pp. 53-54).

25. G.C. Lodge, "Business and the Changing Society," *Harvard Business Review,* March-April, 1974, p. 66.

26. See G. Gilder, *Wealth and Poverty, op. cit.,* pp. 206-216.

27. R. Heilbroner, *Business Civilization in Decline* (W.W. Norton, 1976), pp. 75-76.

28. For one such effort, see E. Mansfield, "Technology and Productivity in the U.S." in M. Feldstein (ed.), *The American Economy in Transition* (The University of Chicago Press, 1980), pp. 563-616.

29. See R. Amara, *The Future of Management: Ten Shapers of Management in the '80s* (Institute for the Future, 1980), p. 6.

30. *Work in America: Report of the Special Task Force to the Secretary of Health, Education and Welfare* (Massachusetts Institute of Technology Press, 1972), p. 13.

31. R.M. Bird, "The Growth of the Public Service in Canada" in D.K. Foot (ed.), *Public Employment and Compensation in Canada: Myths and Realities* (Institute for Research on Public Policy, 1978), p. 32.

32. G. Reuber, "The Role and Size of Government in the Post-Control Period," *Canada's Political Economy* (McGraw-Hill Ryerson, 1980), p. 33.

33. G. Doern, "Regulatory Processes and Regulatory Agencies" in G. Doern and P. Aucoin (eds.), *Public Policy in Canada* (Macmillan, 1979), p. 158.

34. The Economic Council of Canada, *Reforming Regulation* (Economic Council of Canada, 1981).

35. A.M. Maslove, "The Other Side of Public Spending: Tax Expenditures in Canada" in G. Doern and P. Aucoin, *op. cit.,* p. 149. See, also, R.S. Smith, *Tax Expenditures: An Examination of Tax Incentives and Tax Preferences in the Canadian Federal Income Tax System* (Canadian Tax Foundation, 1979); and S. Surrey, *Pathways to Tax Reform: The Concept of Tax Expenditures* (Harvard University Press, 1973).

36. A.M. Maslove, *op. cit.,* p. 154. We can dismiss one causal explanation of expenditures growth in this area that is the favorite argument of neo-conservative writers. These writers have suggested that it is the excessive demand for equality of the economically disenfranchised that has precipitated the massive growth in this sector during the past few decades. Canadian tax expenditure figures do not support this argument. As Maslove and others have shown, "While it does not appear that any strong trends in growth rates by income group exist, there is a clear distributive pattern in favour of higher income groups. Beginning from about $3,000, as annual total income rises, tax expenditures as a percentage of income steadily increase. In dollar terms, in 1976 the average tax expenditure received by a taxpayer reporting income under $5,000 was $75, between $15,000 and $20,000 income it was $694, and for those reporting more than $50,000 of income, it was $6,613" (p. 154-155).

37. For a good discussion, see J. Gillies, *op. cit.*

38. J.K. Brown, *This Business of Issues: Coping With the Company's Environment* (Research Report 758, The Conference Board, 1979), p. 3.

3
The Dynamics of Expanding State Intervention and Public Policy

During the nineteenth century, a salient feature of nearly every aspect of life was the growing presence of business; in the twentieth century, it is the increasing prominence of the State.... The conflict between private and public decision-making is one of the most difficult problems that a market society must face.... Few political issues will be of greater importance for our standard of living in the years ahead.

—Robert Heilbroner

Today government is all-pervasive. It deals with so many facets of our life that regulatory overkill has become a leading political issue.... In fact, the growth of government involvement in business may some day eliminate the free enterprise market economy in the United States.... Corporations have a primary responsibility to fight in the political wars to prevent this fate for United States business.

—L. William Seidman

THE IDEOLOGICAL BOUNDARIES OF THE DEBATE OVER GOVERNMENTAL GROWTH

The substantial growth of government in Western market economies, especially since the end of World War II, has been widely documented.[1] The challenge now is to develop strategies that can reduce both the negative economic impacts of this phenomenon and the propensity of the state to overfeed itself with increasingly large slices of the national economic pie. The single most important step in the development of such strategies is the correct diagnosis of the causes of governmental growth.

The vast majority of studies on governmental growth dispense with causal analysis after a few short cursory remarks. The impression conveyed is that the causes of governmental growth have long been understood, that what is needed rather is an effective action plan on how to stop it. The thesis of this chapter is quite the reverse. Surveys of various action plans worked out by business and government to control governmental growth lead to the conclusion that the architects of these plans have seriously misdiagnosed the causes of the disease they're trying to cure. Without proper diagnosis, the chances are slim for effective remedies. This chapter, then, is an attempt to provide a new diagnostic foundation for effective public affairs action to subdue the overweening appetite of government itself, and to reduce the paralysing effects of this growth on business.

As the comments of L. William Seidman indicate (Seidman, by the way, served as Assistant for Economic Affairs to former President Gerald Ford and was Executive Director of the Economic Policy Board between 1974 and 1977), the growth of government is perceived by a large number of people as an extremely serious challenge to our way of life.[2] Indeed, it is often described as a lethal disease that could eventually destroy the whole social and economic fabric of Western liberal democracies.[3]

One of the leading proponents of this viewpoint is Milton Friedman, who argues that the expansion of governments into traditionally private societal domains has two consequences, "The first is financial crisis...the second [is] loss of liberty and freedom."[4] Pointing to the serious socio-economic problems of New York City, Chile and the United Kingdom, Friedman tells us that the problems of those communities are the necessary products of a long term and misdirected governmental fetish with social-welfare maximization. As far as Britain's future prospects are concerned—and the urban riots during the summer of 1981 no doubt strengthened his case in some circles[5]—Friedman claims that *because of* Britain's high level of public expenditures (according to him total public expenditure in Britain comprises 60 percent of GNP), "...the odds are at least 50-50 that within the next five years British freedom and democracy, as we have seen it, will be destroyed."[6]

Apart from the central argument that governmental growth during the past two decades or so has been socially more costly than beneficial, the neo-conservative opponents of governmental growth share another important debating point: The fundamental *cause* of governmental growth resides in the shifting and short-sighted *values* of citizens in post-industrial societies.[7] According to *Business Week,* for example, it is especially the growing public demand for *economic equality* that serves as "...the greatest single force changing and expanding the role of the federal government in the United States today."[8] To the late Harry G. Johnson, celebrated for his writings on economics, this trend in popular attitudes towards increasing egalitarianism is "...a naive and basically infantile anthropomorphism."[9]

The source of this shift in public attitudes, for many neo-conservatives, is found within the rising influence of a "new class" or "strategic elite" of anti-establishment opinion leaders in most industrially advanced Western societies—specifically, intellectuals, artists, journalists and the leaders of various consumer advocacy groups.[10]

It follows from this that for many neo-conservatives, progress is only possible by recapturing and reshaping the opinion leading centres of our society, rebuilding public confidence in business, and convincing significant segments of the voting public about the hazards of expanding governments. In short, since governmental growth is the product of misguided and elite manufactured ideology, a reduction in the influence and voice of this elite will naturally enough reduce the scope of government.

How accurate an image is this of the causes of expanding public expenditures? And what are the prospects for its subsequent strategy? In the first instance, the above mentioned views about the weight and direction of opinion leading elite influence are either undocumented or are manifestly false. For example, a recent survey of academic opinion vis-à-vis business and the market system in the United States showed that an overwhelming majority—81 percent—of American professors endorse the free-enterprise ideology.[11] The existence of a widespread basis of public support for the free enterprise system has also been documented by the opinion surveys of Yankelovich and others,[12] thereby casting serious doubt on the idea that a massive intelligentsia led and anti free-enterprise shift has taken hold of American public opinion.

Exaggerated claims concerning the depth and direction of the change in public opinion are not the only analytical flaws of the neo-conservative reaction. The major weakness of this approach is that it refuses to acknowledge the role—one way or another—of any other causal force behind state expansion than that of the ideology of misguided self-interest. No serious effort is directed towards discovering or refuting deeper socio-economic forces that may have caused its perceived ideological shift. There is no effort to test the effects of a wide range of environmental forces that, *together with changing values,* could have combined to pull governments (though not necessarily in the correct way) into increasingly expansionist postures. These shortcomings will ensure that the above outlined neo-conservative strategy will not be able to demonstrate anything else than short lived successes. A battle will certainly be won here and there, but the war will be lost.

Friedmanites are not alone in arguing that expanded state intervention is a serious threat to the long term viability of capitalism. This view is also endorsed by most neo-Marxist political economists, albeit with diametrically opposed motives and analytical rationales.[13]

Scholars working within the logic of neo-Marxist political-economy concede that expanded state expenditures, and the general thrust of Keynesian economics, was indeed the only possible short term *liberal, demo-cratic* defense against mature capitalism's inevitable propensity to stagnate. For Marxists, the growth of state intervention is *objectively necessi-tated* by capitalism's diminishing growth rates of aggregate demand, productivity, profits and employment. They add that as capitalism becomes increasingly sluggish, expanded state intervention becomes the only route towards the short term structural revitalization demanded of those econo-mies.[14]

It is important to underscore that for Marxists or neo-Marxists, the objec-tive necessitated growth of state intervention is construed as a *strictly short term remedy*. Though this side of their argument is frequently overlooked by their opponents, neo-Marxists have always believed that expanded state intervention into market economies is, *in the long run,* a highly irrational or contradictory policy measure. Or, as Cy Gonick put it, "The solution to avoiding the Great Depression has helped produce the Great Stagflation."[15]

The neo-Marxist reasoning here is strikingly *similar* to that of main-stream neo-conservatism. Both ideologies believe that expanded state intervention destroys the natural "anti-bodies" protecting the market econ-omy against inefficiency and productivity decline. While for neo-Marxists, the capitalist economic base is quite capable of generating its own contradictions (e.g. monopolistic or oligopolistic production), the perma-nent injection of state expenditures as a corrective device merely accelerates the *long run* collapse of the system. They tell us that as a consequence of expanding state expenditures and intervention, capitalism becomes increasingly flabby and less able to renew itself,[16] and will finally collapse, only to be replaced by an entirely new political-economic configuration called socialism.

The following passage from James O'Connor is an excellent summary of the neo-Marxist position. It is also strikingly similar to the language used by Friedman and his followers:

> The accumulation of social capital and social expenses is a contradictory process which creates tendencies toward economic, social and political crisis.... Because [it] occurs within a political framework, there is a great deal of waste, duplication and overlapping of State projects and services. [In short]...it is a highly irrational process from the standpoint of administrative coherence, fiscal stability and potentially profitable primal accumulation.[17]

One of the essential differences between neo-conservatives and neo-Marxists regarding the question of governmental growth is this: While neo-conservatives perceive governmental growth as a severe threat to capital-ism's survival, they are convinced that this threat can be checked. The reason why governmental growth can, and indeed must be checked, we are told, is because it is a *subjective phenomenon,* precipitated quite simply by the rise of an ill-advised "adversary culture."[18]

Neo-Marxists, agreeing, as we have seen, that the growth of government is a fundamental threat to the survival of capitalism, argue however, that this process can *not* be checked because it is the product of *objective necessities,* i.e., it is derived from the essential dynamics of capitalist political-economic development. Thus while neo-conservatives lament the growth of state intervention and its eventual consequences, neo-Marxists see good cause for rejoicing. For the latter, the universe is clearly unfolding as it should.

What position is taken on the question of governmental growth by those who fall into neither the neo-conservative nor the neo-Marxist camp? The "centre,"[19] put simply, is ripe for new ideas. While neo-conservatives and neo-Marxists have quickly picked up those convenient pieces of the shattered post-Keynesian economic puzzle that fit their preconceived notions, and have quickly tidied up their philosophical backyards, the rest of the economic world is still more or less in disarray.

Notwithstanding its current disarray, the centre is, in my view, the liveliest and likeliest forum for the emergence of a new and feasible alternative. The view from the centre of these two ideological extremes suggests, that while indeed there may be some accidental or "slippery slope" reasons for *some* of the growth of government, in the main this phenomenon was produced by a largely unavoidable and interdependent series of social, economic, technological and political circumstances.[20] This in no way implies that our political leaders are like so many billiard balls shot into different pockets of public spending by various environmental cues. Political leadership, party ideology, social values and culture are indeed very important forces accounting for larger or smaller displacements in the direction of expanded state intervention.

There is no desire here to suggest that one should passively accept a 40 percent public expenditure share of GNP, or that we should consider every single new bureaucratic regulation as inevitable. In short, *if business wants to ensure its future survival and that of the market economy, it must become both more sensitive and action-oriented to the dynamics of those critical socio-economic and political forces that combine to influence the patterns of public spending and of state intervention into corporate domains.*

The challenge for both business and society lies not in the rapid erection of an arbitrary road block in the path of expansionist governments, or in rolling back the aggregate level of current public spending as such by, say, a constitutional amendment. The challenge of the '80s and beyond is to ensure that whenever governments expand *or* restrict their spheres of activity, they should do so only *after* a full environmental impact assessment of those choices has demonstrated that the public well-being will benefit, rather than suffer, from those decisions. Corporate leaders should have the right, along with others, to participate in these policy decisions. It follows then that the challenge is to engineer a fundamental reform of those mechanisms through which our political systems identify, select and transform demands for social action. This issue should be placed at the centre of public debate and scrutiny. Any effort that seeks to misdirect or hinder this critical re-assessment of government's changing role is, in the final analysis, one of the most serious barriers to responsible political involvement on the part of corporate executives and to our long term economic revival.

THE STIMULANTS OF GOVERNMENTAL GROWTH

What then *are* the real sources of governmental growth in our society?

Intensive surveys of the literature have led to this first conclusion: We are still far from possessing a general theory of this phenomenon. All that we have at this point is a vast range of sociological, economic and political rationalizations of some highly complex processes that have contributed individually and in combination to the ebb and flow of state intervention.

While the creation of a general theory is therefore out of reach at this time, there is a strong second best option. Without giving up on the ultimate intellectual task of constructing a general theory of governmental growth, our understanding of this area can still be advanced by cataloguing and monitoring the complex interplay of those *objective forces* that have demanded an increasingly interventionist governmental presence during the past few decades.

The list of the objective forces demanding governmental growth presented below is not exhaustive. Daniel Tarschys, also claiming to provide only a partial catalogue of the causes of governmental growth, has stated, for example, that there are at least seventy-five different processes or events that advance increases in collective expenditures.[21]

While this section focuses on the demands for state intervention, it must be clearly understood that these demands and the state's reactions to them are not related in the form of a simple S-R (stimulus–response) paradigm.[22] The demands—external or internal—for governmental growth are mediated by a whole range of intervening variables *before* they are transformed by political systems into policy programmes. Thus, very significant differences in policy responses can occur not only between different political systems, but even in the life-time of the same political system, as far as the transformation of demands for governmental growth is concerned.[23]

The demands for governmental growth fall into two general categories: 1) socio-economic demands and 2) political-ideological demands.[24] These two general categories are not put forward as primary-secondary forces. The compartmentalization is merely an analytical device and does not suggest that the elements of one group are necessarily more influential than those of the others. The two categories are indeed highly intertwined elements of the same system.

SOCIO-ECONOMIC STIMULANTS

Rising GNP Per Capita

This is one of the earliest causal explanations for the expansion of government. Frequently described as "Wagner's Law of the Increasing Extension of State Activity,"[25] rising per capita GNP is reputed to accelerate the growth of government because of its high propensity to produce (i)**income elastic demands** on the part of consumers. Putting it in less technical terms, this theory suggests that once basic human economic needs for food, shelter and clothing have been satisfied and people move on to higher levels of personal affluence, a whole new range of consumer demands will come to the forefront which presumably only government can satisfy (e.g., demands for more and better education, improved cultural facilities, greater justice, more and better health services and parks, etc.). The nature of many of these "goods and services" is such that they are to be supplied primarily through public rather than private spending. In short, rising GNP per capita will exercise, *for a certain period,* a powerful pull on governments in the direction of increased expenditures because it creates income elastic demands on the part of citizens.[26]

(ii) The demands for governmental growth arising out of expanding GNP per capita can be accelerated by additional and related conditions. One of these can be described as **income elastic attitudes towards taxation.**

This theory simply refers to the idea that "When subsistence needs have been satisfied, citizens are more likely to part with their surplus resources. The government of an advanced society would then be in a better position than that of a poor nation to raise money for public programmes."[27] (Again, the role of intervening variables, or the concept of "threshold" to toleration should not be ignored.)

(iii) The contribution of the **progressive income tax** to the growth of government is similar in that it automatically ensures that as the GNP rises, the revenue base of government will expand at a faster rate than the revenue base of most private income earners.

(iv) The revenue bases of governments in Canada and elsewhere are also profoundly affected by **transformations in economic structures**—such as the rise of foreign trade, the rise of urban commerce, the expansion of economic exchange—and by the escalation in consumption of those retail goods that are subject to the *sales tax*. These transformations provide governments with a wider range of taxing opportunities, or "tax handles," and also produce an accelerated increase in governmental revenues.

(v) If the above processes unfold in a period of **inflation,** the government's share of national income can be even more substantially accelerated. Douglas Auld points out, "As individuals move into higher tax brackets because their money-incomes increase, government can take a larger share as taxes. Because inflation causes people to move into higher tax brackets more quickly, it speeds the growth in government's share. The steady growth of personal income that has occurred over the past 25 years provides a striking example of the effects of this structure in action."[28]

Industrialization

By industrialization, I refer to a process through which first of all, enterprise is separated from the family; secondly, large scale industry becomes an increasingly important form of societal production; and finally, a complex technological division of labour is formed to promote the efficient evolution of this process.[29]

(vi) One of the leading stimulants of governmental growth which is a direct consequence of industrialization is **urbanization.** Urbanization has long been recognized as a process which, by itself, inflates the size and scope of government.[30] The shift of large numbers of people away from the countryside into densely populated urban centres not only increases the relative costs of maintaining services in the diminishing rural population centres, but radically increases urban public sector expenses for such new demands as water supply, sewage systems, garbage disposal, fire and police protection, road and transportation services, and recreational space. It is by no means a coincidence that of the three tiers of government—federal, provincial and municipal—the most rapid public expenditure growth has been at the municipal or local level. (I include here provincial or state transfers to municipalities.)

(vii) The rapid shift of rural populations into an urban setting, the growth of geographic mobility and the **breakdown of the extended family** model (with its built-in tension management mechanisms) has also produced a range of new social problems (crime, alcoholism, juvenile delinquency, divorce, alienation, etc.) that the state is called upon to mediate.

(viii) The separation of enterprise from family and the establishment of large industrial concerns on the basis of both inter-firm and intra-firm **divisions of labour** also accelerates demand for governmental growth. The most obvious examples here are the increasing state-born costs of pro- grammes to cut down on labour market rigidities, to finance specialized professional education and to protect against widespread dislocation that may flow from the failure of a single sub-systemic element. (Unemploy- ment insurance schemes and manpower training programmes are two examples of such defensive mechanisms.)

In conclusion then, the process of industrialization requires the estab- lishment of a complex new infrastructure so as to sustain and enhance itself. Most of the responsibility for this emerging infrastructure is in the hands of public sector suppliers. Or, to put it another way, the unwilling- ness of the private sector to shoulder the excessive and unprofitable burden of putting into place those key services that are essential to sustain the industrialization process, created a vast opening for public sector growth.

Technological Change

Technological change—especially when it unfolds rapidly—is another leading stimulant of governmental growth. As in the previous cases, techno- logically stimulated demands for governmental growth are highly diverse and will stimulate state expansion along a number of different points.

(ix) For example, the introduction of *new technological inventions* such as the automobile, the airplane or various chemical and manufacturing pro- cesses have all sharply increased the agenda and content of state action. Included here are the state-born costs of road construction and mainte- nance, the cost of airports,[31] traffic regulations, safety standards, and mea- sures to guard against some of the harmful **social, physical or envi- ronmental side effects** of new technology.

(x) In increasingly frequent cases, many of the new **technological break-throughs** themselves have become so **costly** to attain that only sustained public financing can lead to their achievement (e.g. resources development, space and communications research, nuclear and solid waste management).

(xi) In an economy such as Canada's, where multinational penetration and foreign ownership is particularly acute, the demands for active state participation in the generation of new technology are especially strong. The perceived reason for this is that parent companies usually retain the functions of developing *innovative technology* for themselves and allow, for the most part, only for the generation of *adaptive technology* in their branchplants. Thus the **branchplant economy** can indeed become a backwater of high technology, from which one of the logical escape routes is significant state support for *private* research and development.[32] (Canada, not coincidentally, has the most favourable tax write-off schemes for private research and development in the world.)

(xii) Technological innovation and especially the introduction of **automation** and robotics can also expand the size of government because frequently it is only through governmental action that newly released and idle manpower can be either protected or retrained.

(xiii) Technological advances in the area of **communications, travel and educational diffusion** have also had a significant impact on the growth of government simply because they increase public awareness about the possibilities of increased socio-economic equality. Or as Daniel Tarschys points out, "The revolution in social communications, particularly the coming of television, has led to increased awareness of the standard of living enjoyed by other segments of society and even in other parts of the world. As a consequence, expectations and pretensions mount and people get increasingly sensitive to injustices in the distribution of public goods. Through information about services provided in other political units, the citizens and their representatives also know more about what there is to get and can thus better articulate and communicate their views."[33]

(xiv) Technology can also increase the size of government, as it were, from the inside. The advancement of professionalism and technological know-how contributes to the development of a better educated, and technically more sophisticated bureaucracy. This not only increases the personal **costs of new bureaucracy** but ensures that this more "sophisticated" apparatus will more thoroughly penetrate its environment.

In conclusion, these various strands of the technological arena constitute, along with other demands, a powerful force for governmental growth.

Market Extension and the Growth of Global Economic Interdependence

(xv) As domestic markets are saturated by suppliers and **foreign trade** becomes an increasingly important contributor to national economic development, governments experience powerful demands to provide not only financial incentives but also financial and regulatory guarantees so as to maintain the stability of this process—if only because dislocations could produce very damaging consequences.

(xvi) The above mentioned process is itself accelerated in the case of *dependent economies.* If national economic well-being is increasingly dependent upon the uncontrollable and unforeseen actions of **foreign economic players,** usually government-dominated players, there is a natural propensity for a dependent economy to institutionalize certain structural guarantees so as to diminish the risks of externally imposed and arbitrary economic processes. Canada is, of course, a good example of such a dependent economy. (Again, the question of how extensively this dependency translates itself into expanded state intervention is only answerable through the analysis of a wide range of intervening variables.)

Economic Stagflation, Market Failures and the Growth of Oligopolistic Production

Under this heading, we find both the Keynesian and the neo-Marxist explanation for increasing state intervention.

(xvii) The Keynesian position may be summarized first. In his *General Theory*,[34] Keynes convincingly buried Say's Law[35]—the central pillar of classical economics dating back to 1803. Say argued, and his view reigned dominant for over a century, that consumers have an infinite desire for and an infinite ability to purchase commodities. Keynes argued, and history demonstrates, that as capitalism moves towards its latter stages of development, its **propensity for continuous inducements of investment declines.** As a consequence, the system is unable to consistently maintain full employment and will demand, therefore, periodic injections of state expenditures to help it ride over the increasingly frequent rough roads that lie ahead.

Keynes' *General Theory* became the central pillar of capitalist economic revival following the Great Depression, and it retained that dominant and unquestioned position until relatively recently.

(xviii) Neo-Marxists partly endorse the Keynesian diagnosis. Indeed, they predate by many decades the Keynesian position concerning the inevitable propensity of capitalism to stagnate. They also argue that economic stagnation can be rectified, on the short term, by increased state expenditures, among other factors. Aside from these two points, neo-Marxists disagree profoundly with just about everything that Keynesian economics proposes.

The neo-Marxist explanation of the *causes* and the *nature* of capitalist economic stagnation differs sharply from the Keynesian approach. The source of the stagnation for neo-Marxists resides in capitalism's drift towards increasing concentration and monopoly, and in the phenomenon of **falling rates of profit**.[36]

For neo-Marxists, the stagnation of capitalism is not a cyclical phenomenon which can be regularly corrected by state spending. They view the stagnation as a perpetually downward slide towards eventual capitalist collapse. It is the increasingly frequent and deepening economic crisis of private accumulation, coupled with an increasingly aggressive or demanding working class, that draws the "relatively autonomous"[37] state into an interventionist posture—first to help out financially in the process of private accumulation, and second to defuse or limit the growing hostility of the proletariat by means of various state financed inducements.

For Marxists, this objectively determined expansion of state intervention— designed to reduce tensions arising from the crisis of accumulation and legitimacy—is the final nail, as O'Connor and others tell us, in the coffin of capitalism. In a truly dialectic fashion, today's solution becomes tomorrow's problem. For a while, the rise in social accumulation is as necessary as was, for example, the rise to prominence of the bourgeois class within the bosom of the feudal system. In the relentless march of humanity, both of those trends constituted, at one time, a step forward. In the long run, however, Marxists argue that these steps become footprints from the past.

Whether one follows a Keynesian position, or various neo-Marxist perspectives, it is indisputable that a slowdown *has* taken place, especially in productivity growth, in all Western economies.[38] The negative effects of this cumulative downturn exercise a powerful pull, once again, on the state to intervene so as to decrease the momentum of this downward slide. (It is, of course, an entirely different question whether the actions of the state, thus taken, diminish or exacerbate the problem.)

Under the general heading of "market failures," there are some additional processes that have accelerated the growth of government during the past few decades.

(xix) While neo-Marxists tend to emphasize the expansion of monopolies and non-competitive markets as important causes of governmental growth, the reverse process also stimulates expanding state intervention. Studies have shown that **excessive competition** often produces a whole range of anomalies (e.g. reduced concern by producers for quality or safety standards, irregularities in compensation for labour, etc.) which in turn sets off demands for external monitoring and control of standards.[39]

(xx) The **growth of externalities** is another motivator of governmental expansion. (The term externalities as earlier described refers to various costs falling on society from the private production and distribution of goods and services.) With the expansion of capitalism, and more specifically, industrial and technological change, externalities increase. This particular form of market failure also acts as a powerful magnet pulling for more and more imposition of corrective measures by the state.[40]

(xxi) Another example of market failure is the breakneck **depletion of non-renewable resources**. Governments are increasingly called upon to intervene in the processes of non-renewable resource management so as to prevent the emergency of a social disaster—or "the tragedy of the commons."[41]

In conclusion, capitalism's propensity towards declining productivity growth, the growth of concentration of capital and oligopolies, and other "market-failures" have together acted as important stimulants of state expansion during the past few decades.

Demographics and Changes in the Labour Force

Two important demographic factors have stimulated the growth of government during the past decades. These are aging and the post-war baby-boom.

(xxii) Longer life expectancy has steadily increased the ratio of non-working to working members of society. The **increase in the relative proportion of pensioners** in our society has been significant and will become dramatic in the future through the combined effects of increased life expectancy, early retirement (if it persists), the maturing of the baby-boom generation and declining birth rates. Whereas, today, the ratio of active workers to retired citizens is six to one, this figure promises to be three to one by the year 2030.[42]

This figure points to an increasingly narrow base of income earners who are going to be called upon to support, *via rising taxes,* the growing numbers of non-income earners. It also promises to bring on a growing wave of new demands on the health care industry, which again is, for the most part, a state-financed concern.

(xxiii) Developments at the other end of the population pyramid, especially the phenomenon of the **post-war baby-boom,** have also accelerated the growth of government by creating increased demands, first in the area of expanded child care services and public education. Later, as this pocket of the population moved into the job market, it set off pressures for increased job training expenditure and unemployment payments. While this force has largely spent itself, it promises to re-emerge, as suggested above, in the form of a "senior-boom" with similar consequences for state expenditures.

(xxiv) Changes in the composition of the labour force, especially the **increasing proportion of female income-earners,** have also exerted and continue to exert demands on state expenditures. As more and more women move into the labour force in North America, they increase demands for expenditures on some publicly financed programmes, such as child care. This shift also exerts pressures on the labour market itself and *can,* along with a number of other factors, contribute to rising unemployment. This increases the level of state expenditures for unemployment insurance payments and job creation programmes. (None of this suggests that working women should shoulder the blame for currently high levels of unemployment and that therefore, women should be deterred via public policy from entering the labour force.)

In conclusion, population growth, demographics and changes in the composition of the labour force are also significant stimulants of extended state activity.

The Relative Price Effect

(xxv) The growth of government has also been pushed forward by the **relatively faster rise of prices in the public sector** than in the private sector. Because public sector goods are produced by monopolistic suppliers, pressures for productivity gains are lower than in the private sector. This lower pressure to maximize productivity produces faster price escalations in the public sector than in the private sector (monopolistic production has the same upward bias on prices in the private sector). Douglas Auld points to yet another source of the differential in public as opposed to private sector productivity gains, by observing that, "It is harder to improve the productivity of the public sector than that of the private sector because labour-saving capital equipment can be applied more easily to a larger proportion of activity in the latter than the former. Two large areas of government spending—health and education—are particularly unsuited to productivity increases."[43]

Situational Forces Affecting Governmental Growth in Canada

We have spoken earlier of such situational forces as economic dependency and multinational penetration that escalate demands for increased state intervention. We can now add to these "situational forces" three additional situations that are peculiar to Canada, and which have also contributed to the growth of the Canadian state: namely, geography, population density and distribution, and economic structure.

(xxvi) The harshness of **Canada's "Northern Frontier"** economy, (xxvii) the vast distances between markets and **poor economies of scale,** and (xxviii) an unusually one-sided **reliance on staples** and hard-to-get natural resources have all demanded a much more active economic role for the Canadian state than is the case in other OECD countries. These situational factors are well known, and their roots in Canada reach back to the time of Confederation and to John A. Macdonald's "National Policy."[44]

These situational factors, together with the other socio-economic forces discussed above, add up to a powerful constellation of demands for governmental growth. One can debate, indeed *must* debate, whether the extent of governmental reaction or its specific forms are proper or not. However, the fact cannot be dismissed that it is *these* socio-economic forces that have propelled governments in the direction of increasing intervention into the private sector.

POLITICAL-IDEOLOGICAL STIMULANTS

As indicated earlier in this study, political–ideological stimulants are not secondary in importance to socio-economic realities. In fact, political and socio-economic forces are closely intertwined, each of them playing a more or less equal role as propellants of governmental growth.

Democracy

(xxix) Of the political–ideological stimulants of governmental growth, democracy and the **widening of popular participation** in political decision-making stands as the most obvious causative factor.

(xxix) One of the earliest advocates of the causal connection between democracy and expanding government was the Italian economist, Francesco S. Nitti.[45] Nitti and some of his followers have argued that if more people are allowed to participate in the selection of government policies, fewer voters will perceive the financing of those policies as a personal economic loss. In other words, *up to a point,* participatory democracy not only contributes to an escalation of demands for state action, but also increases toleration of higher taxes.[46]

(xxx) Another approach to this question is by injecting the variable of **income differentials** into the equation of democracy-led governmental growth. Allan H. Meltzer and Scott F. Richard, for example, have argued persuasively that "Government grows when the franchise is extended to include more voters below the median income.... A voter need only choose the candidate who promises net benefits; majority rule does the rest. ... Although large government poses a threat to many of our freedoms, government grows in every society where the majority remains free to express its will."[47]

(xxxi) The emergence of **egalitarianism** during the past couple of centuries, and its accelerated infusion into the political process during the past few decades is undoubtedly part of the process of government growth and is related to income differentials.[48] It is a truism that the market mechanism is insensitive to the desires and needs of those who are poor. The more wealth one has, the more attentive will the market be to one's desires and personal goals. Thus the market mechanism, as a system responding to public demands and providing rewards, is *inherently loaded* in favour of those members of the public who are the most affluent. *Only* governmental intervention and regulation can correct this one-sided bias of the market system and thereby provide the *equality of opportunity* that all citizens in a democratic order demand.

This external state intervention, propelled by egalitarianism, undoubtedly has had a disruptive impact on the workings and efficiency of the market system. For those who believe that society should live by efficiency alone, the intervention is clearly lamentable.[49] For those who are committed to a more balanced social diet than just efficiency, governmental intervention to provide equality of opportunity is indeed the height of good nutrition.[50]

None of the above is intended to suggest that every increase in governmental intervention takes us one step further towards equality of opportunity, or that every regulatory instrument is for the better. On the contrary, the evidence suggests that while in many cases the *motivation* behind a particular instance of state expenditure rise may indeed be the desire to reduce market imposed social inequalities, the actual policy instrument used does nothing of the kind, and in fact simply retards opportunities to increase economic efficiency.[51]

The trade-off between equality and efficiency, public and private choice, is clearly critical for all societies. The extreme emphasis of one or the other could have a negative effect on both at once. As Arthur Okun observes, "Measures that might soak the rich so much as to destroy investment and hence impair the quality and quantity of jobs for the poor could worsen both efficiency and equality."[52]

In short, while the wisdom of a particular equilibrium arrangement between equality and efficiency can certainly be debated, one cannot argue against the necessity of equal opportunities being injected *by the state* into the mainstream of the market system. This politically motivated necessity undoubtedly contributes to governmental growth.

As indicated earlier, at this point the neo-conservative approach branches out—or more aptly, goes out on a limb—by arguing that it is the excessive demand for entitlements of a powerful new bloc of voters, urged on by a misguided elite of opinion leaders, that is the source of *all* our problems with big government. As indicated throughout this chapter, the stimulants of governmental growth emerge from many corners, including the sheer existence of democracy. While some anomalies in the democratic process itself—for example the frequently contradictory nature of public demands[53]—no doubt contribute to the problem, this is by no means the most significant or exclusive reason why governments have expanded.

(xxxii) The degree of **political competition in a democratic system can also contribute to the growth of government.** If the route towards political office is strewn with numerous obstacles (e.g. many competing parties, a highly organized system of competing pressure groups, minority governments, frequent elections, etc.), these accelerate tendencies on the part of politicians to generate more public goods as a means of gaining voter support.[54]

(xxxiii) Last, but not least, the **widening of political legitimacy** can also fuel the growth of government by providing a more tolerant base (or to use David Easton's terms, wider support channels)[55] for governments as they seek to transform environmental (or internal) demands for expanded state intervention. As Daniel Tarschys points out in this connection, the decline of legitimacy can have the opposite effect:

> Where citizens believe, rightly or wrongly, that there is a great deal of corruption and inefficiency in government operations, they will hardly be enthusiastic taxpayers.... Relative mistrust of politicians and bureaucrats appears to be a pertinent variable when it comes to explaining the level of public spending in different political systems.[56]

Recent decline in public confidence in governments is an important factor to consider as far as future trends in governmental intervention in the United States and Canada are concerned.

Federalism

Federalism is a highly ingenious political device for managing tensions arising from regional and ethnic differentials in a society (some think otherwise). From the point of public expenditures, it can be a costly instrument.

While the data on public expenditures growth in federal as opposed to unitary systems is mixed, there is evidence suggesting that if (xxxiv) the **lines of jurisdiction** between the political units are particularly *blurred* (as is the case in Canada) or if (xxxv) the **competition between political units** is particularly strong (as is the case in Canada), duplication and waste will follow, thereby increasing the aggregate of governmental expenditures.

The fall-out costs of overlapping jurisdictions and excessive political competition are not simply those associated with the maintenance of overlapping bureaucracies (e.g. in agriculture, industry, trade and commerce, immigration, health and welfare, energy and resources, etc.). More importantly, the duplication of bureaucratic functions and the deep-seated political rivalries between centre and periphery are the sources, oftentimes, of highly contradictory government programmes that accentuate the problems confronting it. Jurisdictional quarrels leave many of our political-economic problems unresolved for long stretches of time (the prolonged wrangle over energy policy is a good case in point) thereby increasing economic uncertainties and opening the door to other rounds of contradictory governmental actions.

It should be strongly underscored here, to avoid misinterpretation in the "Great Canadian National Unity Debate," that it is not the *mechanism* of federalism itself that is the principal lever of governmental growth. Rather, it is the poor *tuning* of the federal machine that plays a decisive role. Clearly, if the gears of federalism are worn out and slippery, and if they grate against each other, this will fuel the consumption of governmental expenditures.

Very few citizens would not agree that their federal system is badly in need of a major overhaul. While the need for this overhaul expresses itself not only from economic, but also political and cultural quarters, the correlation between governmental expenditure growth and badly tuned federalism should be more frequently emphasized. *Perhaps if citizens and corporations realized that their higher taxes may be due in part to the anomalies of federalism, they would be less inclined to view constitutional reform as a sterile exercise divorced from their immediate economic concerns.*

The Dynamics of Bureaucracy and Governmental Budgeting

There are also a set of "laws" or characteristics peculiar to government organizations and government budgeting that, together, promote the relatively faster growth of expenditures in public as opposed to private administration.[57]

(xxxvi) One of these central characteristics frequently ignored, is that the public **budgetary process is essentially a political process** and will never be otherwise. While narrow technical cost/benefit considerations do play a role in the process, government budgets are not determined by these forces alone. The dominant force shaping government budgets everywhere is political expediency. The budget is, in effect, a government's response to competing (external and internal) political demands. Or, as Robert Lorch observes, "To a very large degree, when you talk about the budget process, you're talking about the whole political process.... The budget process largely determines who gets what; the dollar sign is a symbol of power.... Power may be divided among several competitors, each clinging to a piece of the decision-making machinery like a dog to a bone...(and) changes in the budgetary process result from changes in power structure."[58]

In short, because the budgetary process itself is particularly sensitive to escalating, and often contradictory, external political demands, and (xxxvii) because **bureaucratic power** itself frequently grows out of the barrel of a large budget, pressures to expand expenditures are stronger in the public sector than they are in the private sector. In the latter, considerations of economic costs/benefits and efficiency play a much more important role, and act as important dampeners of zealous spending.

There are additional factors inherent in the public budgetary process which make it **relatively easier to increase expenditures** in that sector as opposed to the private sector (xxxviii). Because profit is not their "bottom line," because they are monopolistic suppliers of public goods, because their *revenues* are only *marginally dependent on efficiency* and quality of output, and finally, because they have extremely *stable or secure revenue sources,* public agencies face substantially less pressure to keep the lid on costs than private sector firms. Attempts to eliminate this source of public sector budgetary growth by the application of standards developed in the private sector are fundamentally misplaced, and will *never* achieve their intended goal except to a limited extent. Again, as Robert Lorch points out, "Budgeting is at bottom, to repeat, a political process, and anyone who attempts reforms which do not comply with political reality has an uphill battle.... Many beautiful thoughts have been spun about how budgeting 'should be done' without adequate concern whether the idea could possibly work in political reality."[59]

(xxxix) The domination of **rule-fixed** rather than cost-fixed decisions is also an important political source of governmental growth. Federal grants-in-aid, or shared-cost programmes are particularly relevant here. In many cases, the open-ended nature of these programmes ensures that the provincial or state recipients need pay little attention to costs because these will be covered from the federal "rule-fixed" source. Or as Daniel Tarschys and others have documented, "...it can be safely claimed that this separation of fiscal and policy responsibility contributes to the willingness to spend at the regional and local levels."[60]

(xl) The idea of providing bureaucrats with **"tenure"** so as to ensure their political neutrality and to maintain their commitment to the maximization of the public good, rather than to that of their masters, dates back to at least the 18th century. The problem with this principle, which has become deeply entrenched in all Western bureaucracies, is that it contributes to governmental expenditure growth. Bureaucrats are seldom subject to the pressures of job termination, although the Reagan administration has offered a few examples. Even if a particular bureaucratic programme has outlived its usefulness and is terminated (this in itself is a great rarity), the functionaries employed by that programme are seldom released. Instead, these people are often reshuffled into newly created positions in other sectors of the civil service. This reshuffling of bureaucrats, this endless game of "musical chairs," is not without financial costs. In the final analysis, it constitutes a *financing of redundancy.* The added social expenditure is comprised of the salaries of redundant employees, and the costs of needless and wasteful programmes that are frequently set up simply to provide redundant functionaries with something to do.

(xli) The practices of **incremental budgeting and decision-making** are also contributors to the growth of government. As Charles Lindblom and others have argued,[61] incrementalism is the heart and soul of bureaucratic decision-making, and will probably remain so for a long time to come, in spite of efforts in other directions. Incrementalism is a favoured tool because it blends in well with the political realities of the budgetary process and because it is relatively easy to manage. It contributes to governmental expenditure growth, however, because it has an upward bias on spending. Last year's expenditures tend to serve as the base for next year's expenses, and as such, there is comparatively less effort put into monitoring and controlling committed programmes.

In conclusion, while it is certainly a gross exaggeration to assign *exclusive* blame for governmental growth to forces inherent to bureaucracies, it is undeniable that these forces indeed pull much more in the direction of expansion than contraction.

An Additional Political-Ideological Factor
That is Situational to Canada

In the Canadian context, the demands of (xlii) **"nation-building"** undoubtedly have exercised a powerful influence on state expenditures. If left to the forces of the market, natural patterns of cultural, economic and social interaction would have taken Canada into a north-south rather than east-west direction. Had Canadians allowed market forces to regulate these patterns of interaction, Canada, as we know it, would probably not exist today. A passive role by government would have long ago ensured Canada's disintegration.[62] The challenge in Canada is to improve the needed mechanisms of "nation-building" so that they will not only be of a defensive nature but will improve national economic welfare as well.

This argument is not intended as a blanket endorsement of all Canadian governmental policies aimed at "nation-building." The point made is that regulatory powers and expenditures have grown in Canada—for better or for worse—partly because the market system has proved incapable of dealing with the demands of "nation-building." While the choice of regulatory tools and the mix or level of expenditures is vigorously debated, the perceived necessity for emphatic regulatory response by government cannot be denied.

FUTURE TRENDS IN GOVERNMENTAL GROWTH: A CHECKLIST FOR CORPORATE ATTENTION

This chapter's preceding sections have examined a spectrum of technological, economic, social and political factors which have stimulated, in various ways, the expansion of state intervention in Canada and the United States. The objective has been to emphasize that the previous decades of extraordinary governmental growth are not merely the results of subjective causes— e.g. blatant political shortsightedness. This book encourages neither passive corporate submissiveness to growing governmental authority, nor passionate appeals to the public for new faith in old values. Its intention is to provide a more thorough and varied information base about the sources of government growth in order to improve managements' capacities to foresee and affect *future* changes in this area of non-market intervention.

Before a "General Theory" of state intervention can be developed out of the macro processes described above, there must be improved understanding of the micro dynamics of each of these diverse forces. Specifically, more data is required on the transformation process itself through which aforementioned demands are converted into *tendentionally similar, though specifically diverse,* policy results. What factors compel, say, Canada or Germany to move towards expanded state intervention via diametrically opposed expenditures baskets?[63] To put it another way, what factors produce *qualitatively different* profiles for *quantitatively similar* spending aggregates?

Development of rank-order for the above-mentioned macro forces is another subject for study. While the existence of these forces is not in dispute, much more should be known about their relative strengths.

More knowledge about the "life cycles" of each of these processes would also be useful. Up to what historical or developmental point are these forces influential? At which point do they begin to lose their causal influence? While the above may have been the forces stimulating state expansion in the past, will they remain equally powerful in the future? And finally, what are the newly emerging and often countervailing socio-economic and political demands in this area?

All of the above questions point to important and critical areas for future research. The macro analysis presented here can serve as a useful departure point and focus for discussion. Knowledge of these macro forces will compel more caution about the creation of "General Theories" of state intervention. Policy-makers for whom the growth of government expenditures appears to be controllable by a simple act of political will may

Table 3.1 The Future Sources and Direction of Change in Governmental Growth
(+ = increase; − = decrease; ± = stabilize)

According to Current Trends in These Factors of Governmental Growth	Expenditures could	The Relative Size of State		
		Employment could	Regulation could	Tax Expenditures could
1. Income elastic demands	±	±		±
2. Income elastic attitudes to taxation	−	−	±	−
3. Progressive income tax	+	±	±	+
4. Diversification of economic structures	+	±	+	±
5. Inflation	+	±	±	−
6. Urbanization	±	±	±	±
7. Breakdown of extended family	±	±	±	±
8. Division of labour	+	±	+	±
9. Externalities of technology	+	±	+	±
10. High cost of innovation	+	±	+	±
11. Branchplant needs for funding of innovative technology	+		+	±
12. Employment impact of automation	+	±	+	±
13. Demonstration effects of communications media	±	+	±	±
14. Technological costs-benefits of bureaucracy	−	−	±	±
15. International economic interdependence	+	±	+	±
16. Foreign economic penetration (trade-ownership)	+	±	+	±
17. Declining productivity and/or propensity to invest (private)	±	±	±	+
18. Growth of monopolies and the falling rate of profit	±	±	±	±
19. Excessive competition	±	±	±	±
20. Growth of external economies	+	±	+	+

	1	2	3	4
21. Depletion of non-renewable resources	+	±	+	±
22. Increase in relative population size of pensioners	+	±	±	±
23. Post-war baby boom or senior boom	+	±	±	±
24. Growth in proportion of female income earners in work force	±	±	±	±
25. The relative price effect	+	±	±	±
26. Canada's "Northern Frontier"	±	±	±	±
27. Canada's economies of scale	±	±	±	±
28. Canada's Resource Dependency	±	±	±	±
29. Widening participatory democracy	−	−	−	+
30. Income differentials and widening participation	±	±	±	±
31. Egalitarianist ideology	±	±	±	±
32. Increased political party competition	±	±	±	±
33. Political systems legitimacy	−	±	±	±
34. Blurred lines of federal-provincial divisions of power	−	±	±	±
35. Political competition between centre and periphery of federal state	−	±	±	±
36. Political nature of budgetary process	±	±	±	±
37. Budgetary source of bureaucratic power	±	±	±	±
38. Monopolistic nature of bureaucratic services	±	±	±	±
39. Rule-fixed fiscal federalism	±	±	±	±
40. Bureaucratic tenure	±	±	±	±
41. Incremental budgeting	−	±	±	±
42. Demands of Canadian nation building	±	±	±	±
Total factors of:	15 (+) 7 (−) 20 (±)	0 (+) 3 (−) 39 (±)	10 (+) 1 (−) 31 (±)	4 (+) 2 (−) 36 (±)

recognize that far deeper forces are at work. A more thorough public understanding of the diversity of forces that have brought us big government will, in the final analysis, provide an improved capacity first to understand and then to manage the forces and issues that shape both public and private sectors, and hence the lives of people.

With all these comments in mind, I will "stick out my neck" by presenting a range of scenarios for governmental growth during the coming decades. In Table 3.1, listed are all 42 of the previously discussed stimulants of governmental growth, along with extrapolations, into the future. These extrapolations are, under no circumstances, to be seen as *predictions* of the future.[64] Change in all of these realms has not unfolded according to an S–R paradigm, nor will it do so in the future. In short, Table 3.1 is not a *forecast* of what *will* happen 10-20 years down the road. Rather, it is an early warning exercise about the *possible* alternatives facing both public and private sector management.

This Table can serve, moreover, as a reference guide for future corporate involvement. The challenge for corporate decision-makers is to identify and comprehend the leading stimulants of governmental growth, and on *that* basis select action plans that are responsive both to external and internal needs, and which are, moreover, within the reach of the corporation. A corporate strategy based on this approach will be more dynamic and target-oriented than previous approaches. If handled properly and with commitment, such a strategy could pre-empt further escalations in government intervention. *If corporations can get to the causes of state intervention and defuse pent-up pressures in a responsible manner, they will indeed be writing their own future tickets to reduced state interference.* Even in cases where it is found that corporate involvement can *not* prevent state action, advanced knowledge of the terrain, provided by the above approach, will prepare the corporation to adapt more easily to increased regulation, if indeed that becomes inevitable.

Notes

1. A number of studies document this trend, including the following: G.W. Nutter, *Growth of Government in the West* (American Enterprise Institute for Public Policy Research, 1978); D. Auld, *Issues in Government Expenditures Growth* (C.D. Howe Research Institute, 1977); R.M. Bird, *The Growth of Government Expenditure in Canada* (Canadian Tax Foundation, 1970); R.M. Bird and D.K. Foot, "Bureaucratic Growth in Canada: Myths and Realities" in G.B. Doern and A.M. Maslove (eds.), *The Public Evaluation of Government Spending* (Institute for Research on Public Policy and Butterworth and Co. Ltd., 1979); *Redefining Government's Role in the Market System* (The Committee for Economic Development, 1979).

2. Recent surveys by the well-known and highly respected social and opinion research firm of Yankelovich, Skelly and White, Inc., caution us, however, that ". . . there is evidence to suggest that the anti-regulatory mood in the United States is coming more from government leaders themselves than from the public." See, A.H. White and M. Hochstein, "The Climate for Business in the 1980s: New Challenges, New Opportunities" in *Report of the Task Force on Corporate Social Performance* (U.S. Department of Commerce, December, 1980, p. 47).

3. One of the classical early advocates of this "philosophy" is F. von Hayek, the Nobel prize winning economist, in *The Road to Serfdom* (Routledge and Sons, Ltd., 1944). (For one of many ripostes, see H. Finer, *The Road to Reaction*, Quadrangle Books, 1945.) The best known and most articulate contemporary champion of this viewpoint is another Nobel Laureate, M. Friedman. See, for example, his book, *Capitalism and Freedom* (Markham Books, 1972), or his polemic, *Friedman on Galbraith* (The Fraser Institute, 1977). Three additional and interesting reviews of the rise of these sentiments can be found in the following works: J.M. Buchanan, *The Limits of Liberty: Between Anarchy and Leviathan* (University of Chicago Press, 1975); P. Steinfels, *The Neo-Conservatives: The Men Who are Changing America's Politics* (Simon and Schuster, 1979); H.S. Gordon, *The Demand and Supply of Government: What We Want and What We Get* (Discussion Paper No. 79, Economic Council of Canada, 1977), especially Chapter 4; and J. Laxer, *Canada's Economic Strategy* (McClelland and Stewart, 1981), pp. 9-43.

4. M. Friedman, "The Line We Dare Not Cross," *Encounter*, November, 1976, pp. 9-10.

5. Others have argued that the riots were due in large part to the previous years of Friedmanite medication administered by the Thatcher government.

6. M. Friedman, *op. cit.*, p. 9.

7. See, for example, B.M. Johnson, *The Attack on Corporate America* (McGraw-Hill, 1978); P. Steinfels, *op. cit.*; G.C. Lodge, *The New American Ideology* (A.A. Knopf, 1976); N. Chamberlain, *Remaking American Values: Challenge to a Business Society* (Basic Books, 1977); I. Kristol, "About Equality," *Commentary*, Vol. 54, November, 1972; D. Bell, "The Revolution of Rising Entitlements," *Fortune*, April, 1975; M.J. Crozier, S.P. Huntington and J. Watanuki, *The Crisis of Democracy* (New York University Press, 1976).

8. *Business Week*, "Egalitarianism: Threat to a Free Market," December 1, 1975.

9. H.G. Johnson, "Some Micro-Economic Reflections on Income and Wealth Inequalities," *Annals of the American Academy of Political and Social Science*, Vol. 409, September, 1973, p. 54.

10. See, for example, M. Novak, *The American Vision: An Essay on the Future of Democratic Capitalism* (American Enterprise Institute for Public Policy Research, 1978).

11. E.C. Ladd, Jr. and S.M. Lipset, "Professors Found to be Liberal But Not Radical," *The Chronicle of Higher Education*, January 16, 1978.

12. See, for example, A.T. Sommers (ed.), "The Free Society and Planning," *The Conference Board Record,* New York, 1975, p. 4 and A.H. White and M. Hochstein, *op. cit.,* pp. 46-61.

13. For example: P. Baran and P. Sweezy, *Monopoly Capital* (Monthly Review Press, 1966); S. deBrunhoff, *Etat et Capital* (Maspero, 1976); P. Mattick, *Marx and Keynes: The Limits of the Mixed Economy* (Porter Sargent, 1969); James O'Connor, *The Fiscal Crisis of the State* (St. Martin's Press, 1973); A. Gamble and P. Walton, *Capitalism in Crisis: Inflation and the State* (The Macmillan Press, 1976). For two penetrating shorter reivews of the Marxist position, see D.K. Foley, "State Expenditure from a Marxist Perspective," *Journal of Public Economics,* No. 8, 1978, and B. Fine and L. Harris, "State Expenditure in Advanced Capitalism—A Critique," *New Left Review,* No. 98, 1978. For some Canadian contributions to this argument see L. Panitch (ed.), *The Canadian State: Political Economy and Political Power* (University of Toronto Press, 1977); D. Wolfe, "The State and Economic Policy in Canada, 1968-1975" in L. Panitch (ed.), *ibid.*; and also "Mercantilism, Liberalism and Keynesianism: Changing Forms of State Intervention in Capitalist Economics," *Journal of Canadian Social and Political Thought,* Vol. 5, No. 102, 1981, pp. 69-96; R. Deaton, "The Fiscal Crisis of the State and the Revolt of the Public Employee," *Our Generation,* Vol. VIII, No. 4, October, 1972; C. Gonick, *Out of Work* (James Lorimer and Company, 1978) or his *Inflation and Wage Controls* (Canadian Dimension Publications, 1976).

14. See for example G. Williams, "Canadian Industrialization: We Ain't Growing Nowhere," *This Magazine,* March/April, 1975; R. Laxer (ed.), *(Canada) Ltd.: The Political Economy of Dependency* (McClelland and Stewart, 1973).

15. C. Gonick, *Out of Work, op. cit.,* p. 68.

16. For a development of this argument see, for example, C. Gonick, *Inflation and Wage Controls, op. cit.,* p. 28.

17. J. O'Connor, *op. cit.,* pp. 9-10.

18. The term "adversary culture" is one that is associated with L. Trilling. I will discuss this general thesis in some detail below. For a down-to-earth and uncomplicated statement on the subjectively determined, or "adversary culture determined," nature of governmental growth, see *Business Week,* "Egalitarianism: Threat to a Free Market," December 1, 1975. More scholarly treatments can be found in: D. Bell, "The Revolution of Rising Entitlements," *Fortune* April, 1975: I. Kristol, "A Regulated Society," *Regulation,* July/August, 1977; H. Williams, "Egalitarianism and Market Systems," *The Columbia Journal of World Business,* Winter, 1978; and R. Nisbet, *Twilight of Authority* (Oxford University Press, 1975).

19. The word "centre" is neither a particularly elegant nor scientific term to describe the immense space separating the two above mentioned ideological camps. For those who find it difficult to swallow such a huge analytical biscuit, I offer this qualification: The "centre," as used here, does have "left" and "right" boundaries. In other words, for analytical purposes, it can serve as a rallying point either for various shades of social democracy or for more traditional market-

oriented solutions. In the Canadian context, the "centre" can, therefore, accommodate debate and discussion of a wide range of alternatives, including, for example, a new industrial strategy coupled with increased technological development and Canadianization of the economy. More market-oriented solutions would include the introduction of effective anti-combines legislation, the promotion of increased domestic and international competition, reduction of protectionism and cutbacks on all regulatory powers that dampen economic competitiveness. On the first option, see, for example, *Out of Joint with the Times: An Overview of the Canadian Economic Dilemma* (Canadian Institute for Economic Policy, 1979), or J.J. Shepherd, *An Economic Strategy for Canada* (Walter L. Gordon Lecture Series, 1979). For a more market-oriented, competition based counterpoint see: I. Brecher, "Reflections on Being Out of Joint with the Times: An Essay on Canadian Economic Policy," *Essays in Public Affairs,* Vol. 1, No. 1, September, 1980, or his *Canada's Competition Policy Revisited* (The Institute for Research on Public Policy, 1981).

20. There is a large body of literature that supports this vein. The first writer to argue for the inevitability of governmental growth outpacing private sector growth was the German economist A. Wagner, in *Finanzwissenschaft* (1883) and *Grundlegung der Politischen Wissenschaft* (1893). Wagner suggested that public expenditure share of the GNP increases with the growth in the GNP per capita (for an interesting statistical refutation of "Wagner's Law" see, R.E. Wagner and W.E. Weber, "Wagner's Law, Fiscal Institutions, and the Growth of Government," *National Tax Journal,* Vol. XXX, No. 1, 1977). The writings of J.K. Galbraith—albeit from quite a different perspective than Wagner's—are apropos. See his *The New Industrial State* (Signet Books, 1967) or *Economics and the Public Purpose* (Signet Books, 1973). We can include, among Canadian contributors, the above quoted works of D.A. Auld, R.M. Bird, or Barber and McCallum, *op. cit.,* pp. 85-106. For a somewhat less academic, though nevertheless interesting pro-government argument, see also A. Wolfe, "In Defense of the State," *Social Policy,* May/June, 1979.

21. D. Tarschys, "The Growth of Public Expenditures: Nine Modes of Explanation," *Scandinavian Political Studies,* Vol. X, 1975, p. 29.

22. See D. Easton, "The Current Meaning of 'Behavioralism'" in J.C. Charlesworth (ed.), *Comtemporary Political Analysis* (The Free Press, 1967), p. 12.

23. For extended discussions of the conversion process, and the structural-functional dimensions of political systems, see G.A. Almond and G.B. Powell, Jr., *Comparative Politics: A Developmental Approach* (Little, Brown and Company, 1966).

24. I strongly recommend the previously quoted paper by D. Tarschys, *op. cit.,* pp. 9-31. See also D. Butler and B. MacNaughton, "Public Sector Growth in Canada: Issues, Explanations and Implications" in M.S. Whittington and G. Williams (eds.), *Canadian Politics in the 1980s* (Methuen Publications, 1981), pp. 97-102; D.A. Auld, *op. cit.,* pp. 24-34; R.D. Cairns, *Rationales for Regulation* (Economic Council of Canada, Regulation Reference Technical Report No. 2, 1980); and *Responsible*

Regulation (An Interim Report by the Economic Council of Canada, November, 1979), pp. 45-52.

25. For a further discussion, see M. Bird, "Wagner's Law of Expanding State Activity," *Public Finance/Finance Publique,* Vol. XXVI, 1971; S.P. Gupta, "Public Expenditure and Economic Development—A Cross-Section Analysis," *Finanzarchiv,* Vol. XXVIII, 1969, pp. 26-41; V.P. Gandi, "Wagner's Law of Public Expenditure: Do Recent Cross-Section Studies Confirm It?" *Public Finance/Finance Publique,* Vol. XXVI, 1971, pp. 44-56; and R.E. Wagner and W. Weber, "Wagner's Law, Fiscal Institutions and the Growth of Government," *National Tax Journal,* Vol. XXX, No. 1, 1977, pp. 59-68.

26. This process does not have an infinite extension, as effectively demonstrated not only in the writings of such scholars as S.P. Gupta, *op. cit.,* pp. 26-41 or B.P. Herber, *Modern Public Finance* (Richard Irwin Inc., 1967), but also by such real world events as Proposition 13 in California.

27. D. Tarschys, *op. cit.,* p. 24. For a Canadian summary of this phenomenon, see R.M. Bird, *The Growth of Government Expenditures in Canada, op. cit.*

28. D. Auld, *op. cit.,* p. 26.

29. See, for example, R. Aron, *18 Lectures on Industrial Society* (Weidenfeld and Nicholson, 1967); or W.E. Moore, *The Impact of Industry* (Prentice-Hall, 1965).

30. See, for example, A. Brecht "Internationaler Vergleigh der Offentlichen Ausgaben," *Grundfragen der Internationalen Politik II, Leipzig and Berlin,* 1932. For a review of Brecht's ideas, see D. Tarschys, *op. cit.,* p. 11

31. The railways provide an interesting exception that proves the rule: Unlike the automobile industry or the airline industry, the railways must themselves finance the construction and maintenance of roadbeds and terminals—albeit with some state subsidies. This is perhaps one of the most important reasons for the precarious financial state of most private railway networks.

32. For a good discussion of this, see J.N.H. Britton and J.M. Gilmour, *The Weakest Link: A Technological Perspective on Canadian Industrial Underdevelopment* (The Science Council of Canada, October, 1978), and A.J. Cordell, *The Multinational Firm, Foreign Direct Investment and Canadian Science Policy* (Science Council of Canada, December, 1971). For a critique of the Science Council position, see K.S. Palda, *The Science Council's Weakest Link: A Critique of the Science Council's Technocratic Industrial Strategy for Canada* (The Fraser Institute, 1979). For some additional critical views, see J. Jewkes, *Government and High Technology* (Institute of Economic Affairs, 1972) and N.A. Ashford, *National Support for Science and Technology: An Examination of Foreign Experience* (Center for Policy Alternatives, Massachusetts Institute of Technology, May, 1976).

33. D. Tarschys, *op. cit.,* p. 21.

34. J.M. Keynes, *The General Theory of Employment, Interest and Money* (Macmillan, 1960, first published in 1936). For some commentaries and further reflections on Keynes' ideas, the following are particularly useful: D. Dillard, *The*

Economics of John Meynard Keynes (Prentice-Hall, 1948); L. Klein, *The Keynesian Revolution* (Macmillan, 1961); R. Lekachman, *The Age of Keynes* (Random House, 1966); and R. Skidelsky, *The End of the Keynesian Era* (Holmes and Meier, 1977).

35. "Say's Law" is named after the French economist, Jean-Baptiste Say (1767-1832), and dates from the publication of his *Traite d'Economie Politique* in 1803.

36. See K. Marx, *Capital,* Vol. I., Chapter XXV (Progress Publishers, Moscow, 1965) and Vol. III (Progress Publishers, Moscow, 1971), p. 242, among others. For further emphasis on this theory of the falling rate of profit, the following are also useful: P.M. Sweezy, *Modern Capitalism and Other Essays* (Monthly Review Press, 1972), pp. 79-92; P. Baran, *The Political Economy of Growth* (Penguin Books, 1970); D.K. Foley, "State Expenditures from a Marxist Perspective," *Journal of Public Economics,* Vol. 9, 1978, pp. 221-238. While this is not the place to enter into the debate among neo-Marxists, it should be pointed out that some of them such as J. Habermas, reject the inevitability of falling rates of profit. Habermas argues, for example, that the "law of the falling rate of profit" applies only to the phase of liberal capitalism and can, in fact, be reversed in the technologically advanced stages of capitalism. See his *Legitimation Crisis* (Beacon Books), p. 56. (For an interesting analysis of Habermas' views, see J. Sensat, Jr., *Habermas and Marxism: An Appraisal* (Sage Publications, 1979), especially pp. 125-159. For further discussions on the reversibility of the falling rate of profit, see also I. Gough, "State Expenditure in Advanced Capitalism," *New Left Review,* No. 92, 1975; G. Hodgson, "The Theory of the Falling Rate of Profit," *New Left Review,* No. 84, 1974; and B. Fine and L. Harris,"State Expenditure in Advanced Capitalism: A Critique," *New Left Review,* No. 98, 1976.

37. The concept of the "relative autonomy" of the state is expounded at length by a number of Marxist writers, including: L. Althuser, *For Marx* (Vintage Books, 1970); N. Poulantzas, *Classes in Contemporary Capitalism* (New Left Books, 1975); and his *Political Power and Social Classes* (New Left Books, 1973).

38. In the United States for example, productivity per manhour in the private business sector averaged 3.2 percent during 1947-1967. The average annual increase by the late 1960s was down to 1.5 percent, and during the 1970s the average annual rate dipped to 1 percent. On this see, for example, *Manufacturing Productivity Growth 1960-77,* by the Joint Economic Committee, Congress of the United States, 1978; International Monetary Fund, *International Financial Statistics,* Vol. 32, No. 4, April, 1979, pp. 154, 214, 390. For another view, see E. Denison, "The Puzzling Drop in Productivity," *Brookings Bulletin* (The Brookings Institution, 1978); and E. Mansfield, "Technology and Productivity in the United States" in M. Feldstein (ed.), *The American Economy in Transition* (University of Chicago Press, 1980). The phenomenon of decreasing rates of productivity growth are just as evident in Canada, where average annual productivity gains dipped to just a fraction over 0 percent in the 1974 to 1980 period, from a 2.5 percent annual average growth rate between 1950-1974. Forecasts by both the Canadian Conference Board and the Economic Council of Canada indicate that this slowdown is not a short term dip but will be enduring throughout the 1980s. On these, see *A Climate of Uncertainty* (Economic Council of Canada, 1980); H. Sims and J. Stanton, *Recent Changes in*

Patterns of Productivity Growth in Canada (Department of Finance, Ottawa, April, 1980); and H.P. Bones, "Why Has Productivity Slowed Down?" *The Canadian Business Review,* Winter, 1981. Suggestions that declining rates of productivity growth in all of the Western world are in fact largely due to expanded state interventions, are frequent but as yet unsubstantiated. I have not been able to find a single study, apart from categorical assertions, which can conclusively demonstrate such a connection. In West Germany, for example, the average annual increase of industrial productivity during the 1970s was 4 percent, i.e. almost four times as high as that of the United States and yet the West German government absorbs a greater share of the GNP than the United States government. "The truth is that there is considerable uncertainty regarding the contribution of various factors to the observed productivity slowdown," says E. Mansfield, of the University of Pennsylvania, in *Technology and Productivity in the United States, op. cit.,* p. 568.

39. *Responsible Regulation* (An Interim Report by the Economic Council of Canada, November, 1979), p. 47.

40. *Ibid.,* p. 47. See also the following works on this question: K. Kapp, *Social Costs of Business Enterprise* (Asia Publishing, 1963); J.M. Buchanan, and W.C. Stubblebine, "Externality," *Economica,* Vol. 29, November, 1962; C.J. Dahlman, "The Problem of Externality," *Journal of Law and Economics,* Vol. 22, April, 1979; J.H. Dales, *Pollution, Property and Prices* (University of Toronto Press, 1968).

41. G. Hardin, "The Tragedy of the Commons," *Science,* Vol. 162, 1968.

42. J.K. Brown, *This Business of Issues: Coping with the Company's Environments* (The Conference Board Inc., Research Report No. 758, 1979), p. 16. This figure assumes a retirement age of 65. Obviously, if retirement is extended beyond this age and if the trend towards early retirement is reversed, the quoted ratio of active workers to retired citizens will be somewhat different.

43. D. Auld, *op. cit.,* p. 56.

44. The works in this area are numerous. Particularly relevant are: H. Innis, *Problems of Staple Production in Canada* (Ryerson Press, 1933); P. Mathias, *Forced Growth: Five Sources of Government Involvement in the Development of Canada* (Toronto, 1971); J.A. Corry, *Growth of Government Activities Since Confederation* (Rowell-Sirois Commission, 1939); M. Priest and A. Wohl, "The Growth of Federal and Provincial Regulation of Economic Activity, 1867-1978," *Economic Council of Canada, Regulation Reference Working Paper,* 1979.

45. F.S. Nitti developed his thesis in a work published in Italian, dated 1903. For a translation, see C.J. Bullock (ed.), *Selected Readings in Public Finance* (Ginn and Co., 1920), pp. 33-47.

46. This tolerance is clearly not without limits, especially if the burden becomes excessive while simultaneously, the "legitimacy" or credibility of governments with voters is diminished. It would appear that North American taxpayers have, in fact, come very close to *their* limit of toleration and that, in the future, this particular factor will not be of significance as a determinant of governmental growth.

47. A.H. Meltzer and S.F. Richard, "Why Government Grows (and Grows) in a Democracy," *The Public Interest,* No. 52, Summer, 1978, p. 116. Again, this is an interesting category. If income differentials stimulate governmental growth—and the evidence seems pretty solid—then the United States is clearly in for more pressures from this factor in the future. Among industrialized countries, only the French surpass the United States in terms of inequality based on the earnings gap between the top and bottom 10 percent of the population. Germany has 36 percent less inequality and Japan 50 percent less inequality than the United States, yet both have much higher labour productivity growth rates according to M. Sawyer and F. Wasserman, "Income Distribution in OECD Countries," *OECD Economic Outlook,* July, 1976, p. 14. The resolution of the conflict between the "ascendant" factor in governmental growth and the "descendant" factor mentioned immediately above— i.e. declining legitimacy—will bear watching in the future.

48. J. Rawls, *A Theory of Justice* (Harvard University Press, 1971); B. Williams, "The Idea of Equality" in P. Laslet and W.G. Runciman (eds.), *Philosophy, Politics and Society* (Basil Blackwell, 1969), pp. 110-131 and R. Dahrendorf, "On the Origin of Social Inequality" in the same volume, pp. 88-109.

49. For example, I. Kristol, "About Equality," *Commentary,* Vol. 54, November, 1972.

50. K. Polanyi's *The Great Transformation* stands, in my view, as the classic argument in this regard (Beacon Press, 1957).

51. See, for example, A. Armitage, *Social Welfare in Canada: Ideals and Realities* (McClelland and Stewart, 1975); G.L. Reuber, "The Impact of Government Policies on the Distribution of Income in Canada: A Review," in his book, *Canada's Political Economy* (McGraw-Hill Ryerson, 1980), pp. 79-102; W.I. Gillespie, *In Search of Robin Hood* (C.D. Howe Research Institute, 1978); and D. Dodge, "Impact of Tax, Transfer and Expenditure Policies of Government on the Distribution of Personal Income in Canada," *The Review of Income and Wealth,* Vol. 21, March, 1975, pp. 1-52.

52. A.M. Okun, *Equality and Efficiency: The Big Trade Off* (The Brookings Institution, 1975), p. 4.

53. For a good illustration of this point, see A. Blaustein, "Proposition 13—Catch 22," *Harper's Magazine,* Vol. 257, November, 1978, or A. Wolfe, "In Defense of the State," *Social Policy,* Vol. 10, No. 1, May/June, 1979.

54. The classic work on this "thesis" is by A. Downs, *An Economic Theory of Democracy* (Harper and Row, 1957).

55. D. Easton, *A Systems Analysis of Political Life* (John Wiley and Sons, 1965); and *A Framework for Political Analysis* (Prentice-Hall, 1965).

56. D. Tarschys, *op. cit.,* p. 24.

57. See, among others, T. Borcherding (ed.), *Budgets and Bureaucrats: The Sources of Government Growth* (Duke University Press, 1977); A. Downs, *Inside*

Bureaucracy (Little Brown and Co., 1967); D.C. Hartle, *The Expenditure Budget Process in the Government of Canada* (Canadian Tax Foundation, 1977); H.V. Kroecker, *Accountability and Control—the Government Expenditures Process* (C.D. Howe Research Institute, 1978).

58. R.S. Lorch, *Public Administration* (West Publishing Co., 1978), p. 246. This factor, again, can be traced back to K. Arrow's Impossibility Theorem, referred to earlier in this study.

59. Lorch, *ibid.*, p. 246.

60. D. Tarschys, *op. cit.*, p. 25.

61. C. Lindblom, "The Science of Muddling Through," *Public Administration Review*, Vol. 19, Spring, 1959, pp. 79-88, or A. Wildavsky, "Toward a Radical Incrementalism" in A. de Grazia (ed.), *Congress: The First Branch of Government* (American Enterprise Institute, Washington, D.C., 1966).

62. There are numerous studies in this regard, including S.M. Crean, *Who's Afraid of Canadian Culture?* (General Publishing Co., 1976); H. Hardin, *A Nation Unaware* (J.J. Douglas, 1974); A. Rotstein, *Independence: The Canadian Challenge* (Committee for an Independent Canada, 1972); G. Grant, *Lament for a Nation* (McClelland and Stewart, 1967).

63. On the question of comparative public policies the following books are quite useful: R.L. Seigel and L.B. Weinberg, *Comparing Public Policies* (Dorsey Press, 1977) and A.J. Heidenheimer, *et. al.* (eds.), *Comparative Public Policy* (St. Martin's Press, 1975).

64. The following works on the purpose, usefulness and limits of futures research in a corporate setting are recommended: R. Amara and A.J. Lipinski, *Linking the Corporation to the Future* (Institute for the Future, 1977); R. Amara, *Planning, Futures and the Skeptics* (Institute for the Future, September, 1980); S. Enzer, *Exploring Change in the Business Climate* (Center for Futures Research, October, 1980); R. Drobnick, *Emerging Issues: Concepts, Methods and Forecasts* (Center for Futures Research, December, 1980); and S. Enzer, *The Role of Futures Research in Corporate Planning* (Center for Futures Research, March, 1975). For further discussion see also Chapter 6.

4
The Boundaries of
Corporate Social Involvement

*Every corporation should be thought of as a social enterprise
whose existence and decisions can be justified only insofar as
they serve public or social purposes.*
—Robert Dahl

The social responsibility of business is to increase its profits.
—Milton Friedman

During the past couple of decades the terms corporate "social responsibility" and "social involvement" have become deeply embedded in the vocabulary used to discuss business-environmental relations. But while the terms are widely used, their meanings are often mysterious and ambiguous to senior management. How should a corporation guide itself in these realms? What should be its proper stand towards the societal changes enumerated in the previous chapters? Which societal issues should business take under its wings and which ones should it leave to government or others to reconcile? Indeed, how can senior management arrive at a financially optimal blending of its responsibilities to its shareholders and to society at large?

This study advocates that corporate social involvement is not peripheral to corporate strategy but is an essential element of it. Its pursuit is not a moral imperative as such, but a "bread and butter" consideration.

AN OVERVIEW OF THE COMPETING DEFINITIONS
OF CORPORATE SOCIAL RESPONSIBILITY

Until about the middle of the 1960s, surveys indicated that approximately 70 percent of the American population believed that business "strikes a fair balance between the pursuit of profit and the interests of the public." This figure had declined to 33 percent by the mid 1970s, and today it hovers around 15 percent.[1] This dramatic collapse in corporate credibility is not entirely the fault of corporations, but is in fact due to a combination of causes. The recent studies of Seymour Lipset and William Schneider[2] indicate, however, that as far as the public is concerned, the collapse in confidence is due first and foremost to the belief that corporations have become too self-centred and socially careless.

That corporate presidents, public affairs executives and academicians should all have become so mesmerized with the task of trying to define "social responsibility" over the past couple of decades is perfectly under- standable. All recognize the wisdom of Paul Samuelson's remarks: "Once the public comes to believe that what is deemed good for General Motors is no longer good for the public, they will not wait for victory in the voting of shares and proxies. They will strike directly by legislation."[3] Coming to terms with the meaning of "social responsibility" therefore is not just a narrow academic exercise, but is of great *practical* urgency. It is an essential prerequisite to rational corporate decision-making, and is vital to the task of regaining the credibility, the public trust and management control that corporations, as well as other institutions, once enjoyed.

The literature on the subject of "corporate social responsibility" is vast, and its limits are well defined by the positions of Robert Dahl and Milton Friedman, quoted at the beginning of this section.[4] Within these bounds one can find about as many different conceptualizations of "social responsibility" as there are writers.[5]

The reasons for the elusiveness of this term are linked to the broader problem of conceiving a universal theory of the public interest. Kenneth Arrow's Impossibility Theorem[6] coupled with the following comments of Charles Jacob are both helpful at this juncture.

> Many of the policies we would identify as being in the public interest serve precisely the interests of a *partial* public... in short, the public interest turns out to be whatever is in accord with the preconceptions and interpretations of the individual or group invoking its spirit.... While a rigorous definition is *possible,* it would be useless as a practical guide since no consensus among policy makers could be achieved that would agree to the use of its terms.... It is this feature of the concept of the public interest which has provoked many learned essays suggesting that, because of its hopeless generality and vagueness, we might better discard the term altogether and go on to more profitable investigations.
>
> Nevertheless... the idea of the public interest, for better or for worse— and, on the whole, I think, for the better—is here to stay... Ideas—even confused, vague generalities—can have an importance, in spite of their lack of immaculate precision.[7]

The absence of a commonly accepted definition of the public interest makes it impossible to conjure up a *universally acceptable* definition of corporate social responsibility. But just as the idea of the public interest is here to stay, so will the concept of social responsibility—however fuzzy and ill-defined—stay with us for a very long time to come. An overview of the debate concerning corporate interpretations of this term enables us, however, to extrapolate some guidelines that can help corporate strategists in the future.

An important theme of the social responsibility literature is that while for a long time corporations had only one thing to worry about—namely profits—*today,* because of changing societal conditions, they must concern themselves with a range of new socio-political issues in addition to maximizing profits. This "profit-plus" approach has been clearly articulated by George A. Steiner, a well known writer in this field, as follows:

> For two hundred years, business has been asked to achieve one single objective, namely, use scarce resources to produce goods and services that people want at prices they are willing to pay. Today, however, society is expecting business to continue to fulfill that role but also to assume new responsibilities of both a social and political nature. The result is a new role for business, especially the larger corporation, in society.[8]

One may legitimately question whether the economic theory of the firm—which has stressed profit maximization as the *sole* objective of corporations—was *ever* really an accurate description of corporate behaviour.[9]

One of the better known efforts at defining corporate social responsibility in the early 1970s was by the Committee for Economic Development.[10] The C.E.D. argued that corporate responsibility exists on three distinct but interconnected levels, that could be diagramatically represented as three concentric circles (see Figure 4.1).

The inner circle of the diagram represents the basic or "core" mission of the corporation, which entails the efficient and profitable production of goods and services demanded by society, within the confines of the law. If the corporation cannot fulfill its primary mission, it is idle to speak of any other levels of responsibility, for normally such a corporation will simply cease to exist (unless it is subsidized by governments).

The second circle encompasses a different, though related, set of responsibilities. In general, it includes the corporation's responsibilities to all of its *stakeholders* within its total socio-political *as well as* technological-economic realms. External and internal responsibilities exist in such areas as community employment, noise, pollution, job safety, accuracy of information and advertising, equal employment opportunities, investor relations and industrial relations.

The third circle represents, as the C.E.D. puts it, "newly emerging and still amorphous responsibilities that business should assume to become

Figure 4.1 The Classification of Corporate Social Responsibility: The CED Model

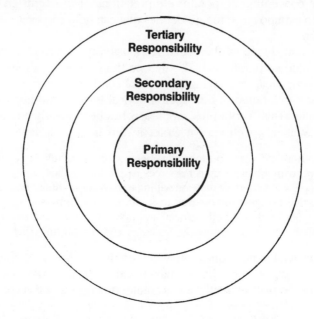

Tertiary
Responsibility

Secondary
Responsibility

Primary
Responsibility

Source: The Committee for Economic Development, New York, New York.

more broadly involved in actively improving the social environment."[11] This third level of responsibility involves corporate participation in the creation of a healthy society (domestic and international). Corporate involvement at this level is frequently, and falsely, described as just plain "do-gooding," as the manifestation of a corporate "soul," as a demonstration of "social duty" or good citizenship. In fact, the model developed by the C.E.D. suggests that responsibility at this level, as at the previous two levels, is inseparable from the *central* economic function of the corporation. The development of a healthy community is not simply a moral imperative but an economic one and should be supported by the corporation for reasons of "enlightened self-interest."

> There is broad recognition today that corporate self-interest is inexorably involved in the well-being of the society of which business is an integral part, and from which it draws the basic requirements needed for it to function at all—capital, labour, and customers.... It is in the *enlightened self-interest* of corporations to promote the public welfare in a positive way. The doctrine has gradually been developing in business and public

policy over the past several decades to the point where it supports widespread corporate practices of a social nature, ranging from philanthropy to investments in attractive plants and other programs designed to improve the company's social environment.... Since major corporations have especially long planning horizons, they may be able to incur costs and forego profits in the short run for social improvements that are expected to enhance profits or improve the corporate environment in the long run.[12]

A number of writers has criticized the above outlined model of social responsibility and its emphasis on "enlightened self-interest" as a guide to action on theoretical, practical and ideological grounds. For example, Lee Preston and James Post argue that the C.E.D. model cannot be considered an effective guide to corporate action because it sets *no operational limits* for that involvement. If social responsibility can mean everything, it can just as easily mean nothing at all and as such, the concept has little theoretical or practical usefulness except as a moral imperative. For Preston and Post, the "fatal flaw" of the C.E.D. approach is "... an absence of boundaries to the scope of managerial responsibility and an absence of criteria for appraising managerial performance."[13]

The concept of corporate social responsibility was given a more realistic or operational interpretation by the Niagara Institute in a 1977 study submitted by it to the Canadian Royal Commission on Corporate Concentration.[14] The authors of the report suggested that it would be better to dispense with the term "corporate social responsibility" because of its moralistic overtones. The recommended usage is social "involvement," "impact" or "performance." These terms, we're told, allow the function to be "delineated on a purely factual and descriptive basis" without "implying any judgement of praise or blame."[15]

The Niagara study distinguishes between "core" and "secondary" corporate involvements. The "core function" contains the basic economic activities of the firm and their immediate socio-political requisites (e.g., respect for zoning by-laws in location decisions). The "secondary" involvement consists of the extended or broader societal impacts of the firm's "core agenda" (e.g., the effects of advertising on lifestyles and corporate response to those consequences).

The boundaries of corporate responsibility are defined in the above approach on an individual basis. "The range of managerial responsibility for any particular corporation should be delineated as sharply as possible to its core activities and their clear and traceable consequences."[16] A deeper social involvement than that is ill-advised, we're told, because of sharply diminishing corporate competence, power and legitimacy into further reaches of society. The model of changing corporate involvement according to the Niagara study is that represented in Figure 4.2.

**Figure 4.2 The Corporation and Its Social Environment:
The Niagara Institute Model**

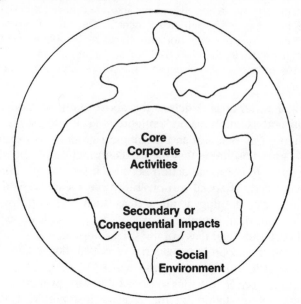

Source: R.T. Mactaggart, et al., *Corporate Social Performance in Canada* (The
Niagara Institute, 1977), p. 14.

The growing concern with the concept of corporate social responsibility
during the past 15 years or so has been criticised from another stance.
Friedman, and others, have been particularly critical of the "Third Level"
involvement as proposed by the C.E.D. They question the right of corporate management to spend stockholders' money on anything else than
profit maximization. Until stockholders grant management the right to
channel their hard-earned cash into areas not directly related to the
increase of financial returns on capital investment, management's "social
responsibility" expenditures will constitute nothing but the height of
irresponsibility.[17]

Increased social involvement by corporations has also been criticised on
the grounds that it is a fundamentally undemocratic tendency which, if carried to its logical conclusion, would result in an odious, self-centred and
socially harmful state of affairs. The argument here is that only governments are entitled to make social decisions. If corporations get into this
act, especially via the "enlightened self-interest" route, this is bound to
result in a submersion of the public interest at the hands of more narrowly

defined concerns. The most articulate statement of this position was by Theodore Levitt in his celebrated essay which appeared in the *Harvard Business Review*:

> With all its good intentions... its proliferating employee welfare programs, its serpentine involvement in the community, government, charitable and educational affairs, its prodigious currying of political and public favor through hundreds of peripheral preoccupations, all these well-intentioned but insidious contrivances are greasing the rails for our collective descent into a social order that would be as repugnant to the corporations themselves as to their critics. The corporation would eventually invest itself with all embracing duties, obligations and finally powers—ministering to the whole man and molding him and society in the image of the corporation's narrow ambitions and its essentially unsocial needs. . . . Government's job is not business and business's job is not government. And unless these functions are resolutely separated in all respects, they are combined in every respect. In the end, the danger is not that government will run business, or that business will run government, but rather that the two of them will coalesce... into a single power, unopposed and unopposable.[18]

The disagreements concerning the meaning and objectives of social responsibility enable us to divide writers on the subject into a number of camps. First, there are the "fundamentalists" of various ideological colours (e.g. Adam Smith, Friedrich Von Hayek, Milton Friedman, Theodore Levitt, Andrew Hacker, Leo Panitch, etc.) for whom only the primary or profit responsibility is legitimate *or* possible. And then there are the so called "revisionist" writers (e.g. Dow Votaw, Prakash Sethi, Lee Preston, Clark Abt, Courtney Brown, Melvin Anshen, etc.), also of various ideological shades, but with a notable absence of Marxists.

The revisionists have come to dominate the literature on social responsibility, not because they are brighter than the fundamentalists, but because the world has changed in their favour. The Marxists are absent from the ranks of the revisionists not because they are unfeeling or socially uncaring, but because they fundamentally disagree with the premise that a privately-owned corporation can simultaneously maximize individual profits and social benefits. This is one antithesis that Marxists simply cannot reconcile. (In practice, such reconciliation would also rule out the necessity of a socialist revolution.)

The dilemmas inherent in the concept of social responsibility have created an additional subdivision, this time within the ranks of the revisionists.

First, there are those whom we can call "process" oriented.[19] They argue that a commonly agreed to or substantive delineation of the boundaries of social responsibility is not possible at this time. Therefore, what the corporation should strive for is a participative-responsive stance vis-à-vis its environment on an evolving or pragmatic basis. The corporation should scan its environment for issues and social forces that are relevant to it and then interact with those forces in an open, two-way fashion. Out of this two-way interaction would emerge the type of involvement that would gain recognition and *support* for the corporation as a socially responsible institution. To use a medical analogy, modern surgery could not have reached its current level of sophistication without going through centuries of primitive trials and errors. In that process a lot of patients died, but in the end, the level of understanding and skill in the medical profession was increased and millions are safe from the ravages of once lethal ailments.

Second, there are those whom we can call "substance" oriented revisionists, of whom Lee Preston and James Post are the leading lights.[20] They see corporate involvement existing only on two levels—the *primary* and the *secondary.* Primary involvement for them consists, by and large, of those central economic functions of the firm that I have elaborated on earlier, and is governed foremost by the mechanisms of the market place. Secondary involvements are all those new activities that the corporation is called upon to pursue in an increasingly interdependent world (e.g. concern with the physical environment, with job safety, humane relationships, equal opportunities in employment, more open communications, open disclosures, etc.).

While in the case of the C.E.D. model, the second and especially the third levels of responsibility are defined as socio-political and only the first level is described in economic terms, Preston and Post rightly point out that "secondary" involvement should include both social and economic activities. Or as they say, "... the concept of secondary involvement, which implies the pursuit of effects and implications to *their* ends, whether nearby or remote, economic or social, provides a more useful terminology and approach."[21]

The other distinguishing feature of the Preston-Post approach, again to its credit, is that it dispenses with the C.E.D. model's suggestion that for corporate involvement, literally the sky is the limit. They have made an important effort to cap the proverbial gush in the direction of social responsibility by dispensing with the phrase altogether (calling it public responsibility) and by arguing that *public policy* is the substantive limit for corporate social involvement. Or to quote them:

> What goals and criteria should guide managerial behavior within the legitimate scope of corporate responsibility? Our answer is that appropriate guidelines are to be found within the framework of relevant public policy.[22]

To be sure, Preston and Post do not reject the "process" approach out right. They argue rather that the process approach could be usefully augmented by their "substantive" approach so as to close the circle on this debate. They feel that their solution to this problem still enables the corporation to fashion its "own agenda of social action based upon its situation and activities. It rejects the notion that there is a single social performance agenda for all corporations, and denies that the firm should develop an accommodating response to whatever social issues may be raised; [thus] large areas of the social landscape are simply out of range of the legitimate power of the corporation."[23]

While Preston and Post have undoubtedly moved the debate to a higher plateau, and while they have cleaned out many of the weeds cluttering this whole field, they have not, in my judgment, produced an operational theory of corporate involvement.

First of all, their conceptualization of public policy is so broad that in the final analysis policy is indistinguishable from its environment. Thus, the corporate executive, waiting to be pointed in the right direction towards a more limited scan of his or her surroundings, will still ride hill and gully over a very broad environmental terrain.

The second problem with this approach is that it presents an image of the policy process that is both idealistic and unrealizable. Note:

> The point is that the public policy process is, in our society, the means by which *society as a whole articulates its goals and objectives,* and directs and stimulates individuals and organizations to contribute to and cooperate with them. Hence, appropriate *guidelines for managerial performance are to be found* not in the personal visions of the managers themselves or in the special interests of any particular pressure group or constituency, but rather, *in larger society.*[24]

As Kenneth Arrow, for example, has shown, society "as a whole" cannot have goals, nor could it articulate them "as a whole," especially in a democracy such as ours. Public policy, rather, is a reflection of the relative power position of groups and interests within a particular society at various moments in time. The degree to which "society as a whole" is *seen* to be discounted from the policy process and the perception of just who is included or excluded in the calculus of consent, are often determined by ideological considerations masquerading as objectivity. Neo-conservative writers today argue that the public policy process in America has discounted the interests of the business community during the past couple of decades. They argue that the process has been one-sidedly dominated by the advocates of the "adversary culture"—i.e. by liberal academicians, journalists, and their anti-establishmentarian camp followers in pursuit of government handouts. Or in David Vogel's words,

> A loose coalition of middle-class based consumer and environmental, feminist and civil rights organizations, assisted on occasion by organized labor, aided by sympathetic media and supported by most of the intelligentsia, were able to influence both the terms of public debate and the outcomes of governmental policy in a direction antithetical to the interests of business.[25]

The other side of the ideological fence argues equally forcefully, and with a heavy mix of rhetoric and statistics, the thesis so neatly phrased by Elmer Schattschneider:

> The flaw in the pluralist heaven is that the heavenly chorus sings with a strong upper class accent. Probably about 90 percent of the people cannot get into the pressure system.[26]

The case against those who urge that corporations should become politically more active in the public policy process in order to regain their hard-earned place in society's esteem, is strongly put by Andrew Hacker as follows:

> Corporations... are not voluntary associations with individuals as members, but rather, associations of assets, and no theory yet propounded has declared that machines are entitled to a voice in the democratic process.... When General Electric, American Telephone and Telegraph, and Standard Oil of New Jersey enter the pluralist arena we have elephants dancing among the chickens.[27]

For these critics, then, the suggestion that corporate social involvement should take its cues from public policy means that corporations will continue to play a one-sided game due to their alleged domination of the policy process.

For neo-conservatives, the opposite conclusion follows. Since they see the policy process as a one-sided reflection of the values of an adversary class or culture, responsiveness to those values, and to public policy in general, is tantamount to an abrogation of corporate responsibility. Rather than taking their cues from the process, the corporation is urged by Vogel, and others, to wade right into the process so as to re-inject *its* values and demands more effectively into that system.[28] Preston's and Post's effort to represent this process as a "value free" exercise just does not work, even if they rename social responsibility as public responsibility. ("We choose the word *public* rather than *social* [responsibility], of course, in order to stress the importance of the public policy process, rather than individual opinion and conscience, as the source of goals and appraisal criteria.")[29]

In short, let's not kid ourselves. Corporate leaders have opinions, values and attitudes just as anyone else does, and of course they want to inject those values into the political system on issues they consider to be of vital interest. They have their own vision of "the just society," of the role of business within that society, and of the wisdom or lack thereof of their adversaries. The corporation is not an inanimate machine and it does not cater to the needs of inanimate entities as suggested by Hacker. Corporations, rather, are associations of human beings in pursuit of objectives that are important to their members.

Whether or not corporate executives tolerate dissent from their rank and file, however important that consideration may be, is not the question here. There are many political parties in liberal democracies whose internal procedures for selection of party policy are anything but broadly based. Yet such parties are not barred from policy involvement. (Indeed, the notion of rank and file control over policy making inside most political parties is as mythical as is the idea that shareholders determine corporate strategy.) The severity of sanction used by many political parties or unions against members who attack the "party line" is well known. And how representative are many of the "consumer interest" groups that claim to speak on behalf of all consumers in the policy-making arena? If it is legitimate for organized labour to finance, support and control candidates and parties of its own (e.g. the British Labour Party or the New Democratic Party in Canada), why should it be illegitimate for business to do the same, as long as clear-cut guidelines on financing and involvement are established?

The point about policy participation is that if an association's objectives are legal, if those objectives are perceived as useful by society (e.g. the generation of goods and services, income and employment) and if the achievement of those objectives is conditioned by public policy, that association, be it a corporation or a consumer advocacy group, has every right to participate in the policy process.

The democratic solution to the problem of unequal access to power is *not* to disenfranchise the advantaged party but to provide improved access to the disadvantaged through new rules, checks and balances. The objective is to prevent *any* special interest or coalition from monopolizing the process by which societal priorities are identified and pursued. Most important of all, if large segments of society elect to withdraw from the political arena—for whatever reasons—or if they allow themselves to be pushed aside by special interests, they should not be surprised if at times they end up like "chickens dancing among the elephants." While such a dance is in the interest of neither party, society in the final analysis, suffers the most from its negative effects.

In short, the idea that corporations have no right to participate in the policy making process is untenable on the grounds of its subjective bias. Equally untenable is the image of corporate responsibility according to which corporate leaders objectively take their cues for responsible action from an objective societal welfare maximizing process, in which they are self-interested participants. The latter proposal is too fragile an analytical biscuit to swallow in one piece.

So then, what options are open to the exasperated corporate leader who is being whipped in the opinion polls for being socially irresponsible, who is feeling the hot breath of government down his back,[30] and whose cry is: "How is such responsibility defined? Is it the responsibility of corporations to solve all of society's social problems left unanswered by government? Or merely to try to do so? Or merely to try to solve some of the problems? Which ones? How much?"[31] Common sense answers are clearly imperative.

AN AUDIT-BASED APPROACH TO
CORPORATE SOCIAL INVOLVEMENT

The essential prerequisite of successful corporate strategy is for senior management to recognize that demands for corporate social involvement, however defined, are not going to dissipate in the future. Be it "social responsibility" or "social performance," the concept has become deeply engrained in the minds of corporate constituents and is now a permanent part of the vocabulary of exchange between corporations and their environments. If it has not already been assigned a permanent place on the corporate agenda by the forces outlined in the previous chapters, it will most certainly become so situated in the future.

The latest corporate survey conducted in Canada in this area fully corroborates these points.[32] Ninety-three percent of the respondents to that survey indicated that public expectations of corporate social performance are not decreasing and indeed, 83 percent stated that such demands will increase in the future. Similarly, 95 percent of the respondents stated that their companies' social performance efforts will not decrease in the future, while 82 percent expected increasing efforts in the years to come[33] (see Table 4.1).

There is no place to hide from the above reality. Rather than fighting a rearguard action against corporate social involvement or simply allowing societal changes to buffet the corporation at random, senior management must legitimize this activity as an important component of corporate strategy. Social involvement, in other words, should be designated by senior management as a "core" rather than "peripheral" element of the corporate

Table 4.1 Public Expectations and Management Efforts Regarding Social Performance in Canada

	Percentage of Respondents			
Behaviour	**Increasing**	**Not Changing**	**Decreasing**	**No Response**
Public expectations regarding corporate social performance	83.3	9.8	3.8	3.0
Corporate management's efforts regarding social performance	81.8	12.9	4.5	.8

Source: Hal Schroeder, *Corporate Social Performance in Canada: A Survey* (Lethbridge: University of Lethbridge, 1983), p. 7.

strategic culture. Given this realization, it then becomes imperative that some form of social audit be instituted by which the corporation systematically analyses its socio-political environment and injects the results of that analysis into its strategic decisions, goals or objectives.

The American Institute of Certified Public Accountants presented a very useful depiction of "corporate social audit" which will be applied in this section.[34] Social audit, they say, refers to:

The development of information about the social impacts of a company's present actions;

The establishment of objectives, plans, and standards of desired social performance; and

The subsequent determination of the effectiveness of efforts to achieve them.[35]

The Institute's very detailed review of problems and opportunities in this realm concluded that "There is little likelihood that a system will be developed in the foreseeable future that can measure the social impacts of business actions with anything approaching the refinement of financial accounting systems. Nevertheless, substantial strides can be expected to result in more useful social information. [And] Social information should be considered to bear the same relationship to corporate decision-making and performance in the social arena as financial information bears to decisions and performance in the financial field."[36] Given these benchmarks, the *framework* for injecting social involvement into corporate strategy—i.e. into the determination of what the nature of the corporation should be and how that is to be achieved—can be presented as follows:

1. The critical first step to corporate social performance is the drive to produce goods and services that are demanded by people, in a manner that is consistent with public policy, profitable, and of the highest quality. Societal reputation is not achieved through inefficiency, low productivity, dependence on government handouts, or through the manufacture of goods and services that reflect artificially induced needs and are of shoddy quality. The massive consumer dissatisfaction with the American automobile industry during the 1970s, for example, stems from the perception that the industry cannot or does not manufacture attractive, low priced, fuel-efficient and reliable cars as well as the Japanese. No amount of political action, grass-roots activity, advocacy advertising and the myriad of other issues management tools will turn this credibility problem around, until the primary corporate "raison d'être" itself is fully confronted and its problems resolved. Improved productivity, efficiency, innovation and product leadership could substantially reduce the sagging credibility of business in America today. (As we have seen in previous chapters, many of these objectives are no longer attainable by strict economic technological tools and do in fact require socio-political guidance.)

2. Once we have come this far towards responsible behaviour—and it is surprising in how many cases step number one will indeed suffice—we need to ask:

- Is the achievement of the corporation's central or core mission dependent on secondary involvements?
- Is the corporation capable of defining and implementing these secondary moves in a manner that will be deemed legitimate and of *mutual benefit* to it and to society?

This second step, simply put, is a systematic assessment of corporate *needs* and *capabilities* for involvements above and beyond the strict economic-technological ones related to the pursuit of its primary mission. In this assessment, or audit, of corporate social involvement needs and capacities, the following steps are particularly important:

a. Measure and analyse the *sensitivity* or exposure of current and expected corporate profits *and* corporate operations (from the top to the bottom of the company) *to socio-political issues and forces* (domestic and international). It is important to know here which profit centres are most sensitive to socio-political forces, and which socio-political forces are the most relevant to profit centres at each level.

The environmental analysis that will determine this should be incremental rather than zero-based. In other words, it should take its primary targeting cues directly from the core activities of the firm. The nature of the business, the characteristics of its products, services and operations will guide the environmental analysis process to identify the critical socio-political dimensions of corporate profitability and operations.

b. Measure and analyse the major socio-political *impacts* (including feedback) of current and alternative corporate strategies. This analysis should identify not only the *currently* significant social impacts of corporate operations from the top to the bottom of the organization. It should also attempt to forecast significant future societal impacts of current and contemplated corporate designs.

c. Assess all past and current corporate *socio-political programmes,* from the top to the bottom of the corporation. Know at which levels, where, through whom, and with what *frequency and effectiveness* the corporation has involved itself in the socio-political realm. Taking a cue from organizational theory, it is important to recognize here that *informal* corporate-environment linkages are as important to this inventory as the formal ones. It may be that the audit of formal communications or interaction channels will not show significant socio-political involvements. But if the senior division manager says, "I'm on first name basis with the mayor, with my congressman and with community leaders, and I speak to them quite often about all kinds of things," some socio-political involvement obviously exists, even if it is not formally assigned. This step of the audit will also tell you what gaps, if any, exist between current needs and current performance. The gap, needless to say, can be open-ended. The corporation may find that its needs are not being met by current public affairs activities and thus it may opt to invest more time and resources into the function. In the reverse, this audit may also turn up all kinds of socio-political activities at various levels of the firm, which the corporation quite simply does not need, and which it could eliminate at a considerable financial saving. Whichever the result, this audit clearly is an indispensible element of responsible fiscal management.

Finally, this audit should not only examine the adequacy of in-house programmes and resources but should also evaluate the usefulness and costs of all of the external resources that the corporation relies on in this area (e.g. consultants, trade associations, business associations, scientific associations, etc.).

d. On the basis of the above, estimate the capacity of the corporation to affect or influence the critical socio-political issues facing it on the short, medium and long term. What are the feasible options? How can they be achieved? At what costs and benefits? A corporation may find that it is highly sensitive to certain public issues but if its capacity to influence or change those issues is non-existent, it will be wasting its resources to try. In short, *estimate the financial costs and benefits* accruing to the corporation from different types and levels of *future* socio-political involvement in conjunction with established needs, resources and capabilities.

3. After taking the steps outlined in the audit above, senior management should draft a *Social Performance Policy Statement*. This statement, which should be short, lays out the broad parameters of corporate socio-political involvement, and serves as the basic policy guide for management action. The policy statement should not be carved in stone, and should not define highly specific areas. It should be annually fine tuned and should guide the fundamental socio-political activities of the organization.

4. Only following on the heels of this analysis, should the corporation develop the appropriate public affairs structure needed to sustain and support its "core" and "secondary" involvement. *Departments, units, roles*, the designation of officers, responsibilities, programmes and lines of communication (external and internal) should be established strictly on the basis of the above outlined audit rather than on the basis of some externally suggested model. (Those should be used only as general roadmaps from which a company should deviate as prudence requires.) The organizational model that works for one corporation may be totally inappropriate for another. The same goes for the level of socio-political involvement. Thus, to the initial question of whether there is one best way to structure and manage public affairs and corporate responsibility, the answer is, "No." *The best public affairs model is the one that works.*

5. Once an audit has shown that corporate profits, operations and general viability are closely interlinked with socio-political issues, and that capacity exists or can be feasibly designed to manage this linkage, one key decision must be implemented, if it has not already been done so, by the head of the corporation: *this management function must be moved from the periphery to the centre of corporate decision-making.* Public affairs and corporate responsibility considerations must take their place, along with management of finance, marketing, research and development, etc., *in the strategic planning process.* And moreover, such considerations must permeate the operations of the organization from the top to the bottom—or wherever along the hierarchy the audit has indicated there to be a need for interpenetrating capabilities. The comments of Courtney C. Brown are germane:

> Until the performance of its social responsibilities becomes as much a part of a corporation's business as its production and distribution of goods and services, the analysis of alternative options for organizing the social responsibility function will remain a sterile exercise. When social responsibility is peripheral, decisions on how to organize its administration will be both difficult and trivial.[37]

6. The final commandment in this audit process is to *repeat the whole exercise regularly, at least once every two or three years.* The environment does not stand still. Institutions which do not adapt can be caught flat-footed with "mud on their faces." The public affairs audit should become a habit, like regular medical checkups. By regularly reassessing corporate-environmental linkages, and the thrust and effectiveness of corporate strategies vis-à-vis these linkages, the corporation will provide itself with an insurance policy against socio-political surprises that could, if left unmanaged, jeopardize the viability of the organization.

The steps outlined above contribute a common sense, though by no means easy, framework for injecting social involvement into corporate strategy. (More discussion of some of the difficulties entailed in this process and suggested ways of overcoming them are presented in the following chapters.) These steps are in fact essential elements of any rational decision-making process. It may be surprising to learn, however, that the vast majority of Canadian and American corporations, as well as most other institutions, which together spend enormous sums of money on public affairs management, seldom utilize any kind of audit-based approach in this area. The approach outlined above is rigorously applied by management in other areas of corporate decision-making, yet it is frequently ignored in the management of public affairs. At present, the average corporation's public affairs involvement is still very much a function of individual horizons, internal corporate politics, internal marketing skills and just plain "Does the Boss like or dislike this stuff?" This ad hoc approach, in the face of expanding governments, growing public interest group challenges, and the "crowding-in" of external issues is patently irresponsible, both to society and the best interests of the corporation. Hal Schroeder's recent survey of Canadian corporate social performance demonstrates that social performance measurements systems are very rarely used. "Less than four percent of the responding corporations are at present conducting regular social audits. The same number at present have plans underway to introduce social audits.... The indication is that only a small percentage of Canada's major corporations will be conducting regular social audits in the foreseeable future."[38] (The usage of the term "social audit" in Schroeder's survey appears to coincide only with element 3 of the earlier quoted A.I.C.P.A. classification. This significantly narrower usage, therefore, substantially understates the utilization role of "social audit" by Canadian corporations. For example while only 3.8 percent of Schroeder's respondents indicated that their corporations pursue regular social audits, 83.3 percent state that they conduct formalized impact assessment of corporate strategy alternatives on the physical environment and 70.5 percent stated that they pursue *formalized social impact assessment* of corporate strategy alternatives.)

Table 4.2 The Utilization Rate of Social Performance Measurements by Corporations in Canada

Measurements	Percentage of Respondents		
	Yes	No	No Response
Regular social audits at present	3.8	93.9	2.3
Planning regular social audits	3.9	82.7	13.4
Using social performance criteria in evaluating individual managers	30.3	59.8	9.8

Source: Hal Schroeder, *Corporate Social Performance in Canada: A Survey* (Lethbridge: University of Lethbridge, 1983), p. 12.

It is certainly recognized, and I concur, that the rigorous standards of financial auditing cannot be applied to the social realm. The advocacy of an audit-based approach to corporate social involvement does not imply that the foundations of this audit be made identical to currently used financial accounting systems. The above outlined framework is not an "ideal system" but "an initially achievable system" of social auditing.[39] The linking of specific measurement devices, such as those developed by the A.I.C.P.A., to this framework, and the adoption of a more systematic approach, is both attainable and financially desirable.

Not to assume the *necessary* socio-political responsibilities because of nagging uncertainties about the frequent "unpredictability" or "softness" of this exercise is difficult to comprehend. Risk lies at the heart of the business enterprise. The acceptance of risk-taking at the primary level of corporate involvement and fear of risk to the extent of producing paralysis at the secondary level, is illogical and self-defeating. The vast majority of corporate failures and financial losses are reducible to miscalculations at the primary level. Financial losses to the corporation stemming from secondary level involvements are most often due not so much to imprecisions in allocation decisions as to the absence of such decisions in general. In short, inadequate management and hesitation or outright refusal to assume responsibilities at the secondary level, even when needs and capacities have been defined, is a recipe for both bad business and an unhealthy social environment. It is wrong not because it flies in the face of some moral or ethical principles but because it is the chief source of growing institutional paralysis and decay. The adoption of a "revisionist" (rather than "fundamentalist") position towards corporate social involvement not only makes good financial sense but could pave the way for a less adversarial, less self-centred, more cooperative set of social relationships. As laid down in our opening paradigm, and as argued throughout this study, this new relationship between institutions, groups, governments, etc., is the key to success and survival in the age of scarcity and interdependence. From these conclusions, public affairs and its ties to corporate strategy will derive their main sources of strength.

Notes

1. A.H. White and M. Hochstein, "The Climate for Business in the 1980s: New Challenges, New Opportunities" in *Business and Society: Strategies for the 1980s* (Report of the Task Force on Corporate Social Performance, U.S. Department of Commerce, December, 1980), p. 47.

2. S.M. Lipset and W. Schneider, *The Confidence Gap: How Americans View Their Corporations* (Macmillan, 1981).

3. P.A. Samuelson, "The Businessman's Shrinking Prerogatives," *Business and Society Review,* Spring, 1972, p. 38.

4. R.A. Dahl, "A Prelude to Corporate Reform," *Business and Society Review,* Spring, 1972. M. Friedman, "Milton Friedman Responds," *Business and Society Review,* Spring, 1972, as well as his article "The Social Responsibility of Business is to Increase its Profits," *The New York Times Magazine,* September 13, 1970.

5. Some of the better works which also provide a guide to the literature and critical comments on the works of others are the following: M. Anshen (ed.), *Managing the Socially Responsible Corporation* (Macmillan, 1974); M. Beesley and T. Evans, *Corporate Social Responsibility: A Reassessment* (Croom-Helm, 1978); C. Brown, *Beyond the Bottom Line* (Macmillan, 1979); The Committee for Economic Development, *Social Responsibilities of Business Corporations* (The Committee for Economic Development, 1971); J. Hargreaves and J. Dauman, *Business Survival and Social Change* (Associated Business Programs Limited, 1975); L. Preston and J. Post, *Private Management and Public Policy: The Principles of Public Responsibility* (Prentice-Hall, 1975); D. Votaw and P. Sethi, *The Corporate Dilemma* (Prentice-Hall, 1973); R.T. Mactaggart, *et. al., Corporate Social Performance in Canada* (The Niagara Institute, 1977).

6. K. Arrow stated in this theory that while individuals may be theoretically capable of making rational choices, the democratic collectivity, because it is a composite of competing or contrasting values, desires, and needs, is unable to provide for collective rationality. Or as he puts it, "There can be no constitution simultaneously satisfying the conditions of Collective Rationality, the Pareto Principle, the Independence of Irrelevant Alternative, and Non-Dictatorship," in "Values and Collective Decision-Making," *Philosophy, Politics and Society,* Vol. III, edited by P. Laslett and W.G. Runciman (Basil Blackwell, 1969), p. 228. For an extended discussion, see K. Arrow, *Social Choice and Individual Values* (John Wiley, 1951).

7. See C. Jacob, *Policy and Bureaucracy* (D. Van Nostrand, 1966), pp. 192-93.

8. G.A. Steiner, "An Overview of the Changing Business Environment and Its Impact on Business" in L.E. Preston (ed.), *Business Environment/Public Policy* (1979 Conference Papers, American Assembly of Collegiate Schools of Business), p. 14.

9. For an excellent critical review, see E. Furubotn and S. Pejovich, "Property Rights and Economic Theory: A Survey of Recent Literature," *Journal of Economic Literature*, December, 1972, pp. 1137-1162.

10. Committee for Economic Development, *op. cit.*

11. *Ibid.*, p. 15.

12. *Ibid.*, pp. 27-33.

13. L.E. Preston and J.E. Post, *op. cit.*, p. 53.

14. R.T. Mactaggart, *et. al., op. cit.*

15. *Ibid.*, p. 12.

16. *Ibid.*, p. 15.

17. M. Friedman, "Milton Friedman Responds," *op. cit.*

18. T. Levitt, "The Dangers of Social Responsibility," *Harvard Business Review*, September-October, 1958, pp. 41-47. Another useful review in this vein is by W. Baumol, R. Likert, H. Wallish and J. McGowan, *A New Rationale for Corporate Social Policy* (Lexington Books, 1970). For stronger statements of this thesis, from a Marxist perspective, see L. Panitch, "The Development of Corporatism in Liberal Democracies," *Comparative Political Studies*, Vol. 10, No. 1, April, 1977 and P. Schmitter, "Still the Century of Corporatism," *Review of Politics*, January, 1974. A similar theme is found in A. Hacker's *The Corporate Take-Over* (Harper and Row, 1964).

19. The works of P. Sethi, D. Votaw, C. Abt, T. Jones and F. Steckmest belong here.

20. L.E. Preston and J.E. Post, *op. cit.*

21. *Ibid.*, p. 96.

22. *Ibid.*, p. 57.

23. L.E. Preston and J.E. Post, "Private Management and Public Policy," *California Management Review*, Vol. 23, Spring, 1981, p. 57.

24. L.E. Preston and J.E. Post, *Private Managment and Public Policy, op. cit.*, p. 102.

25. D. Vogel, "The Power of Business in America: A Re-examination" (Typescript, 1982), p. 2. The same thesis is advocated by M. Novak, in *The American Vision: An Essay on the Future of Democratic Capitalism* (American Enterprise Institute for Public Policy Research, 1978).

26. E.E. Schattschneider, *The Semi-Sovereign People: A Realist's View of Democracy in America* (Holt, Rinehart, 1960), p. 35. For some Canadian illustrations, see R. Mahon, "Canadian Public Policy: The Unequal Structure of Representation" in L. Panitch (ed.), *The Canadian State* (University of Toronto Press, 1977); D. Olsen,

The State Elite (McClelland and Stewart, 1980); J. Richards and L. Pratt, *Prairie Capitalism: Power and Influence in the New West* (McClelland and Stewart, 1979); W. Clement, "The Corporate Elite, the Capitalist Class and the Canadian State" in L. Panitch, *op. cit.*

27. A. Hacker, *op. cit.,* pp. 7-8.

28. E. Grefe, *Fighting to Win: Business Political Power* (Harcourt, Brace, Jovanovich, 1981); Institute for Political Involvement, *A Report on the Prospects for Increased Involvement of Business People in the Canadian Political System* (Institute for Political Involvement, April 1978); P. Pare, "Political Involvement: From a Necessary Evil to a Management Skill," *Canadian Banker and ICB Review,* Vol. 85, October, 1978; I. Shapiro, "Business and the Public Policy Process," Address before the Chicago Chapter of the Planning Executives' Institute, May 9, 1979; P. Sethi, "Serving the Public Interest: Corporate Political Action Strategies for the 1980s," *Management Review,* Vol. 70, March, 1981; D. Vogel, "Business's 'New Class Struggle,'" *The Nation,* December 15, 1979 and his, "The Power of Business in America: A Re-examination," *op. cit.;* and G. Keim, "Foundations of a Political Strategy for Business," *California Management Review,* Vol. 23, No. 3, Spring, 1981.

29. L.E. Preston and J.E. Post, *Private Management and Public Policy, op. cit.,* p. 102.

30. And the innocent enough sounding Task Force launched by President Reagan in the United States at the end of 1981 on "Private Sector Initiatives" may also be part of the equation calling—indeed possibly invoking—greater corporate responsibility.

31. C.A. Abt, "The Social Audit Technique for Measuring Socially Responsible Performance" in M. Anshen (ed.), *Managing the Socially Responsible Corporation, op. cit.,* p. 95.

32. H. Schroeder, *Corporate Social Performance in Canada: A Survey* (University of Lethbridge, 1983).

33. *Ibid.,* p. 6.

34. The American Institute of Certified Public Accountants, *The Measurement of Corporate Social Performance* (American Institute of Certified Public Accountants, 1977).

35. *Ibid.,* p. 6.

36. *Ibid.,* pp. 7-10.

37. C.C. Brown, "Organizing for Socially Responsible Management" in M. Anshen (ed.), *op. cit.,* p. 36.

38. H. Schroeder, *ibid.,* p. 11.

39. On the distinction, see The American Institute of Certified Public Accountants, *op. cit.,* pp. 15-29.

5

The Components of the Public Affairs Function

The buck does not stop in the public affairs department.

—Anonymous

DELINEATING THE TURF

Once senior management has established that socio-political information is essential to the development of sound corporate strategy, the obvious question is, who will be mandated to gather and integrate that information? Should there be a separate public affairs department? Should this responsibility be designated to the public relations people, to corporate planners, or to marketing? If a separate department is set up, should this department be given access to all domains of the corporate environment, or should it be excluded from certain sectors? Of the myriad of environmental issues facing the corporation, which are the ones particularly germane to public affairs management and which are not? If the jurisdiction of the public affairs department is to be selective, what is to be the basis for this selectivity?

Answers to the above questions are obviously required. Survey results clearly demonstrate that the trend both in the United States and Canada is to establish distinct public affairs departments, units or their equivalent, and to delegate to these departments a number of responsibilities created by the socio-political environment of the corporation.

My survey of Canadian corporate behaviour showed that 68 percent of the responding firms have established distinct public affairs departments and that over half of these units have been set up since 1971 (see Table 5.1).

As far as the environmental jurisdiction of these departments goes, there is a great deal of variation from company to company. With increasing frequency, the corporate environment itself is portrayed as consisting of a four-dimensional matrix of forces—namely, the social, the economic, the political and the technological, applicable to both a domestic and an international setting.[1]

One can bicker endlessly over whether a particular issue is really part of the social, rather than the political environment. So, while the drawing of

Table 5.1 Percentage of Responding Canadian Corporations that Have a Distinct Public Affairs Department, Unit or the Equivalent

Response	Over All Response	Top 100 Firms
Yes	68.3	79.0
No	31.7	21.0

precise demarcation lines between these four environmental states is clearly impossible, the quadrant approach is nevertheless a useful ordering device:

1. In general, the *social environment* consists of social values, cultural characteristics, societal inequalities, education, demographics, lifestyles, etc.
2. The *economic environment* contains such key factors as capital, resources, labour, unemployment, inflation, productivity, GNP, etc.
3. The *political environment* consists of the executive, legislative, judicial and bureaucratic branches of the state, state regulatory bodies, political parties, pressure groups and the like.
4. The *technological* realm includes new product lines, research and development, innovations, automation, technical management of computerized information and so on.

As outlined in the introduction, the various segments of the environment are in a state of constant interaction, never in a static relationship with one another. None of these environment segments is of prior or of secondary importance, because causation is circular. The relationship between business and its environment can therefore be represented by Figure 5.1.

Surveys and interviews among members of the public affairs community reflect widespread uncertainty about which segments of the above outlined environmental quadrant really fall into the public affairs department's purview. While most executives are pretty sure that they have a clearcut mandate to monitor social and political trends, they are very uncertain about their involvement with technological and economic trends. In many cases, top management is equally ambiguous about this question. This uncertainty is the principal cause of recurring "turf battles" between public affairs units and other corporate departments. These battles are set off whenever public affairs units, in hot pursuit of socio-political intelligence, wander into the technological-economic realms of the corporate environment. Such "meanderings" immediately touch off an alarm in the heads of other line managers who are fearful that their traditional turfs are being invaded by outsiders. The ensuing conflicts seriously restrict the capacities of the corporation to develop or pursue new strategies towards their changing environment.

Figure 5.1 Business and Its Environments

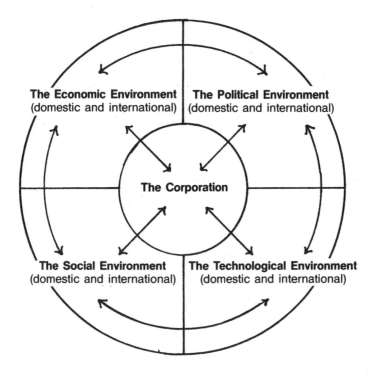

Such negative consequence for corporate performance is even more debilitating when public affairs units are explicitly *barred* by top management from including economic-technological trends on their analytical agenda. This exclusion is usually due to the argument that responsibility for monitoring these trends falls within the purview of other, long established units, such as finance, marketing, strategic planning or research and development.

The negative consequence flowing from the restricted or fuzzy environmental targeting of public affairs units can, however, be rectified by senior management. The approach to causation elaborated on in the introduction and above, can be particularly helpful at this point. If causation is circular, then clearly, the management of relations between the corporation's changing social-political environment cannot be optimized, and socio-political trends cannot be properly spotted unless and until shifts in the economic and technological realms are fully integrated into the calculus of change.

Political ideas, new social values and new public expectations do not simply leap out of the mind-sets of individuals confined to the socio-political arena. These new socio-political forces are in fact closely connected to and conditioned by changing economic and technological circumstances. The growing public concern with environmental protection, shifts in governmental regulation, or in egalitarian values could not have been forecast nor fully understood without reference, for example, to technological variables. Indeed, as suggested earlier, one of the main reasons why public affairs professionals, corporate planners and senior executives *are* experiencing difficulties in coping with the above noted changes is that they have not recognized the vital role of economic-technological elements in the overall equation of societal change.

The conclusion drawn from this observation for management is as clear as it is significant. The public affairs unit's contribution to the development of a new corporate strategy is only partly a derivative of strict socio-political analysis. To be genuinely effective, these corporate units must have access to and professional competence in integrating economic and technological factors into their socio-political prognostications.

This has some logical, and perhaps unpopular, staffing consequences. Senior management must ensure that its public affairs personnel possess sound business-economic and technological competence, and are also good purveyors or communicators of socio-political intelligence. Public affairs professionals frequently lament the socio-political "ignorance" of senior management. They often neglect to realize, however, that their own deficiencies in business-economic knowledge are as important barriers to effective corporate performance as are the socio-political analytical shortcomings of their superiors.

The above points are not designed to suggest that technological-economic forecasting/monitoring should be "taken over" by public affairs departments or that the public affairs professional should serve as a parallel or duplicating source of advice to the C.E.O. on the organization's technological-economic alternatives. This is not at all what public affairs is or is becoming. The point to stress is that if public affairs units or professionals are to optimize their contribution, they must be able to swim in technological-economic waters. More precisely, they must have the capacity to understand how socio-political objectives *and* changes are conditioned by technological-economic variables and vice-versa, and they must have the authority and competence to advise or act in these areas.

In short, the suggestion that public affairs units or professionals should bypass economic and technological issues and simply focus on socio-political matters betrays a profound ignorance at management levels about the dynamics of socio-political change. The translation of this misdirected approach into management practice leads to recurring waste, to misallocation of scarce resources, to strategic mistakes and in the final analysis, to diminishing profitability.

Once the question of which segments of the environment are germane to public affairs is clarified, exploration is required into the depth and width of the penetration into *each* of these sectors of the environment by the designated corporate unit. We need also to ask whether the extent of this penetration is constant or variable for all organizations over time. In other words, is there *one best way* of structuring and organizing the public affairs function? Is there such a thing as the poor man's "public affairs Cadillac" that can transport the corporation to and from its environment efficiently and at significantly reduced costs?

The flippant answer to the last question is that if one can afford it, why not travel in style? A number of large corporations are indeed doing just that. They employ literally an army of public affairs professionals and researchers, scanning just about anything in the universe that moves. Similarly, there are large corporations that employ only a handful of public affairs professionals, yet are as effective in managing their relations with their socio-political environment as the highly staffed corporations. As in so many things, size is not necessarily a sign of virtue. In the following sections, we shall examine the clientele and the wide-ranging services that can be provided by corporate public affairs.

THE SERVICES AND CLIENTELE OF CORPORATE PUBLIC AFFAIRS DEPARTMENTS

The Basic Mandate

The tasks of public affairs management vary greatly from corporation to corporation. Differences in corporate size, resources, the nature of the business itself, the attitude of senior management, the qualities of the practitioners themselves, the needs and capacities of the corporation in the public affairs realm and the lack of a generally acceptable organizational model, or unwillingness to accept one, are but some of the causes of the absence of organizational uniformity.

As stated earlier, there is no "one best way" to organize or manage this management function. The best way is that which works. This is not to say that corporations can't learn from each other's experiences, or that the quest for generalizations—the hallmark of scientific methodology—should be put aside in the academic pursuit of this area. Quite the contrary, heightened theoretical sophistication is an essential prerequisite for the future development of this management field. The point to remember, however, is that the manner in which this function is to be exercised is very much conditioned by the internal "culture" of the firm, and by the nature of the unique linkages between a specific firm and its environment. Wholesale transplants of organizational models from one corporate setting into another are, therefore, seldom possible. The wiser inventors of models readily accept this.

Keeping this warning in mind, the tasks that are commonly shared by all mature public affairs units or their equivalent can nevertheless be outlined as follows:

1. *To help identify and anticipate* emerging socio-political pressures upon the corporation as well as to help identify and anticipate the internal and external socio-political impacts of corporate economic-technological behaviour;

2. *To help monitor* continuously the behaviour of all those socio-political forces, issues, groups and personalities that have a bearing upon the economic-technological viability and legitimacy of the corporation (internal and external);

3. *To help set priorities on* importance of the above derived socio-political forces, issues, groups and personalities as far as corporate involvement is concerned (internal and external);

4. *To help educate* management at all levels of the corporation about the ways in which socio-political forces limit or enhance corporate economic strategy—and hence profits—and to sensitize corporate decision-makers to the socio-political impacts of their policy choices. This educational function is designed to improve the decision-making capabilities of management and will provide a more rational and effective strategy for the future;

5. *To help develop corporate action plans and response mechanisms* that reduce the divergence between corporate behaviour and socio-political change. These action plans should include both internal changes and their impacts on corporate behaviour as well as efforts to influence external socio-political trends;

6. *To participate directly in or to interact with* those external socio-political processes (government, the media, pressure groups, academia, unions, political parties, etc.) that have an important influence upon the operations and playing field of the corporation (often called net-working); and

7. *To help develop internal and external communications programmes* to support and sustain the activities and response mechanisms outlined above.

The corporate public affairs *officer*, first of all, provides advisory services to senior management colleagues and to corporate line-managers on relevant socio-political issues. The role is that of a catalyst of change, both inside and outside of the corporation. The public affairs officer performs a liaison role with relevant internal and external groups with the objective of bridging the gap between the corporation's economic-technological thrust and its socio-political milieu.

The corporate public affairs *function*, on the other hand, includes both the public affairs officer *and* other operating managers who work together and caucus to achieve the above mentioned "bridging" of corporate economic-technological forces with socio-political change. (This "job description" may help clarify the image of public affairs in the minds of senior officers.)

Whereas during the early stages of this management approach, corporate public affairs *officers* tended to carry the main burden of responsibility for this task, in the latter phases the responsibility is more evenly distributed between the public affairs department and other operating units in the corporation. In other words, while in the initial phases of this managerial revolution, corporate public affairs departments (or units) may experience a rapid acceleration in size, personnel, budgets and jurisdictional responsibilities, during the latter phases of the revolution, there is a pendular swing back. The function becomes more diffused, and more evenly distributed between the centre and periphery of the corporate entity. Or as some enlightened public affairs officers define their role: "Our task is to work ourselves out of a job."

As stated above, corporate public affairs management is a catalytic agent for both internal and external change, in roughly equal proportions. The sections below survey the target constituencies for public affairs involvement both within and outside of the firm, and comment on the kinds of exchanges public affairs tends to pursue with these constituencies.

The Internal Clientele

The role of the public affairs unit *within* the firm is to advise the chief executive officer, top management, line officers, planners, communicators and employees about socio-political forces or issues that are pertinent to the economic-technological well-being of the firm (see Figure 5.2). The aim is to inject an increasingly important dimension into the traditional strategic and decision-making processes of operating and staff units throughout the corporation, from the C.E.O. to the shop floor. This aim can be achieved *directly* and *indirectly*. The direct approach sees the public affairs unit as the exclusive agency specializing in socio-political intelligence, the results of which it injects into various operating-staff cultures. Increasingly, however, the indirect approach is being used. In this case, the public affairs

Figure 5.2 The Internal Clientele and Services of the Public Affairs Department

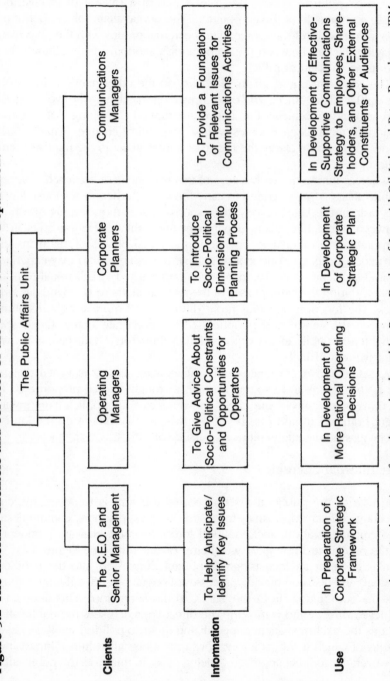

Source: A somewhat revised version of a schema developed by Peter Bartha of Imperial Oil Ltd. and Peter Broadmore, IBM Canada Ltd.

unit plays the role of a *facilitator, helping* to increase the public affairs capabilities of line managers, acting as counsel to operating managers and planners as *they* fuse socio-political considerations into their day-to-day activities.

The External Clientele

The external clientele of public affairs is represented in Figure 5.3. A brief commentary on each of these external target areas follows:

a. External Stakeholders "Stakeholders" is an umbrella term to refer to all those individuals or groups that have a "stake" in the welfare of the corporation or who are affected one way or another by corporate activities. Generally, internal stakeholders are employees, unions and various management sectors. External stakeholders include, among others, suppliers, creditors, shareholders, institutional investors, customers and affected local community groups. Vis-à-vis external stakeholders, corporate public affairs has a frontline responsibility. These groups have a vested interest in and involvement with the corporation. It is the responsibility of public affairs management to keep abreast of the changing concerns and needs of this constituency, to keep it continuously updated about corporate plans, objectives and activities, and generally to create harmonious interactions between the corporation and these groups.

To illustrate, one of the key components of the "external stakeholder" population is the community or municipality in which the corporation is located. Participation in the management of community affairs or community relations, as most surveys indicate, is indeed one of the leading responsibilities of public affairs departments in Canada and especially in the United States. Table 5.2 lists the various community relations activities of Canadian firms and also shows their perceived significance or usefulness.

b. Special Interest Groups Special interest groups are also referred to as public interest groups, or single-issue pressure groups. Into this general category fall all those groups that are organized to apply pressure upon governments, public opinion and the corporation in specific areas that relate to the production and distribution function (consumer protection, environmental protection, equal employment opportunities, etc.).

The impact of special interest group behaviour on business has grown enormously over the past twenty years.[2] Studies show, for example, that most of the consumer safety and health laws passed in the United States during the past couple of decades are directly due to the lobbying efforts of these groups. Indeed, there are those who suggest that tracking public interest group behaviour provides a better "read-out" of impending public policy changes than does public opinion polling.[3] For these reasons then, it

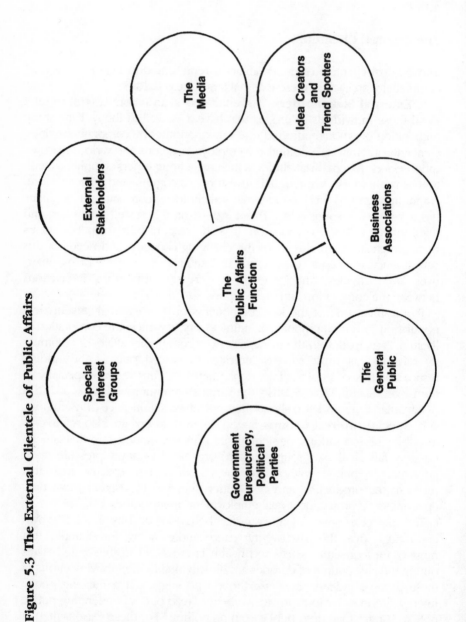

Figure 5.3 The External Clientele of Public Affairs

Table 5.2 Community Relations Activities of Canadian Corporations and Their Perceived Significance

Activity	Highly Significant			Insignificant	
	1	**2**	**3**	**4**	**5**
Active management participation on boards of community projects, charities, etc.	12.0	31.6	36.1	15.0	5.3
Financial support for local community groups, associations	18.0	36.1	30.8	12.0	3.0
Corporate advertising in local media	3.0	10.5	18.0	41.4	27.1
"Open-house" days for members of the community at large	3.8	14.3	26.3	23.3	32.3
"Open-house" days for community opinion leaders	8.3	15.9	27.3	20.5	28.0
Advertising of corporate support for local community projects	1.5	9.0	25.6	30.1	33.0
Management speaking tours in local community or schools	3.8	14.3	21.8	36.8	23.3
Inviting regular community group feedback on corporate behaviour	3.0	15.8	12.8	27.8	40.6
Hiring policy favoring residents of local community	10.6	17.4	29.5	16.7	25.8
Scanning and prioritizing local community issues for corporate response	6.0	18.8	22.6	29.3	23.3

Percentage of Respondents Consider This to Be

Mean Ranking of the Above	Mean Score
1. Financial support for local community groups, associations	2.459
2. Active management participation on boards of community projects, charities, etc.	2.699
3. Hiring policy favoring residents of local community	3.295
4. "Open-house" days for community opinion leaders	3.439
5. Scanning and prioritizing local community issues for corporate response	3.451
6. Management speaking tours in local community or schools	3.617
7. "Open-house" days for members of the community at large	3.662
8. Corporate advertising in local media	3.789
9. Advertising of corporate support for local community projects	3.857
10. Inviting regular community feedback on corporate behaviour	3.872

Table 5.3 Government Relations Activities of Canadian Corporations and Their Perceived Significance
(includes municipal, provincial, federal and international levels)

	Percentage of Respondents Consider This to Be				
	Highly Significant			Insignificant	
Activity	1	2	3	4	5
Systematically anticipating legislative and regulatory trends	34.8	23.5	27.3	12.9	1.5
Projecting favourable corporate image to rule-makers	26.3	34.6	29.3	8.3	1.5
Working to reduce level of government regulation in the company's economic sector	11.4	22.0	42.4	18.2	6.1
Keeping governments advised on a regular and systematic basis about company's special needs	24.8	33.1	25.6	11.3	5.3
Alerting governments to possible impacts of various legislative scenarios upon the company	34.1	34.8	23.5	6.1	1.5
Working to create a more favourable political climate for free enterprise in general	13.6	28.0	33.3	19.7	5.3
Scanning existing and future governmental legislation for provisions that would increase the company's business opportunities	12.0	25.6	35.3	24.1	3.0
Voluntarily advising governments on how to improve the quality of regulation	5.3	27.5	29.8	32.1	5.3
Developing and proposing new alternatives for improving business-government relations within company's sector of the economy	11.4	26.5	34.1	20.5	7.6

Mean Ranking of the Above	Mean Score
1. Alerting governments to possible impacts of various legislative scenarios upon the company	2.061
2. Systematically anticipating legislative and regulatory trends	2.227
3. Projecting favourable image to rule-makers	2.241
4. Keeping governments advised on a regular and systematic basis about company's special needs	2.391
5. Working to create a more favourable political climate for free enterprise in general	2.750

Table 5.3 continued

Mean Ranking of the Above	Mean Score
6. Scanning existing and future governmental legislation for provisions that would increase the company's business opportunities	2.805
7. Working to reduce level of government regulation in the company's economic sector	2.856
8. Developing and proposing new alternatives for improving business-government relations within company's sector of the economy	2.864
9. Voluntarily advising governments on how to improve the quality of regulation	3.046

is in the vital interest of the corporation to establish contact and information *exchanges* with all those interest groups that have an influence or potential influence on corporate activities. This provides the corporation both with an early warning system about impending socio-political change and with an opportunity to broaden the information resources of the public interest group. As a consequence of this interaction, the corporation should be in a better position to both anticipate the future and to reduce the likelihood of being falsely attacked.

c. Governments, Bureaucracies, Political Parties Interaction with political parties, bureaucracies and governments at local, regional, national and international levels is one of the most important concerns of corporate public affairs management.[4] The increased influence of public policy on corporate behaviour during the past few decades, and the potentially disruptive consequences of even the most innocent of governmental measures make it the vital interest of business to maintain open lines of communication with all those officials, departments and politicians whose actions can directly or indirectly affect corporate well-being. The corporate strategy here should be one of trying, first of all, *to understand* the multiple pressures that bear upon government, *to learn* of the possible directions of future public policy, *to participate* in its formation, and *to inform* government decision-makers about the realities of corporate life. Out of this information exchange will emerge a more stable, less disruptive and less adversarial relationship as well as more enlightened public policies. This will benefit both business and society as a whole.

Tables 5.3 and 5.4 illustrate the government relations activities of Canadian corporations.

d. The Media For the vast majority of the public, the mass media— television, radio, newspapers or magazines—are the major external sources of information about the world we live in, and specifically about the role

Table 5.4 The Major Mechanisms Used by Canadian Corporations in the Management of Federal Government Relations

Mechanisms	Percentage of Respondents	
	Use It	Don't Use It
Trade Association(s)	95.4	4.6
Frequent visits to Ottawa by senior executives	94.6	5.4
The Ottawa Office	34.1	65.9
Government relations consultants situated in Ottawa	49.6	50.4
Plant visits by members of Parliament	68.2	31.8
Speakers' bureaus	51.6	48.4
Advocacy advertising	43.3	56.7

played by business in that world. The media are not simply one of the most important sources of public information about corporate behaviour, but are, in fact, a powerful socializing instrument, shaping social values, attitudes, beliefs and opinions.

Given the media's pivotal role, it is not surprising that good media relations are vital to the well-being of the modern corporation. Effective media relations can serve the corporation as an important source of information about changing public perceptions and needs. Media relations can also serve as an important channel of information *from* the corporation to the public in general. Corporate credibility and legitimacy can both be enhanced by carefully *planned, systematic, open* and *informative* media programmes and these should become important components of the public affairs mandate of modern, dynamic corporations.

e. Business Associations Most corporations belong to at least one trade or business association (e.g. National Association of Manufacturers, Chambers of Commerce, Federations of Small Business, Bankers Associations). These associations can be of great importance to the corporation from a public affairs standpoint. First of all, associations can serve as important sources of research and information about socio-political issues relevant to their members. Such research services could significantly reduce the financial burden upon individual corporations which are otherwise compelled to conduct their own, and often, duplicative, socio-political analyses. Effective relations with business associations also provide the corporation with a "loudspeaker." Through its associations, the corporation can rally support for its socio-political strategies, and inject these strategies into the public policy process with greatly enhanced power or credibility. The old adage that there is strength in numbers is nowhere more relevant than here. For many corporations, a full public affairs management programme is both humanly and financially out of reach. The establishment of public affairs services by the firm's trade association can significantly enhance the effectiveness of members.

f. Relations With Idea Creators and Trend Spotters Into this constituency fall all those opinion leaders—in the media, research institutes, academia, government, or wherever—who individually, and through their disseminating vehicles (the classroom, the scientific press, television, etc.) exercise a significant influence on public opinion and on the diffusion of new socio-political ideas. Once again, the relationship here should be *two-sided*. On the one hand, an effective network in this area can substantially enhance the corporation's environmental scanning capabilities. Being plugged into the sources of new ideas (think tanks, policy institutes, academia, etc.), the corporation can gain a much better handle on emerging issues and on socio-political trends. These connections also provide the corporation with opportunities to inject its own "messages" directly into the process of idea creation and dissemination. Through these processes, the corporation improves its own as well as society's learning capabilities, and provides for a more informed and balanced progression of the ideas that will shape our future.

g. The General Public The final critical contact point for public affairs involvement is at the level of the general public. To suggest that public opinion is the major engine of public policy—even in our present era of frenetic political surveys—is an exaggeration. Public opinion nevertheless sets the framework, the tone or the limits for most legislative action. Advance knowledge of these limits, and of the public's attitudes, beliefs and values concerning matters of vital interest to the corporation, is an extremely important "window" on the public policy process.[5] Through this "window" the corporation can gain an early warning capability about emerging policy trends, and thereby be better prepared for future eventualities. Close contact with public opinion enhances corporate strategic planning capacities, provides support in all of the above mentioned areas (e.g. media relations, government relations, etc.) and can serve as a guide for corporate social involvement.

The general public serves not only as a tremendously important *source* of information for corporate strategy but also as a critical *vehicle* through which the corporation itself can influence the processes and direction of those socio-political changes that are vital to its interests. Effective communication of corporate views, realities and concerns to the public is, therefore, vital. Direct communications with the public must be as carefully planned and orchestrated as any other corporate activity. The corporation must identify the priorities of its target audiences, conduct research on the perceptions, knowledge and attitudes of those target groups, and formulate its messages on the basis of those assessments.

A manipulative approach in this area is a risky and counter-productive exercise. A single incident of false information can do irreparable long term harm to corporate credibility, and can seriously constrain the effectiveness of corporate involvement at all of the other levels we have discussed above. Manipulative communications programmes have a tendency to be transparent. Once such programmes have been identified as fragile or misleading, the media, special interest groups and other opinion leaders will ensure that the transgression is magnified many times over, thus casting a cloud over any subsequent corporate strategy.

The above pages have sketched out the internal and external clientele of corporate public affairs management, and have emphasized that interaction with these clients need not be centralized and, indeed, is more likely to be effective if it is diffused in an intelligent and coordinated manner through various layers of the corporate entity. The final mix of public affairs centre-periphery prerogatives is to be determined on an individual basis. It depends to a great extent on the nature of the issues affecting the corporation, the nature of the business, and the personalities and capacities of the people staffing the critical contact points. These intervening variables may demand either a strongly centralized approach, or a substantial degree of decentralized involvement—albeit with a central strategic overview.

The significance of the external and internal clients on the above checklists is not uniform. In most cases, corporate capacities and needs are selective and only a part of the above activities are pursued. In some cases, relations with the general public will be particularly important, while in other cases this involvement may be less so. In some cases, government relations will be the corporate lifeline; in others, such connections are sheer fluffery.

A recent survey of corporate public affairs behaviour in the United States conducted by the Public Affairs Research Group of Boston University (see Table 5.5) provides a good snapshot of the current "incidence" of many of the above mentioned activities.

The Boston University survey is a useful data base for analysis of corporate public affairs behaviour in the United States. As with any pioneering venture, however, it raises important new questions. One in particular which the Boston Survey has not addressed, perhaps by intention, is the extent to which the various public affairs missions belong to the jurisdiction of public affairs departments. In other words, we do not know whether the 71.5 percent of the public affairs units which listed "corporate contributions" within their domain have full, or partial jurisdiction over this matter. In the area of "advertising," the survey does not distinguish among product advertising, issue advertising and advocacy advertising. It does not reveal whether public affairs units play a leading or supportive role. Similar points

Table 5.5 The Functions Which United States Corporations Consider to be Within the Province of Public Affairs

Activity	Percentage of Respondents	
	Yes	No
Community relations	84.9	15.1
Government relations	84.2	15.8
Corporate contributions	71.5	28.5
Media relations	70.0	30.0
Stockholder relations	48.5	51.5
Advertising	40.4	59.6
Consumer affairs	38.5	61.5
Graphics	33.5	66.5
Institutional investing relations	33.5	66.5
Customer relations	23.8	76.2
Other	26.3	73.7

"Other" includes grass-roots lobbying and political action committees.

Source: Public Affairs Research Group, *Public Affairs Offices and Their Functions* (Boston University, 1981), p. 3.

could be made about "graphics," "stockholder relations," "consumer affairs" and others on the list. In short, the degree of centralization or decentralization of the function is not apparent from the survey.

My survey of Canadian corporations generated some additional data in this domain and throws some light on the *level of involvement* of public affairs departments in the above areas. Tables 5.6, 5.7 and 5.8 provide figures for leading and supportive public affairs roles and a ranking of these activities by firms in Canada.

CONCLUSIONS

Earlier in this book, public affairs management was described as a process by which a corporation *anticipates, monitors* and *manages* its relations with those social and political environmental forces that shape the company's operations and environment. The figures in Table 5.6, 5.7 and 5.8 demonstrate that in Canada, at least, apart from a couple of activities—namely communications with the media and with the public at large—corporate public affairs departments do not have a monopoly over this management activity. While there was a sharp increase in the past decade in the number of corporations that have set up distinct public affairs departments to deal with the "crowding-in" of external issues, most departments *share* the function with other corporate units. This trend appears to be similar to that in the United States.

Table 5.6 Activities Pursued by Canadian Corporate Public Affairs Departments: Leading and Supportive Roles

	Percentage of Respondents			
Activity	P.A. Plays Leading Role	P.A. Plays Supportive Role	P.A. Plays No Role	No Such Activity at Company
Corporate donations	62.5	24.0	9.4	4.2
Monitoring-anticipating social-political changes	57.3	38.5	3.1	1.0
Involvement in local community affairs	35.4	56.3	5.2	3.1
Product advertising	16.0	33.0	38.3	12.8
Advocacy advertising	30.9	19.1	9.6	40.4
Communications with the public	83.3	16.7	0.0	0.0
Communications with the media	86.5	12.5	1.0	0.0
Communications with employees	56.3	35.4	8.3	0.0
Communications with financial stakeholders	39.1	37.0	9.8	14.1
Federal government relations	50.0	43.8	6.3	0.0
Provincial government relations	53.1	40.6	5.2	1.0
Municipal government relations	24.2	53.7	16.8	5.3
International government relations	6.5	31.2	29.0	33.3
Measurement by corporate social impact	44.1	31.2	9.7	15.1
Developing corporate responses and strategies towards changing external issues	37.9	57.9	2.1	2.1
Implementing corporate responses and strategies towards changing external issues	31.9	56.4	6.4	5.3
Developing programmes to increase the public affairs skills of line managers	53.7	25.3	9.5	11.6
Development of corporate strategic plans	7.4	76.8	12.6	3.2
Conducting in-house research on socio-political trends and issues	42.6	26.6	14.9	16.0

Table 5.7 Ranking of Activities in Which Public Affairs Departments Play a Leading Role in Canada

Activity	Percentage of Responding Departments with Leading Role
1. Communications with the media	86.5
2. Communications with the public	83.3
3. Corporate donations	62.5
4. Monitoring and anticipating social-political changes	57.3
5. Communications with employees	56.3
6. Development of programmes to increase public affairs skills of line managers	53.7
7. Provincial government relations	53.1
8. Federal government relations	50.0
9. Measurement of corporate social impact	44.1
10. Conducting in-house research on social and political trends and issues	42.6
11. Communications with financial stakeholders	39.1
12. Developing corporate responses and strategies toward changing external issues	37.9
13. Involvement in local community affairs	35.4
14. Implementing corporate responses and strategies towards changing external issues	31.9
15. Advocacy advertising	30.9
16. Municipal government relations	24.2
17. Product advertising	16.0
18. Development of corporate strategic plans	7.4
19. International government relations	6.5

Table 5.8 The Ranking of Key Supportive Roles Performed by Canadian Public Affairs Departments

Activity	Percentage of Responding Departments Playing a Supportive Role
1. Development of corporate strategic plan	76.8
2. Developing corporate responses and strategies towards changing external issues	57.9
3. Implementing corporate responses and strategies towards changing external issues	56.4
4. Involvement in local community affairs	56.3
5. Municipal government relations	53.7
6. Federal government relations	43.8
7. Provincial government relations	40.8
8. Monitoring and anticipating social and political change	38.5

In connection with the question of how corporations structure or organize themselves to pursue the public affairs function, it is also important to recall that while 31.7 percent of the corporations that participated in the survey for this study do pursue public affairs activities, they have not established a separate department or unit by that name.

The absence of exclusive jurisdiction by public affairs departments over most elements of the public affairs function is an indicator of widespread organizational diversity. It also testifies to a principle that we have laid down earlier—namely, that this function must permeate both line and staff management throughout the firm. At the same time, this diversity and desirability of sharing of the function presents an important coordinating challenge to senior management. Indeed, it requires direct and close control by the chief executive officer. While there is no single organizational model dominating the field,—the best model being that which works—the significance of the overall function to corporate strategy is indisputable. Coordinating the various levers of public affairs and ensuring that they all pull together to assist corporate strategy is a top-management priority. The person who can make this happen is, in the words of George A. Steiner, "The New CEO."[6]

Notes

1. Ian Wilson, senior management consultant with Stanford Research International, is one of the earliest and most systematic advocates of this approach. See, for example, his "Environmental Analysis" in K. Albert (ed.), *Business Strategy Handbook* (McGraw-Hill, 1982), or "Environmental Scanning and Strategic Planning" in L.E. Preston (ed.), *Business Environment/Public Policy: 1979 Conference Papers* (American Assembly of Collegiate Schools of Business, 1980).

2. Some of the more interesting works on *how* to manage in this terrain are the following: B. Crew, "How U.S. Companies Tackle the Pressure Group Challenge," *Industrial Management*, December, 1978, and January, 1979; E. Ladd, "How to Tame the Special Interest Groups," *Fortune*, October 20, 1980; F. McLaughlin, "Public Interest Groups" in J. S. Nagelschmidt (ed.), *The Public Affairs Handbook* (AMACOM, American Management Associations, 1982); S. Greysar, "Does Consumerism Have a Future?" A paper prepared for the October 5-6, 1980 Conference on "The Future of Consumerism" sponsored by the Center for Business and Public Policy, College of Business Management, University of Maryland, 1980; J. Place, "Special Interests: Democracy or Disaster?" *Journal of Commercial Banking and Lending*, Vol. 62, July, 1980.

3. J. Holcomb, "Anticipating Public Policy: An Interest Group Approach," *Public Affairs Review*, Vol. I, 1980.

4. Indeed, one could write a book on strategies and tactics in this area. There are a number of works that do that. In the Canadian context, Jim Gillies' book is

recommended: *Where Business Fails: Government Relations at the Federal Level in Canada* (Institute for Research on Public Policy, 1981); see also J. Faulkner, "Business Government Relationships in Canada," *Optimum*, Vol. 7, No. 1, 1976; Institute for Political Involvement, *A Report on the Prospects for Increased Involvement of Business People in the Canadian Political System* (Institute for Political Involvement, Toronto, 1978); R. MacLaren, "Firefighting or a Systematic Relationship," *Business Quarterly*, Vol. 41, Winter, 1976; D. Thain, "Improving Competence to Deal With Politics and Government: The Management Challenge of the 1980s," *Business Quarterly*, Vol. 45, Spring, 1980.

Among American studies: E. Grefe, *Fighting to Win: Business Political Power* (Harcourt, Brace, Jovanovich, 1981); J. Aplin and W. Hegarty, "Political Influence: Strategies Employed by Organizations to Impact Legislation in Business and Economic Matters," *Academy of Management Journal*, Vol. 23, September, 1980; E. Epstein, "The Emergence of Political Action Committees" in H. E. Alexander (ed.), *Political Finance* (Sage, 1979); R. Godown and J. La Mere, "P.A.C.'s: Channels for Corporate Action," *Industrial Development*, July, 1979 and G. Keim, "Foundations of a Political Strategy of Business," *California Management Review*, Vol. 23, Spring, 1981.

5. On the uses of survey research see D. Bates "Using Polls," *Public Relations Journal*, Vol. 37, March, 1981; R. Zentner, "Survey Research" in J. S. Nagelschmidt (ed.), *The Public Affairs Handbook, op. cit.*; G. Molitor, "The Hatching of Public Opinion" in R. J. Allio and M. W. Pennington (eds.), *Corporate Planning Techniques and Applications* (American Management Associations, 1979).

6. G. Steiner, *The New CEO* (Free Press, 1983).

The Driving Forces of Corporate Public Affairs

If an organization is heading in the wrong direction, the last thing it needs is getting there more efficiently.
—B.B. Tregoe and J. W. Zimmerman

Ay, now I am in Arden; the more fool I: when I was at home, I was in a better place: but travellers must be content.
—William Shakespeare, *As You Like It*

ENVIRONMENTAL ANALYSIS, ISSUES MANAGEMENT AND PUBLIC AFFAIRS RESEARCH

Throughout interviews, and on the conference circuit, I have often been approached by people in search of the perfect environmental forecasting system with which they could close the door, once and for all, on uncertainty and thus provide their corporation with a smooth and predictable ride into the future.

There is no such key to be found. Those public affairs professionals who persist in searching for the instrument that will eliminate environmental turbulence are destined to do so forever.

This categorical assertion should not suggest that the pursuit of improved environmental analysis and forecasting is futile. On the contrary, such a quest is one of the leading tasks of public affairs management, as the previous chapter indicated. The point to realize is that the future does not exist beyond the horizon, stored in a warehouse and awaiting our key to unlock it. A new future is created every minute of every day by human beings interacting with each other under constantly varying social, technological and economic circumstances. And chance itself remains one of the key players in this process. Even the best environmental analysis system will not eliminate environmental turbulence and surprises.

The purpose of environmental analysis, as Liam Fahey and others have aptly stated, is not to reduce environmental uncertainty as such, but to "enhance the organization's capability to *handle* environmental uncertainty."[1] Or as Ian Wilson also stresses:

> In an uncertain environment we can never truly know the future, no matter how much we may perfect our forecasting techniques. It is highly misleading, therefore, to claim (or believe) that environmental forecasting can predict *the* future. What it can do—and do effectively—is to help us clarify our assumptions about the future, speculate systematically about alternative outcomes, assess probabilities and make more rational choices.[2]

This chapter makes no effort to produce a "state-of-the-art" model of environmental forecasting, because there is no single model that can be totally validated. Myriads of models compete for the coveted title, but the "best" model is always the functional expression of corporate needs, capacities and environmental dependencies.

A review of the various competing models could fill the pages of a relatively thick book and will not appear here. The "state-of-the-art" of environmental analysis would capture nothing but a blur. As Wayne Boucher, one of the leading practitioners of this art, so aptly said of forecasting ". . . all books are necessarily out of date long before they are published, the current technological literature is fragmented, and the true 'state-of-the-art' is known only to its practitioners."[3]

The set of guidelines and recommendations that follow on how to proceed towards increasing sophistication in this realm is based on surveyed experience and interviews. The first step to sophistication is to clarify the meaning of "scanning," "monitoring" and "forecasting."[4] "Scanning" refers to a radar-like activity by which the corporation attempts to detect and identify unforeseen obstacles to its strategy. "Monitoring" refers to a different kind of activity. Here the corporation keeps track of previously identified obstacles, and continuously calculates its relationship to those obstacles over time. "Forecasting" is an exercise by which the corporation *projects* a scenario of the terrain that lies beyond its monitoring and scanning capacities. The forecast itself is a projection, in most cases, from the scanning and monitoring data base.

These then are the three distinct, though interdependent, probing mechanisms of environmental analysis. How extensively management adapts to each of these functions is largely a question of its socio-economic terrain, of the speed with which management chooses to move in whatever direction, and of the resources it has at its disposal.

In Chapter 5, we saw that 95.8 percent of the responding public affairs departments to my survey were involved in some form of monitoring and anticipating socio-political change. The same percentage was also involved in *developing* corporate responses-strategies towards changing external issues. A slightly smaller percentage of the responding departments—88.3 percent—stated that they were also involved in the *implementation* of the corporate responses-strategies towards changing external issues.

Tables 6.1, 6.2, and 6.3 provide a read-out of current and projected Canadian corporate practices in the realm of environmental analysis, issues management and public affairs research. These tables demonstrate the peaceful coexistence of a wide range of environmental analysis and issues management techniques currently in use or being contemplated by Canadian corporations. These results are quite similar to data recently collected from corporations in the United States.[5] The combination of "currently used" and "projected use" figures from the above tables shows a very high—75-85 percent—frequency of use ratio.

The mechanisms ranked least significant are:

1. The use of full-time issues manager(s)—59.1 percent of respondents saw no need for it.
2. Location of issues management and corporate planning function in one body—60.5 percent of respondents saw no need for it—and
3. Using institutionalized interdepartmental issues committees—50.8 percent of respondents saw no need for it.

As far as assessing their corporations' effectiveness in selected environmental analysis and issues management areas, Tables 6.4 and 6.5 show that Canadian respondents considered themselves to be most effective in a monitoring mode and least effective in integrating issues analysis into the strategic planning process.

In order to improve performance in these areas and in public affairs research in general, some additional guidelines are clearly in order. Of particular importance is the question of how to enhance the contribution of environmental analysis and issues management to the corporate planning process. (This last point will receive detailed discussion in the section immediately following.)

Those wishing to get a better handle on forecasting techniques may find the typologies that were developed by Selwyn Enzer of the Center for Futures Research to be particularly useful.[6] According to Enzer, one can identify five different types of forecasting models. These models are:

1. Scientific predictions
2. Quantitative models
3. Extrapolative models
4. Reasoned opinions, and
5. Speculations

Table 6.1 Current and Projected Environmental Analysis, Issues Management and Research Mechanisms Utilized by Canadian Corporations

	Percentage Respondents Reporting		
Issues Management Mechanisms	Currently Used	Not Used But Considering	Not Used and See No Need
Use of full time issues managers	12.1	28.8	59.1
Ad hoc attention of decision-makers to the business implications of public issues	70.1	19.7	10.2
Institutionalized and systematic scanning of public issues that are relevant to the company	60.9	27.1	12.0
Institutionalized and systematic scanning of public issues that are relevant to the business sector	63.4	22.1	14.5
Institutionalized and systematic scanning of major short term strategic issues (major impact over 1-5 years)	57.1	29.3	13.5
Institutionalized and systematic scanning of major long term emerging issues (5-15 year impact frame)	31.8	44.7	23.5
Quantitative assessment of economic and financial impact of public issues on company	47.3	33.6	19.1
Identification and analysis of corporate response alternatives to public issues	55.3	30.3	14.4
Active participation of relevant line and staff officers in corporate issues programmes	56.2	28.5	15.4
Using institutionalized, inter-departmental issues committees	16.9	32.3	50.8
Formal integration of quantitative issues analysis into corporate planning process	25.4	45.2	29.4
Informal corporate planning guidance from issues impact analysis	51.2	31.4	17.4
Location of issues management and corporate planning function in one body	8.4	31.1	60.5

Table 6.2 The Ranking of Currently Used Environmental Analysis, Issues Management and Research Mechanisms by Canadian Corporations on the Basis of Frequency of Use

Ranking	Percentage of Respondents Currently Using
1. Ad hoc attention of decision-makers to the business implications of public issues	70.1
2. Institutionalized and systematic scanning of public issues that are relevant to business sector	63.4
3. Institutionalized and systematic scanning of public issues that are relevant to the company	60.9
4. Institutionalized and systematic scanning of major short term strategic issues (major impact 1-5 years)	57.1
5. Active participation of relevant line and staff officers in corporate issues programmes	56.2
6. Identification and analysis of corporate response alternatives to public issues	55.3
7. Informal corporate planning guidance from issue impact analysis	51.2
8. Quantitative assessment of economic and financial impact of public issues on company	47.3
9. Institutionalized and systematic scanning of major long term emerging issues (5-15 year impact frame)	31.8
10. Formal integration of quantitative issues analysis into corporate planning process	25.4
11. Using institutionalized, inter-departmental issues committees	16.9
12. Use of full time issues manager(s)	12.1
13. Location of issues management and corporate planning function in one body	8.4

Table 6.3 Three Leading Contemplated Environmental Analysis, Issues Management and Research Mechanisms by Canadian Firms

Ranking	Percentage of Respondents That Currently Do Not Use But Consider Using This Mechanism in the Future
1. Formal integration of quantitative issues analysis into corporate planning process	45.2
2. Institutionalized and systematic scanning of major long term emerging issues (5-15 year impact frame)	44.7
3. Quantitative assessment of economic and financial impact of public issues on company	33.6

Table 6.4 Perceived Effectiveness of Canadian Corporations in Selected Environmental Analysis, Issues Management and Research Areas

Issues Management Areas	Very Effective 1	2	3	4	Ineffective 5
	Percentage of Respondents Consider Themselves to Be				
Anticipating issues	7.0	27.3	52.3	12.5	0.8
Monitoring issues	18.9	39.4	31.5	8.7	1.6
Prioritizing issues	16.4	33.6	32.0	15.6	2.3
Quantifying issue impact	4.7	19.7	40.2	29.1	6.3
Integrating issue analysis into strategic planning process	4.7	15.7	39.4	30.7	9.4
Managing issues	7.1	22.0	46.5	22.0	2.4

Table 6.5 Corporate Effectiveness Ranking in Selected Environmental Analysis, Issues Management and Research Areas

Ranking of Approaches	Mean Scores
1. Monitoring issues	2.346
2. Prioritizing issues	2.539
3. Anticipating issues	2.727
4. Managing issues	2.906
5. Quantifying issue impact	3.126
6. Integrating issues analysis into strategic planning process	3.244

In the terrain that public affairs finds itself, scientific predictions, quantitative models and even extrapolative models are frequently difficult to apply. Or, as Enzer points out:

> In most areas of change, particularly those which are unquantifiable and those which involve social changes, our lack of theoretical understanding frustrates any attempt to construct meaningful analytic models for projecting future trends. Typical examples of such areas are in changes in values, human behavior, new technologies and many others. These are areas in which there is sufficient qualitative understanding to permit some insightful commentary, but not enough to create an explicit model; hence, we must resort to the use of the integrative models of reasoned opinion and speculation here.[7]

The precision of "reasoned opinion and speculation" can vary tremendously from case to case. Tightening the margin of error in this area is of vital concern to public affairs practitioners. There are literally hundreds of charts, checklists, and guidelines that are available to help in this regard. Two of the more interesting ones are those suggested by Peter Bartha of Imperial Oil Ltd. (as shown in Figures 6.1 and 6.2).[8]

The challenges for environmental analysis resist, however, even the most sophisticated of all possible checklists. The most important challenges to overcome are:

1. Where do we set the limits of our scanning-monitoring system? How do we decide what data to look at and what to ignore?
2. Who decides what is or is not important? Who should be entrusted with the task of scanning and monitoring?
3. How does one interpret the results of scanning-monitoring systems? What is the significance or meaning of the data as far as corporate viability and credibility are concerned?
4. How does management rank the importance of issues? And how does it set priorities on the diverse range of events, issues and information collected by the scanning, monitoring and forecasting techniques?
5. Having ranked issues in terms of corporate priorities, what kind of programmes and policies should management pursue in each area?

Sound judgment, rather than mathematical formulae, should be the first rule of response to these challenges. Sound judgment can also be augmented by the following guidelines:

In setting boundaries of the scanning-monitoring system, it is essential to establish some form of public affairs audit as described in Chapter 4 of this study, and to act according to that initial assessment. External consultants can advise on the audit and the subsequent establishment of scanningmonitoring limits. Whether internally defined or derived with help of consultants, the scanning-monitoring system must be *holistic*—i.e. it must reach into *all* four of the societal quadrants outlined in Chapter 5. The advice of Ian Wilson is once again appropriate:

> The essential function of environmental analysis is to contribute to the identification and assessment of the strategic *issues* confronting the business. From a planning point of view, the essential question is: what are likely to be the positive or negative impacts of macro-environmental forces on the micro-environment of the business? This suggests defining issues as opportunities or threats, and adopting a matrix approach to issue identification.[9]

The "reach" finally determined should be clearly articulated. It should be

Figure 6.1 The Public Affairs Research Process

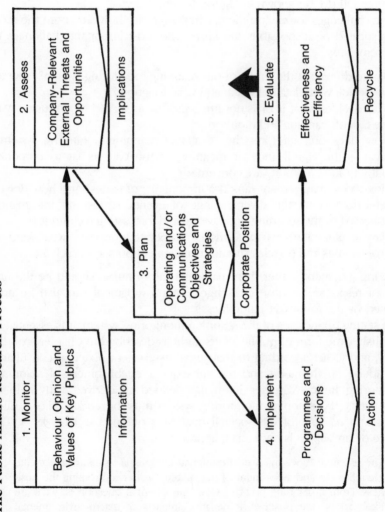

Source: Peter Bartha, Imperial Oil Ltd.

Figure 6.2 Environmental Monitoring-Analysis System

Grouping	Monitoring Data Base	Research/Analysis Techniques
1. Public —General —Key Segments	—Attitudes —Knowledge Level	—Surveys —Special Studies
2. Media —Print —Electronic	—News —Editorials —Features	—Content Analysis —Contact Programme —Editorial Briefings
3. Thought-Leaders —Organized Groups —Academics —Activists	—Position Statements —Publications —Conferences	—Literature Search —Surveys —Contact Programme
4. Government —Politicians —Civil Servants —Advisors	—Policy Statements —Background Studies —Legislation	—Legislative Review —Issue Analysis —Contact Programme

Source: Peter Bartha, Imperial Oil Ltd.

written in the form of a scanning agenda and should be regularly tested for relevance.

Who should be charged with the pursuit of this function? Practice, once again, differs. In some cases, this scanning-monitoring function is highly centralized, and is vested in a small central research team reporting to a senior officer. In other cases, the responsibility is widely dispersed in the form of a TAP (Trend Analysis Program) or TEAM (Trend Evaluation and Monitoring) approach.[10] There are cases where this function, in its entirety, is contracted to external consultants, or to trade and business associations. One interesting, flexible and relatively inexpensive method is QUEST— Quick Environmental Scanning Technique—developed by the Center for Futures Research at the University of Southern California.[11] This system is built on the assumption that top management has already some view of the dynamics of the changing corporate environment. The system is designed to produce, through various specified stages, a shared executive view of the trends and events that will have critical implications for the organization's strategies and policies.

Correct interpretation of the data gathered by scanners and monitors is also critically important. Incomplete or careless diagnosis at this point will nullify the most valiant efforts at subsequent phases of the environmental analysis process and thereby derail future corporate strategy. For this reason, the seasoned public affairs executive frequently calls for a "second opinion"—from consultants, research institutes, trade associations or other sources—so as to sustain the diagnosis against possible miscalculations.

A number of devices can be utilized to place priorities on corporate action, some of which are given as examples in Figures 6.3, 6.4, 6.5 and 6.6.

The final step and often the most difficult one, is to select the appropriate response mechanism, or "issue action program," to deal with the identified challenge. Here, decision-makers must often set their own precedents and

Figure 6.3 Impact and Probability Occurrence Matrix

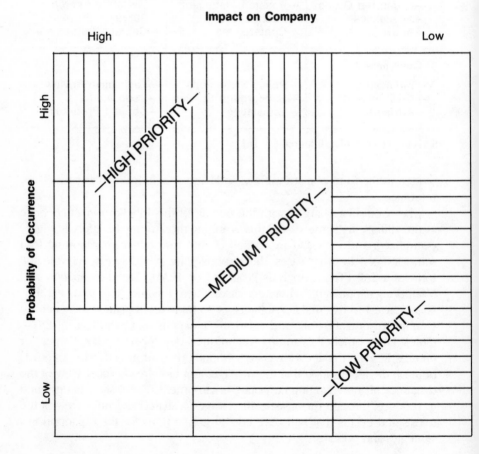

Figure 6.4 Importance and Leverage Matrix

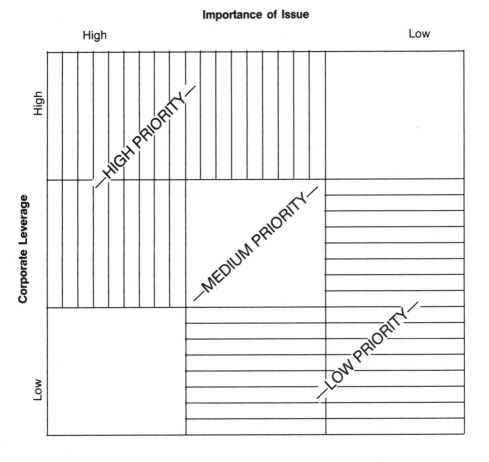

Importance of Issue

Figure 6.5 Simplified Priority Score Grid

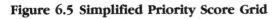

Issues	Probability	×	Importance	=	Priority
X	10		8		80
Y	5		7		35
Z	9		2		18
Etc.	—		—		—

Scale: High = 10
          Low = 1

Figure 6.6 Complex Priority Score Grid

Issues	Time Factor	Probability	Impact on Corporation	Gale Scale	Priority Score
X	5	5	10	4	1000
Y	5	5	8	4	800
Z	2	3	7	4	128
Etc.	—	—	—	—	—

Scales:

Time Factor:	0-1 Year = 5 points 2-5 Years = 2 points 6-10 Years = 1 point	(Assess date by which either societal pressure or legislation/regulation may have changed the "rules" so that the corporation must change the way it acts)
Probability:	1-5 points	(Probability of "rule" change as defined above)
Impact on Corporation:	1-10 points	(Major or minor effects on corporate costs/revenues/plans/policies)
Gale Scale:	1-4 points	(Assesses probable media political/public interest on the issue, for or against)
Priority Scale:	(Derived by multiplying the four preceding factors. To be used only in selecting issues for further research, analysis, preparation of public affairs strategy)	

Source: Public Affairs Department, Royal Bank of Canada.

exert leadership. Generalized solutions to highly particularistic problems rarely work.

A prevalent misconception in this area is that slavish application of some formalized process will inevitably provide the correct answers. This perception, widespread as it is, is unrealistic. Prudence and pragmatism are of high premium here, and there is a need to upgrade performance in additional areas that we shall now examine.

LINKING PUBLIC AFFAIRS TO
STRATEGIC PLANNING

In preceding sections and chapters of this book, we saw that managements' "theater of war" has changed sharply during the past decade-and-a-half.

Interviews throughout the United States and Canada, my own surveys and those of others, have proved that two of the leading challenges to executives are: 1) to engineer a better "match" between corporate competencies and environmental opportunities; and, 2) to link public affairs management to strategic planning.

The Boston University survey, for example, showed that while a very high proportion of public affairs departments in the United States participate in their corporation's strategic planning processes (see Table 6.6), only 3

Table 6.6 The Ways in Which Public Affairs Influences and/or Affects Corporate Planning in the United States

The Nature of the Public Affairs In-Put into Planning	Percentage of Public Affairs Respondents Perform These Activities
Identify public issues for corporate attention	92.8
Set or help set priorities for these issues	78.5
Identify public issues for department, division and/or subsidiary attention	74.2
Set or help set priorities for these issues	64.8
Provide forecasts of social/political trends to the corporate planning office	74.1
Provide forecasts of social/political trends to departments, divisions and/or subsidiaries	73.0
Review corporate plans for sensitivity to emerging social/political trends	69.1
Prepare a narrative section regarding future social/political trends which is included with directions for preparing corporate plans	57.8
Review department, division, and/or subsidiary plans for sensitivity to emerging social/political trends	55.0

Source: Public Affairs Research Group, *Public Affairs Offices and Their Functions* (Boston University, 1981), p. 18.

percent of the responding executives consider this participation as an important part of their overall responsibilities.[12]

My survey showed that Canadian public affairs managers perceived themselves to be least effective in their contribution to strategic planning and that their highest priority was to improve this linkage (see Tables 6.3 and 6.5 above). Seventy-six point four percent of the respondents to my survey questionnaire stated that public affairs managers should play a more significant role in their corporations' strategic planning processes.

Before one can design improved linkages between public affairs and corporate strategy, it is imperative to know the reasons why performance in this area is so weak. Why is it, for example, that only three percent of the public affairs executives in the United States consider their strategic planning responsibilities to be of current importance? Is this low score a function of frustration? Is the input into planning considered unimportant because senior management, or the planners themselves, do not take the public affairs contribution seriously? Is it because the input channels from public affairs to planning are not deep enough or pervasive enough? Does the public affairs professional feel unable to contribute usefully to the planning process? It is important to have correct answers to these questions. Analysis of data pertaining to these questions suggests that the leading causes of limited success in the public affairs-strategic planning interface are:

1. *The range of issues* identified by most socio-political scanning is so *vast*—the number of factors running into the hundreds at times—that the strategic planning body is simply unable to transform these inputs and thus ignores most of them.
2. Many of the factors brought forward to the planning body by public affairs scanners are of a *qualitative* or *soft* nature. Traditional strategic planners react first and foremost to signals that demonstrate measurable or calculable impacts on corporate finances and assets. In its early stages, the public affairs input into planning has been *less than successful in providing financial cost-benefit data* for its various scenarios. In other words, the difficulty public affairs has in reducing to dollars and cents the impacts of its various socio-political strategies precludes it from being taken seriously by the planning body.
3. Strategic planning is a fusion exercise through which specialized financial, marketing, research and development, etc., considerations are brought together into a focused strategic thrust. During the initial phases of its development, conventional public affairs tends to have few, if any, linkages to any of the above mentioned corporate units that relate directly to the planning process. The *absence of a pre-plan caucus*

between finance and public affairs, for example, tends to shut out public affairs considerations at the critical planning stage.

4. Line or operating executives and, in many cases, the *senior management* group of the corporation, often *do not understand public affairs* and look upon its practitioners as "new kids" on the block, who have yet to prove their worth. This lack of appreciation or distrust is not infrequently the direct consequence of the inability of public affairs officers to speak the language of finance, business or management.

No doubt other factors may also restrict the role of public affairs in the strategic planning process. Yet the four constraints listed here appear to be the most serious and prevalent. Together they have combined to restrict the optimized use of the public affairs tool in many corporations and are, in fact, restricting the opportunities of the corporation itself to reap the full benefits of effective public affairs use. Overcoming such constraints is therefore a major challenge both for the public affairs profession and for business in general.

The guidelines, referred to earlier, are now timely.[13]

1. First of all, public affairs must sharply *curtail the number of factors* it introduces into the planning process at any one time. This self-imposed restraint avoids the chance of overloading the planning mechanism with socio-political information and increases the absorption rate of public affairs data.

2. Public affairs officers must learn to *"speak the language"* of finance, marketing, accounting and other *key business sectors.* They must learn to "caucus" with these operating departments in the language that these departments understand. *Thus,* public affairs will be perceived as meaningful. In turn, the public affairs officer will become more sensitive and knowledgeable of the "business" side of the profession.

3. Public affairs must translate its leading socio-political variables into at least some degree of *financial cost-benefit terms.* It must make every effort to quantify the external socio-political impacts of corporate policies and actions, and vice-versa, in order to facilitate the entry of those variables into the planning and action process.

4. For public affairs to be taken seriously at the planning level, the *function must be diffused* throughout the corporation (without, however, abandoning a central strategic coordinating presence). Line managers or operating managers throughout the corporation should be given responsibilities and be held accountable for public affairs know-how. Once these managers have recognized that public affairs is a relevant and significant factor in their operations, *they* will carry this conviction into the planning process, and thereby legitimize, from the "bottom up," the linkage of this function with strategic planning and policy action.

5. The legitimization of the function "from the bottom up" has been identified in the previous point as an important means of linking public affairs to corporate planning. However, *"top down" involvement is equally important.* The *central* public affairs staff must help all segments of the corporate hierarchy to identify major socio-political considerations within *their* realm of responsibility. In other words, there must be a high degree of "counter planning" by the central public affairs unit that will directly tie in with the previously mentioned "upward" public affairs enrichment process. Ian Wilson has pioneered a framework for this "top down" process that is useful (see Figure 6.7).

6. In order for steps one through five to succeed, the corporate *chief executive officer and senior management must be fully committed*, both in word and deed, to the importance of the public affairs function. One way to ensure this understanding and executive involvement is to establish an interdepartmental Public Affairs Planning Committee, staffed by *senior corporate officers*, that is mandated to monitor and enforce each of the steps outlined above.

7. Finally, for public affairs to become a serious factor in the management planning and action process, it must *increase* its *analytic rigour.* The research basis, the scanning, monitoring and forecasting techniques, and

Figure 6.7 A Matrix Approach to Issue Identification

Micro-Environment \ Macro-Environment	Trends/Events/Developments			
	Social	Economic	Political	Technological
Markets				
Customers				
Employees				
Competitors				
Technology				
Materials/Supplies				
Production				
Finances, Shareholders				
Public/Government Relations				

Source: I. Wilson, "Environmental Analysis" in K. Albert (ed.), *Business Strategy Handbook* (McGraw-Hill, 1982).

the general analytical support system of *this function must be profession-ally developed and presented.* Whether this analytical support is drawn from the outside—trade associations and consultants—or strictly from within, "seat of the pants" flying will defeat the purpose. One reason why this book is also directed to senior corporate officers is to give this advice: Putting responsibility for the public affairs function into the hands of dilettantes is like putting finance into the hands of an office boy. In many cases, senior management does recognize the need for a more systems-oriented public affairs involvement, but then engages in a self-defeating exercise by poor staffing and by forcing the function to report to individuals who are simply not equipped to understand or maximize the opportunities available to the company.

Similarly, senior management sometimes delegates selection of the public affairs officer to middle managers unqualified to judge the qualities required. In short, by *demanding and increasing the profession-alism of public affairs,* senior corporate officers can improve the quality of its output and thereby demonstrate that public affairs must be taken seriously by strategic planners and vice-versa.

Public affairs is already connected to the strategic planning process in some form or another in an increasing number of corporate cases. The challenge facing the modern corporation is to breathe life into this linkage and to ensure that the connection will be substantive rather than merely symbolic. This objective can be realized through the steps outlined above.

A particularly important step is to increase the competence of *operating managers* in socio-political domains. Point four stressed the need to diffuse the function and to build social performance criteria into the overall performance-compensation evaluation system of managers. Expanded public affairs competence of operating managers will enhance the overall strategic capacities and performance levels of the corporation. The diffusion of this competence can also reduce central staff expenditures, consulting costs and generally improve corporate capacity to deal with the complexi-ties of socio-political change, the "crowding-in" of external issues and interdependence. Some guidelines to diffuse public affairs throughout the organization are now in order.

INCREASING THE PUBLIC AFFAIRS CAPABILITIES OF OPERATING MANAGERS

A recent survey of American trends by the Conference Board in New York,[14] as well as my own analysis of Canadian corporate behaviour, strongly underline the need for effective new measures in this area. As two executives surveyed by the Conference Board remarked,

> Those being groomed for the top are not being prepared for the world they will have to deal with. . . . The world is drifting and business is not quite keeping up.[15]

> The changing business environment has had a very big impact on the company—there's no doubt about that—but not on management development programs.[16]

The figures from the Conference Board survey provided in Table 6.7 demarcate the current and future public affairs management development trends for firms in the United States.[17] My survey of Canadian corporations found that 37.4 percent of the respondents have already put such programmes into place while 42.0 percent are actively considering such programmes. In other words, almost 80 percent of Canadian firms see a need for developing the public affairs competence of their line managers (see Table 6.8).

Table 6.9 demonstrates the frequency of public affairs criteria used in management appraisal systems by Canadian firms.

Of the firms which indicated that they use public affairs criteria in management appraisal, 43.5 percent thought these criteria carried little weight in their company's promotion-reward system. Only 4.3 percent thought that significant weight was attached by senior management to such competence in evaluating performance.

Table 6.11 also throws some light on the perceived weight that will be attached to public affairs competence in future management appointments in Canada.

As indicated earlier, almost 80 percent of the firms surveyed in Canada reported a need for developing the public affairs competence of their executives. A significant number of these firms have already put in place programmes to achieve this objective. These programmes are diverse and are listed together with their frequency of use in Table 6.12. It is clear that the corporation wishing to improve public affairs competence of managers can do so in many ways. Concentrating exclusively on one or two methods is not recommended. The greater diversity in training methods, the greater likelihood that public affairs will penetrate the surface of traditional management culture and practice.

In a recent lecture to the Public Affairs Council, Dean David Blake of Northeastern University, astutely summarized the preconditions for success of the above outlined programmes and for gaining wider acceptance for public affairs by operating managers. These preconditions are:

Table 6.7 Perceptions by Surveyed Executives of Developmental Activities and Needs Within Their Companies

Aspects of Public Affairs Competence in Senior Managers	Percent of Surveyed Executives Who Believe that the Aspect of Competence...		
	Is Now Being Developed	Merits Increased Attention or Emphasis	Is Not Now Being Developed and Does Not Merit Increased Attention or Emphasis
Knowledge or understanding:			
—of the social, economic and political environment in which business operates	68	54	10
—of legislative, regulatory and judicial processes and political trends	65	55	9
Skill or ability:			
—to "listen"—give heed to unfamiliar or competing viewpoints, values and interests	36	47	36
—to communicate company policies and views effectively, both internally and externally—directly and through the media	67	57	8
—to negotiate and interact effectively with individuals and groups, both internally and externally	42	42	41
—to deal with hostile groups or confrontation	26	48	44
Managerial perspectives and sensitivities:			
—appreciation of the relationship of public affairs to strategic planning	39	64	18
—sensitivity to how company decisions will affect and be perceived by various internal and external publics	47	59	20
—alertness to change in the social, political and economic environment	49	52	19
—readiness or willingness to "get involved"—to play an assertive, proactive role	43	54	22

Source: Seymour Lusterman, *Managerial Competence: The Public Affairs Aspects* (The Conference Board, Report No. 805, 1981), p. 33.

Table 6.8 Perceived Need to Improve Public Affairs Skills/Knowledge of Operating Managers in Canada

Responses	Percentage of Respondents
Yes, there is a need and we have programmes in place	37.4
We see no need for any programmes at this time	20.6
We have no programmes in place at this time, but we see a need for them	42.0

Table 6.9 The Frequency of Use by Canadian Firms of Formal Public Affairs Criteria in Management Appraisal Systems

Responses	Percentage of Respondents
Yes, we use this approach	16.2
We don't use this approach and we see no need for it	36.2
We don't use it currently, but see a need for it	47.7

Table 6.10 The Significance Attached to Formal Public Affairs Criteria in Management Appraisal Systems in Canada

Responses	Percentage of Respondents Using Criteria
Low significance	43.5
Moderate significance	52.2
High significance	4.3

1. If line managers are to utilize the new tools of public affairs, these tools must be in fact *relevant* to the operating manager's job.
2. In addition to seeing relevance, the operating manager must be filled with a sense of *ownership* of these new managerial tools. This sense of ownership is best achieved by ensuring that the line manager is an active participant in the public affairs planning process of the corporation. (Operating management involvement in an issue task force is a useful educational device.)
3. In order to enhance the "absorption" of this new management technology, a central public affairs staff must assist-support operating managers

Table 6.11 Perceived Weight Attached to Public Affairs Competence in Future Management Appointments in Canada

Management Position	Little or No Weight	Some Weight	A Great Deal of Weight
Chairman (if not C.E.O.)	11.8	40.9	47.3
Chief executive officer	4.9	40.7	54.5
President (if not C.E.O.)	6.7	43.8	49.4
Chief operating officer	11.2	51.7	37.1
Vice chairman	24.6	46.2	29.2
Executive vice president	10.9	54.3	34.8
Chief financial officer	36.7	55.5	7.8
General counsel/corporate secretary	32.0	49.2	18.9
Human resources/personnel managers	12.4	58.1	29.5
Marketing managers	21.8	54.6	23.5
Manufacturing managers	48.6	48.6	2.8
R&D managers	52.3	41.1	6.5
Planning managers	22.3	55.4	22.3
Head of group, division or subsidiary	11.9	57.6	30.5
Plant or facilities managers	30.8	52.1	17.1

by making the function as *comprehensible* as possible. Communications networks between the periphery and centre of the corporation must be readjusted to allow for responsiveness and feedback. Central staff must also be at the service of operating managers, providing meaningful advice and information so as to sustain the learning process.

4. Finally, line managers must also feel that there is a *pay-off* to their efforts. They should be able to see the positive *results* of their new involvement; they should be encouraged to persist, and should be helped to realize that the pursuit of public affairs does make a positive contribution both to the corporation and to their own career aspirations.

The diffusion of public affairs throughout the corporation, the institution-alization of the function and supportive management development systems require both careful planning and active chief executive officer support. None of these can be imposed from above (for long) but must be expanded by participation from below. If the operating manager can develop a "stake" in the process, the overall exercise will be considerably more successful.

THE INTERACTION OF PUBLIC AFFAIRS AND PUBLIC RELATIONS

One of the most frequently raised and often hotly contested issues in this management area is whether public affairs is an activity distinct from public

Table 6.12 Programmes Used to Develop the Public Affairs Competence of Operating Managers in Canada

Programmes	Percentage of Respondents Answering	
	Yes	No
Providing public affairs courses, seminars, workshops, in-house	72.0	28.0
Encouraging line managers to attend externally offered courses, conferences, workshops on public affairs	64.0	36.0
Utilizing internal newsletters and related communications vehicles to communicate public affairs information to managers	78.0	22.0
Bringing in public affairs experts from outside the company to address or meet with company managers	46.9	53.1
Rotating or assigning managers to periods of full time duty in certain jobs within the company (e.g. public affairs)	18.8	81.3
Making or approving full time assignments, leaves, or loans of managers to outside ventures	26.5	73.5
Assigning managers to standing company committees that deal largely or solely with public affairs issues	40.0	60.0
Assigning managers to special company committees or task forces having public affairs missions	68.0	32.0
Giving managers other special assignments or responsibilities with public affairs content or character	79.6	20.4
Including public affairs responsibilities among those on which managerial performance is appraised	60.0	40.0
Special provisions for public affairs activity in compensation system	14.3	85.7
Initiating special measures for self-development through reading or other means	49.0	51.0
Encouraging managers to participate in public affairs or community activities on a voluntary, after hours basis	85.7	14.3

relations. The question is of considerable importance, not simply as an academic exercise, but also as a means of clarifying lines of managerial jurisdiction, the designation of operational tasks and the specification of qualifications required to fulfill those tasks with effectiveness and efficiency.

Answers to the question of the precise differences between these two functions elicits a range of responses, some quite emotional. Public affairs, for some, is simply a handy new label for an activity that, during the 1960s, public opinion came to perceive as a manipulative exercise. Large segments of the public see "P.R." pejoratively, associating it with "hype," with sheer image making, and with a one-sided concern with media relations.

Because of this tarnished image of public relations, many firms are simply dropping the label and replacing it with public affairs. The latter term apparently does not strike the same negative response. In other words, it appears to be good public relations to use the term "public affairs"—even though, in many cases, the actual activities pursued under this new label are much the same as before.

Others may use the terms interchangeably, while emphasizing that the orientation of public relations in the modern corporation must be altered. The more traditionally rooted example of this otherwise innovative approach stresses that the function must advance both the *image* and the business *strategy* of the corporation, and that it must be upgraded in stature by being plugged straight into the C.E.O.'s office.[18] The bottom public relations line at this point, however, is still one of *outward* and one-way communications, of getting the message out, and giving only secondary attention to bringing external messages back into the corporation. There is often very little awareness among traditional public relations practitioners of the "participatory" or interactive side of corporate relations as outlined in the preceding sections, or of the various socio-political dimensions that this particular corporate function should tap during the strategic planning of corporate economic-technological policies.

The above points are also supported by a survey of members of the Public Relations Society of America a few years ago. That survey demonstrated that the top ranking concerns of *public affairs*—e.g. community relations, government relations, investor relations—were close to the bottom of the interest scale of *public relations* professionals.[19]

A more advanced form of the revised public relations paradigm is that suggested by Jerry Amernic:

> The whole concept of PR has changed from a function whose major purpose was to create goodwill to an operation involving a three-step cycle. First, there is the public affairs arm which studies the environment and any existing pressures; next, the response mechanism to answer those pressures; and finally, the actual communications programs themselves.[20]

A similarly transformed image of public relations is found in a review put forward by Stephen A. Greyser.[21] Here the division-line between the two functions is literally non-existent, owing to the designation of a much broader role for public relations.

A useful distinction between traditional public relations and public affairs is that which Peter Broadmore of IBM Canada has put forward. According to

Table 6.13 The Public Relations/Public Affairs Spectrum

From	To
internally-driven	externally driven
reactive	proactive/interactive
now-oriented	futures oriented
concerned with facts	concerned with issues
produces communications	produces intelligence
event management	process management
managed disclosure	open disclosure
bureaucratic	participative

Source: Peter Broadmore, IBM Canada, Ltd.

Broadmore's schema, the ideal-types of these two functions are distinguishable from each other by a series of contrasting orientations (see Table 6.13). This schema does not foreclose the possibility of public relations becoming public affairs; it simply draws attention to the sharply contrasting characteristics of *traditional* public relations and *contemporary* public affairs management practices.

Traditional public relations skills are by no means illegitimate, and may co-exist with newly established corporate public affairs units. The way in which the "turf" is shared between these two units varies from corporation to corporation. In some cases, the two functions are located in separate and distinct departments; in other cases the functions are fused. The executive wishing for guidance in this area should follow the rules of pragmatism. Or as Richard Armstrong of the Public Affairs Council so aptly put it:

> Public affairs people and public relations people are going to be working more closely together in the future, whether they want to or not. And some of the bickering that has taken place in the past 20 years is going to become irrelevant, because the senior vice presidents in charge will not tolerate any lack of cooperation. . . . Top management will judge both public affairs and public relations on the basis of performance and results, not on the basis of titles or job description.[22]

A review of trends in public relations-public affairs suggests that demarcation lines between these functions are increasingly blurred. A growing number of public relations professionals are re-orienting themselves from a reactive (or proactive) communications specialization into an interactive and public issues-based stance. This reorientation is breathing fresh air into the public relations profession, and is providing it a more solid, issues-based foundation. This trend is particularly noticeable in Canada. Unlike the United States, where public affairs for the most part grew out of lobbying or

Table 6.14 The Professional Background of Senior Canadian Public Affairs Officers

Background Prior to Work in Public Affairs	Percentage of Respondents
Legal department	3.2
Finance	9.7
Marketing	8.6
Public relations	46.2
Active politics/bureaucracy	8.6
Mass media	2.2
Other	21.5

government relations activities, in Canada, the roots of public affairs lie within public relations. As Table 5.3 showed, communications with the media and communications with the public are the two leading elements in the overall mission of Canadian public affairs departments.

In the United States, the public affairs function, especially during its initial phases, was heavily staffed by professionals with a legal background. In Canada, as Table 6.14 shows, the most frequent professional background of public affairs executives is that of public relations.

These divergent roots of American, as opposed to Canadian, corporate public affairs are largely due to the differences between the political systems of the two countries—one presidential, the other parliamentarian. The government relations component of public affairs in Canada has always been a more modest, less structured and relatively less important (though not unimportant) element of the public affairs mission than that in the United States because of the lesser propensity of Canadian legislators to influence public policy or to be swayed by lobbies. The relatively greater weight of public relations components in the overall corporate public affairs function in Canada, and the closer interplay between these two realms has ensured that outdated, and at times even offensive, elements of public relations will sooner end in Canada. To put it another way, Canadian public relations has tended to be somewhat quicker off the mark in recognizing the need for two-way communications between corporations and their environment, and has moved earlier towards an issues-oriented, interactive approach, working in tandem with public affairs, than is the case in the United States. (It would be an exaggeration to suggest, however, that this new interactive public relations approach has come to dominate the profession in Canada. On the contrary, the traditional public relations approach, while somewhat less prevalent in Canada than in the United States, is still dominant.)

One innovative and sophisticated fusion of public relations and public affairs is that developed by David Grier, a senior public affairs executive at the Royal Bank of Canada. In Grier's schema, the public relations roots of public affairs are clearly visible. His approach names *one* of the important designated functions of corporate public affairs as "reputation management." A strong, cohesive and sustained corporate reputation (say with shareholders, community leaders, employees, government officials, other corporate decision-makers, the public at large, etc.) is assumed to be an essential condition for business prosperity. The greater the dependency of business prosperity on reputation, the more significant a role will public affairs assume in the strategic planning processes of the firm. Corporate reputation, according to Grier, is not a commodity that one can buy simply by investing heavily into communications management, perception manipulation or advertising. *The main founts of corporate reputation are corporate character and action.*

Given these assumptions, Grier suggests that the combined public affairs-public relations function should first of all assist management to develop a set of "reputation objectives" (e.g. to be the most productive, innovative, professionally managed firm in the market; to produce goods that are of consistently high quality and are responsive to human needs; to exercise utmost care in product safety or environmental protection, etc.). These "reputation objectives" must, of course, flow from (or at least be completely consistent with) the firm's strategic business objectives. Secondly, the public affairs unit in Grier's analysis monitors and analyses:

- the gap between public perceptions and actual corporate performance levels along each reputation objective; and
- the gap between actual corporate performance and the targeted reputation objective.

In the final phase of the joint public affairs-public relations mandate, senior management is assisted in the development and delivery of *action plans and programmes* designed to move both public perceptions and corporate performance closer to the targeted reputation ideal.

The specific steps in this "gap analysis" process are illustrated in Figure 6.8 and are as follows:

1. Set reputation objectives—"desired perception" goals.
2. Identify relevant target groups—"publics."
3. Research public *perceptions.*
4. Assess how the *reality* of corporate performance differs from "desired perception" goals. Conduct "gap analysis" to determine:
   a) performance gap, and
   b) perception gap.

Figure 6.8 Illustration of the Gap Analysis Process in Public Affairs

Reputation Goal: To achieve a situation where Canadians believe that:

"Corporation XYZ is a leader in environmental protection and concern."

Target Groups: Governments, Media, Environmental groups, Community groups

Current Situation Point Scale:

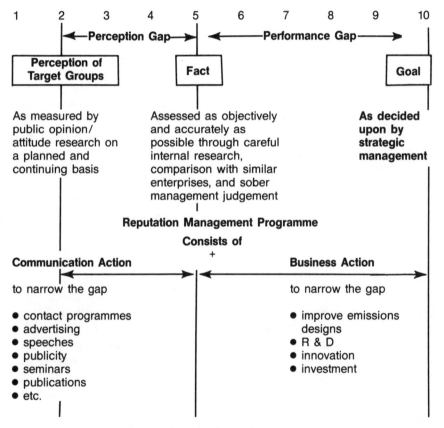

Source: David Grier, The Royal Bank of Canada

5. Devise and implement business actions to narrow performance gap.
6. Devise and implement communication actions to narrow perception gap.
7. Evaluate and report on a regular basis.
8. If necessary, revise strategic business goals.

In Grier's system, the public affairs unit works in close consultation with the corporate strategic planning group, with unit managers and with public relations to achieve programme objectives. Overall responsibility for the programme, including the establishment of reputation goals, is the responsibility of *strategic management*. Public affairs units and issues management task forces serve at this stage in an advisory-resource capacity. (Note: public policy committees, at Board of Director levels, can have a profound influence on the enthusiasm of management for effective public affairs programming.)

Within the framework of the reputation management programme, public affairs advises operating management on the design and implementation of *business actions* aimed at narrowing the performance gap. These actions are integral elements of corporate business plans. Within the framework of the strategic reputation management programme and shorter term business plans, the public affairs unit, working with operating management, designs and delivers *communications actions* aimed at narrowing the *perception gap*.

In closing then, corporate practices have shown that significant differences between traditional public relations and contemporary public affairs do exist. But it is also evident that the more recent, interactive, issues-based approach in public relations shares much in common with public affairs and indeed, at times is indistinguishable from public affairs.

To the degree that this is accurate, the questions of boundaries, divisions of labour, and lines of jurisdiction are not terribly important. In the final analysis, what matters is that if the corporate public affairs audit—as outlined in Chapter 4—demonstrates a need for various components of a public affairs mission, the corporation should pool the knowledge and skills of its professionals—regardless of titles or labels—so as to achieve the targeted mandates as effectively as possible.

CONCLUSIONS: THE TRANSITION FROM ADOLESCENCE TO MATURITY—A SUMMARY OF THE STAGES IN THE DEVELOPMENT OF CORPORATE PUBLIC AFFAIRS

Surveying the evolution of the public affairs function in Canada and the United States over the past 20 years enables us to compile a checklist of the

Table 6.15 The Adolescent/Mature Spectrum of Corporate Public Affairs

Adolescent	Mature
1. Public affairs function enjoys only a limited degree of internal legitimacy. Senior management does not fully understand its uses and is skeptical about its effectiveness—though it tolerates it. Public affairs officers, therefore, are engaged in excessive internal proselytizing at the expense of external-internal action programming.	1. The function has the full support and understanding of senior management and is perceived to be as legitimate an element of corporate strategy as is finance, R&D, accounting, marketing, etc. This acceptance produces a decline in proselytizing and an increase in the utilization of diverse and analytically sophisticated external-internal action programmes.
2. Public affairs officers pursue contacts and relations with external groups/individuals on an irregular basis, surrounded in secrecy and based on personality, style and informal connection.	2. Public affairs officers liaison with external groups in a systematic, open and institutionalized basis. The interaction is grounded on objective analysis, mutual interest, and formalized procedures.
3. The public affairs programme is basically reactive to external challenges and is seen as crisis management. It is a firefighting approach to socio-political events.	3. The public affairs programme is essentially that of relationship management, whereby interaction-interpenetration with key external-internal groups is the rule rather than the exception. The programme is one step ahead of issues, rather than behind them. It serves as management's "eyes and ears" into its socio-political environment, helping to narrow the divergence between corporate strategy and environmental change.
4. Public affairs is a line function. The public affairs unit is the only source and executor of the corporation's socio-political plan.	4. Public affairs is a staff function. Rather than the sole creator and executor of corporate social responsiveness, the officer is a catalyst, a facilitator, a cajoler, of socio-political involvement, wherever it may be needed throughout the organization.
5. Public affairs is a centralized function with little room for participation in the process by local or middle level managers.	5. Public affairs is diffused so that in addition to its central staff, local and middle level operating managers are active participants in the development and delivery of public affairs programmes.
6. Public affairs is an "add-on dimension" to strategic planning. It is peripheral to the central strategic planning and asset management function.	6. Public affairs is institutionalized and closely tied to the strategic planning process.

Table 6.15. continued

Adolescent	Mature
7. The information sources and the analytical tools of public affairs are eclectic and are largely qualitative.	7. The information sources are focused and are based on systematic environmental scanning, social audit, issues management and planning techniques that utilize quantitative measures as much as possible.

characteristics that distinguish the mature public affairs variant from its adolescent relative (see Table 6.15).

I should caution, that this checklist is not intended to suggest that after 20 years of growth, the mature version of this function has come to dominate corporate practice. On the contrary, even today, the adolescent variant is its most prevalent form both in Canada, and to a somewhat lesser extent, in the United States. Certain corporate characteristics—such as size, relative share of the market, degree of susceptibility to government regulation and product line—however, are key intervening variables here. The large oligopolistic or regulated firm whose products touch on a diverse range of socio-political sensitivities is much more likely to be pursuing the mature version of the function than the small (or medium sized) competitive and unregulated corporation. Here as elsewhere, however, there are exceptions to the rule.

Another point to bear in mind is this: The frontiers of adolescence-maturity are not drawn along a straight line in corporate practice. The analysis of corporate management behaviour suggests a "mix" rather than an "ideal type" configuration. In some aspects of the function, there is considerable maturity, while in others the function is still in its adolescent stages. Table 6.15 nevertheless is a useful instrument, for it captures the essential trends under way in this important area of corporate management.

Selection of the appropriate public affairs mode, as we have emphasized throughout, reflects individual corporate-environmental interdependencies, strengths, weaknesses and demands. As stated earlier, there is no ideal public affairs model that can be uniformly applied by all corporations. Long term success depends on total commitment from the chief executive officer, on the selection of the *appropriate* programme vehicle, and on the diffusion throughout line and staff of the principles that are outlined in these sections. The integration of these processes into corporate strategy, their energetic support by senior management, and the utilization of *appropriate* "state-of-the-art" planning vehicles will significantly enhance the viability of corporations affected by the forces of interdependence and environmental change.

Notes

1. L. Fahey, W. R. King and V. K. Narayanan, "Environmental Scanning and Forecasting in Strategic Planning—The State of the Art," *Long Range Planning,* April, 1981.

2. I. Wilson, "Environmental Analysis" in K. Albert (ed.), *Business Strategy Handbook* (McGraw-Hill, 1982).

3. W. Boucher, "Forecasting" in J. S. Nagelschmidt (ed.), *The Public Affairs Handbook* (AMACOM, American Management Associations, 1982).

4. In this area I have benefitted significantly from the advice of I. Wilson of SRI— one of the leading lights in the field of environmental analysis.

5. See, for example, the Boston University survey and J. K. Brown's studies for the Conference Board, *This Business of Issues: Coping with the Company's Environments* (Research Report No. 758, 1979) and *Guidelines for Managing Corporate Issues Programs* (Research Report, No. 795, 1981).

6. S. Enzer, *The Role of Futures Research* (Center for Futures Research, Graduate School of Business Administration, University of Southern California, March, 1975).

7. *Ibid.,* p. 8.

8. For an excellent discussion, see P. Bartha, "Managing Corporate External Issues: An Analytical Framework," *Business Quarterly,* Fall, 1982.

9. I. Wilson, *op. cit.*

10. *Ibid.,* p. 17.

11. B. Nanus, *Quest—Quick Environmental Scanning Technique* (Center for Futures Research, Graduate School of Business Administration, University of Southern California, August, 1979).

12. Public Affairs Research Group, *Public Affairs Offices and Their Functions* (Boston University, 1981), p. 25.

13. Some of the useful "how to" works on this topic are the following: R. Aldag and D. Jackson, "Planning for Corporate Social Actions," *Managerial Planning,* Vol. 29, September/October, 1980; L. Fahey (et. al.), "Environmental Scanning and Forecasting in Strategic Planning—The State of the Art," *op. cit.;* J. Fleming, "Linking Public Affairs With Corporate Planning," *California Management Review,* Vol. 23, Winter, 1980; J. Higgens and D. Romano, "Social Forecasting: An Integral Part of Corporate Planning," *Long Range Planning,* Vol. 13, April, 1980; M. Kastens, "Why and How of Planning," *Managerial Planning,* Vol. 28, July, 1979; H. Klein and W. Newman, "How to Integrate New Environmental Forces Into Strategic Planning," *Management Review,* Vol. 69, July, 1980; G. Means, *Integrating Public Issue Analysis into Corporate Planning: Fundamental and Advanced Techniques* (Sage, 1980); and J. E. Post (et. al.), "The Public Affairs Function in American Corporations: Development and Relations With Corporate Planning," *Long Range Planning,* Vol. 15, No. 2, 1982, pp. 12-21.

14. S. Lusterman, *Managerial Competence: The Public Affairs Aspects* (The Conference Board, Report No. 805, 1981).

15. *Ibid.,* p. 33.

16. *Ibid.,* p. 34.

17. Another very useful schema is by F. Steckmest, "Career Development for the Public Policy Dimension of Executive Performance," *Public Affairs Review,* Vol. II, 1981, pp. 84-87.

18. See for example, D. Eisenstadt, "P.R. and the Corporation: Making Them Work Together," *Metropolitan Toronto Business Journal,* Vol. 72, No. 2, March, 1982, or his, "The Growing Corporate Status for P. R. Role" in *Financial Post,* July 7, 1979; also in this vein, "P. R.'s Validity Will Be Put to the Test in a Decade of Change," *Marketing Magazine,* Vol. 84, July 16, 1979 and "Top 12 P.R. Challenges for 1980," *Public Relations Journal,* Vol. 36, February, 1980, and D. Fetherling, "New Image of Public Relations" in *Canadian Business Magazine,* December, 1979.

19. J. A. Morisey, "Will the Real Public Relations Professional Please Stand Up," *Public Relations Journal,* December, 1978.

20. J. Amernic, "Public Relations Status Report," *Business Journal,* July/August, 1979, p. 31.

21. S. A. Greyser, "Changing Roles for Public Affairs/Public Relations," *Harvard Business School Bulletin,* January/February, 1981.

22. R. Armstrong, "What is Public Affairs?" in J. S. Nagelschmidt (ed.), *The Public Affairs Handbook, op. cit.,* pp. 6-7.

7

The Emerging Public
Affairs Curriculum

The Universe is an infinite sphere, the centre of which is everywhere, the circumference nowhere. . . . In space, the Universe encompasses me and swallows me like a dot; in thought I encompass the Universe.

—Blaise Pascal

IS THERE AN EDUCATIONAL CHALLENGE?

In previous chapters, we examined how corporate strategy is increasingly influenced by a new constellation of societal forces. The remaining task is to examine the educational challenge posed by the realities outlined earlier. How responsive are educational institutions to changing organizational-environmental relationships? Do universities and other educational institutions understand, support, and prepare students for the roles demanded by the new managerial revolution? What are the perceived educational demands in this area and what can be done to satisfy these demands? What should be the basic components of a public affairs curriculum? And finally, what are the constraints upon our educational institutions that limit their responsiveness, and how can these constraints be removed?

The corporate survey questionnaire for this book was sent to a group of professionals, many of whom are pioneers in this rapidly expanding management field. Their responses pertaining to education are highly relevant to the curriculum-makers in our institutions of higher learning. As stated earlier, approximately 95 percent of the respondents agreed with the definition of public affairs provided in the survey questionnaire. Sixty-seven point four percent of the respondents had no knowledge whatsoever of *any* university programme in Canada catering to their field (see Tables 7.1 and 7.2). A whopping 78.4 percent of the respondents believe that Canadian universities are not sufficiently responsive to the growing educational demands of Canadian corporations in the area of public affairs management. Some conclusions follow logically:

1. It is quite clear that institutional public affairs education at the university level, perhaps more so in Canada than in the United States, has

159

Table 7.1 Awareness of the Existence of Canadian University-Based Public Affairs Programmes by Canadian Public Affairs Managers

University Programme	Number of Respondents Identifying This Institution	Percentage of Total Respondents Aware of This Programme
University of Manitoba	1	0.7
University of Ottawa	1	0.7
University of Western Ontario	4	2.87
University of British Columbia	1	0.7
Concordia University	3	2.15
Mount St. Vincent University	8	5.75
York University	7	5.03
Université de Montreal	2	1.43
Haute Etudes Commerciale	1	0.7
University of Calgary	1	0.7
McGill University	1	0.7

Table 7.2 Perceived Responsiveness of Canadian University-Based Public Affairs Programmes to Corporate Needs

Percentage of respondents that felt universities were sufficiently responsive	21.6
Percentage of respondents that felt universities were not sufficiently responsive	78.4

been untutored and negligent about professional requirements. In an age of high unemployment, especially among the young, this is particularly worrisome.

2. Those universities that claim to have educational programmes in institutional public affairs are failing to communicate their scholarship and existence to a very important clientele.

3. In the opinion of those who work in the private sector vineyard, the general usefulness of Canadian academic public affairs *programmes* leaves a lot to be desired. Paradoxically, all this may even be good news for academia, for clearly there's no way to go but up.

There is, of course, another possible conclusion which many academicians will no doubt favour. They can choose to dismiss the criticisms of their corporate clientele as misguided and based on false expectations. Oftentimes, academicians, especially those in social sciences-humanities, may say that corporate complaints about their programmes constitute only an effort on the part of the business community to reshape the university to suit its exclusive desires. These academic defenders of tradition frequently point out that the primary mission of the university is not to seek relevance, but to search for eternal truths and theoretical knowledge. The role of the university, they expound, is not to train people for professions or jobs, but to stimulate the capacity of students to engage in critical thinking.

Ironically, this "function" of the university is seldom, if ever, made clear to the incoming student by academic recruiters desperate to sign up as many students as possible in order to counteract falling enrollment and departmental budgets. Thus students often learn too late, and usually after graduation, that their acquired knowledge and skills are not employable. Curiously enough, it is only at this point that academia really levels with its young proteges to ask—"But what did you expect? Surely not a job? Don't you know that the role of the university is not to train but to educate?"

This is obviously not the place to engage in a polemic on what the purpose of the university is or ought to be, or how one should reconcile competing demands for relevance and critical thinking. My own position is that without critical thinking one can not be relevant and conversely, critical thinking without a foundation of relevance is a "pie in the sky." Philosophy, literature, the arts, and the humanities in general, are *all* relevant to the quest for survival in economic or technological domains. Indeed, the disciplines of economics, management, engineering, or any of the "hard" sciences that do *not* provide themselves and their students with a liberal arts foundation face most squarely the prospects of becoming irrelevant. In short, relevance and critical thinking are not seen here as polar opposites but as inseparable entities. This value premise, again, profoundly conditions the programme designs to be presented in sections of this chapter.

In the United States, and especially in Canada, the challenges to public affairs education are enormous and include both theoretical and applied domains. Indeed, these challenges, as a recent conference of European and North American deans of business schools concluded, is a global phenomenon: "Socio-economic changes will become so complex and come with such rapidity in the decades ahead that student profiles may be altered and measurement and testing techniques may have to be drastically revised."[1] Similar sentiments were expressed by the Educational Innovation Committee of the American Assembly of Collegiate Schools of Business in 1975:

> Corporations today are operating under a totally different set of public expectations, guidelines and laws than they were twenty years ago. . . . The rules, regulations, and game plans by which American managers must operate today are dramatically changed from the bottom line management philosophy of even a decade ago.[2]

A survey of educational responsiveness to these calls for reform, however, cannot but agree with Francis Steckmest's remarks: "Managements are confronted with a hodgepodge rather than well-conceived programs of education, training and experience."[3]

A REVIEW OF CANADIAN AND AMERICAN EDUCATIONAL AND RESEARCH PROGRAMMES

In order to facilitate the presentation, the following three modes of public affairs education will be examined: the business school, the interdisciplinary social science based public affairs school and the off-campus approach.

The Business School Approach

Academicians working within the business school setting tend, almost unanimously, to agree that "the natural academic home for public affairs should lie in the study of management policy."[4] While the validity of this proposition may be questioned, it is undeniable that virtually all of the pioneering academic work on this subject during the past decade or so has been done by management policy professors.[5] This is not at all to suggest, however, that business schools have given appropriate weight to this educational component in their overall curricula. Indeed, the business school response, according to Harvard University President Derek Bok, has been far from satisfactory: "While many chief executives actually spend up to half their time on government, regulatory and community affairs, most business school curricula pay little attention to relevant public policy issues."[6]

These observations are even more applicable to Canada. While federal and provincial governments in Canada together spend a larger share of the GNP and have adopted a substantially more interventionist posture than that found in the United States, and while "social responsiveness" on the part of Canadian executives appears to be running somewhat ahead of the United States,[7] Canadian business schools, with a few exceptions, and not counting some solid individual scholarly efforts, have literally turned a blind eye to this educational area. Apart from a couple of bright lights (say, the University of Western Ontario, or York University), the typical Canadian business programme is a dark place indeed for those wishing enlightenment about the dimensions of this critical management area.

The surveys of Rogene Buchholz in the United States show that most American business schools offer *one or two courses* in the public policy-business environment area.[8] At the undergraduate level in the United States,

33.6 percent of the business schools do not require *any* such courses to be taken by their students. Forty-six percent of the schools require that undergraduates take *one* such "environmental" course during their studies. A further 16.8 percent require that undergraduates take *two* of these courses. At the graduate level, 30.4 percent of schools in the United States make no formal requirements upon their students in public policy-business environment. Fifty-four percent of the graduate programmes require that students take one course from this field, while a further 11.6 percent require that two public policy courses be taken in the graduate programme. Buchholz's study showed that 44.2 percent of the infrequently offered undergraduate public affairs courses in the United States are *required,* while 55.8 percent are *electives.* At the graduate level, 45.7 percent of the courses offered must be taken by students while 54.3 percent are optional.[9]

The total educational activity in the United States, as shown in Table 7.3, is quite impressive, however, and suggests a considerable body of academic research and teaching.

While the figures in Table 7.3 suggest a sizeable teaching and research component in public affairs, the fact of the matter is that in the United States one-third of the business school population is *not* required to take any of the courses offered. The remaining two-thirds of the students are required to take only one such course, or at most two, during their formal academic preparation for a career in business.[10] Given the dramatic changes in the way that business must operate, it is surprising to find that the educational profile of the American MBA, and especially that of its Canadian counterpart, has not changed noticeably over recent years. In short, while

Table 7.3 The Dimensions of the American Business School Response

Item	Numbers
Total number of public policy-business environment courses	1,019
Total number of required undergraduate courses in field	252
Total number of elected undergraduate electives	318
Total number of required graduate courses	205
Total number of elected graduate courses	244
Total number of faculty teaching in this field	1,130
Total full-time faculty teaching full-time in area	334
Total full-time faculty teaching part-time in area	572
Part time faculty	180
Graduate student teachers	44

Source: R. Buchholz, *Business Environment/Public Policy: A Study of Teaching and Research in Schools of Business and Management* (American Association of Collegiate Schools of Business, 1979), p. 98.

the global output is certainly increasing, one must remember, as Richard Armstrong and Michael Jones remind us, that "...the nation's business students are not introduced fully to contemporary public affairs in one or two courses on the 'business environment.'"[11]

Some teachers may hypothesize that the business school is responding to needs in this area in an unseen way—that is, by integrating public affairs materials into traditional or functional business courses (such as into finance, marketing and accounting). This, some would argue, may explain the rather slow and sluggish institutional responsiveness at the *specialized* course level. Such a hypothesis may also lead to a belief that since the mature public affairs function is being diffused throughout the corporation, business schools should do the same by diffusing public affairs content into functional courses.

These arguments cannot stand up to serious analysis. While there *is* evidence of the integration of public affairs material into courses at the functional level, this is done in an extremely superficial and haphazard fashion. The integration appears to be more a token than a substantive readjustment of the traditional course content.

According to Buchholz, the overwhelming evidence suggests that business schools cannot meet the demand by ". . . a few additions to the typical business policy course or courses in the functional area."[12] While such integrative approaches are clearly important and must constitute one of the frontiers of educational reform, it is of vital importance that the business school curriculum contain *more* courses at both the undergraduate and graduate levels in which "environmental and public policy material are combined in a single comprehensive required course."[13] Future prestige of business schools, and indeed their relevance, will be measured by their responsiveness to this felt need.

Analysis of the American and Canadian business school approaches towards public affairs education suggests that while academic and student interest in this area is growing, at faculty levels there is as yet only a very shallow recognition that public affairs is a distinct field of study, comparable to marketing or finance. The opportunities to specialize in public affairs at the business school level are extremely limited and frequently discouraged. While in 1982, eighteen schools in the United States offered a major or concentration in the public policy-business environment area (see Table 7.4), these programmes are still facing many challenges in successfully integrating the wide range of knowledge *and* skills needed in public affairs management. In many cases, the programmes are reasonably successful in sensitizing students to *some* of the important environmental constraints facing managers, yet students often are not provided with clinical training in the *technical skills* needed to manage in such environments.[14]

Schools of business have numerous hurdles to cross in public affairs education. They include:

a. Business schools must *interact,* to a greater extent than they have up to now, with schools of government, institutes of public administration and the social sciences in general in order to meet new needs.

b. *Case study material,* especially in Canada, is urgently needed. Teachers in this subject area in Canada are faced with a virtual desert. Strenuous efforts must be made to compile Canadian case study material for the various components of this function.[15]

c. There is still a shortage of *rigorous conceptualization.* The analytical framework and the materials presented in most business school courses on public policy, for example, are often a mish-mash of unrelated elements.

d. The *international dimensions* of the corporate socio-political environment must be integrated into the business school curriculum.

e. *Faculty development:* there is a serious shortage of faculty competent to teach and pursue research in the field.[16]

Table 7.4 U.S. Business Schools Offering A Major or Concentration in the Public Policy/Business Environment Area

A. Schools with a Bachelor's Public Policy Major

> Georgetown University
> University of Miami, Florida
> Memphis State University

B. Schools with a Master's Public Policy Major

> Pacific Lutheran University, Tacoma, Washington
> University of Texas at Dallas
> Boston University
> Boston College
> George Washington University
> Jackson State University, Jackson, Mississippi
> University of Miami, Florida
> University of California, Berkeley
> Williamette University, Salem, Oregon
> University of California, Irvine

C. Schools with a Doctoral Public Policy Major

> Texas Tech. University, Lubbock, Texas
> University of Massachusetts
> University of California, Berkeley
> University of Washington
> University of Pittsburgh

Soruce: R. Buchholz, *op. cit.* p. 36.

f. While there is not much danger of programme duplication or overkill, especially in Canada, there is cause, in both countries, for concern about the *absence of standardized educational approaches* in this field. The application of professional standards and accreditation would do much to streamline and focus efforts and would greatly enhance the pedagogical development of this important managerial area.[17]

g. The *"skills" side of public affairs management* deserves much greater emphasis. Introducing business students to some elements of the social sciences, and to the dynamics of societal change, are steps in the right direction, but further steps are needed. In particular, students should be given the opportunity to focus on *how* organizations and their changing environments interpenetrate, and especially on *how* this interpenetration or interdependence could be better managed.

This list of constraints or challenges that business schools face in the area of public affairs education is by no means exhaustive. They are mentioned with increasing frequency in the works of a number of new studies aimed at revitalizing the traditional MBA. Sal Divita, for example, has lucidly argued that there are two particularly important educational needs that MBA programmes must address: "the development of personal decision-making skills," and, "development of a broader perspective of the corporate world."[18] Divita argues that it is especially important that writing and communications skills, knowledge of international affairs, business-government relations, and the social sciences be integrated into the MBA curriculum. On the prospects of change, Divita is not optimistic. He identifies the built-in inertia of business schools as the principal agent of resistance:

> The managerial milieu of our business schools is not a mechanism that allows the institution to be responsive to change—and certainly not with dispatch. Too often, change, however small, is considered threatening by the faculty and/or administration. Thus, we have a condition that maintains the status quo more than it produces responsive behavior. The schools, then, constitute a formidable barrier to effecting change as are the actions or inactions of the corporation.[19]

The barriers to innovation that Divita points to are certainly not unique to business schools and are found throughout our universities and colleges.

The Interdisciplinary Social Science-Based Public Affairs School

The opening chapter mentioned that the traditional social science-based academic usage of public affairs—as distinct both from the common sense and institutional meaning of the term—is highly eclectic and randomly structured. There are interdisciplinary schools of public affairs that teach nothing but communications skills, and others by the same name which consist, by and large, of political science or of urban studies. The traditional social science-based, interdisciplinary approach has had no discernible focus. It is, by and large, the creature of university politics, on-tap resources, personalities and chance.

This does not denigrate the efforts or the academic legitimacy of people working within this tradition. As already noted, *some* of the variants of the interdisciplinary approach have indeed attained a high level of focused sophistication. The accreditation and professionalization of public adminis-tration schools via the National Association of Schools of Public Affairs and Administration is a case in point. There are, moreover, literally thousands of academicians in Canada and the United States who pursue extremely important and relevant research in various aspects of public policy. These efforts are generally housed either in a specific discipline (e.g. political science or economics) or in interdisciplinary public policy institutes. Such interdisciplinary policy studies are very valuable and cannot be dismissed as irrelevant either on practical or on theoretical grounds.[20] *The point is, however, that the focus of existing social science-based public affairs schools in the United States and Canada is not that which the overwhelming proportion of public affairs practitioners—in business, government or labour—consider to be the essence of their profession.*

Public policy institutes or interdisciplinary schools of public administra-tion tend to focus upon problems pertaining exclusively to public sector management. (See for example the accreditation guidelines of NASPAA.) The concern of these educational bodies with the interlinked dimensions of institutional public affairs management as outlined in this study, has been non-existent, or is at best marginal. While these interdisciplinary, social science-based bodies provide valuable contextual support for corpo-rate public affairs, and are significant sources of new knowledge about forces shaping our society, they have not served (nor have they been intended to serve) as guideposts to the new managerial revolution. Surveys and interviews of public affairs managers, even in the public sector, have found that the expertise and knowledge required by their profession is not forthcoming from our presently instituted interdisciplinary schools. They demonstrate in short, that the programme responses of these schools are inadequate. They spotlight a number of challenges and constraints that interdisciplinary schools in particular must overcome as they pursue the tasks of public affairs programme development. Some constraints follow:

a. The first and most vivid shortcoming of existing social science-based interdisciplinary schools is the *absence of focus* on public affairs as a management function. Only limited attention is paid to the dynamics of organizational-environmental relationships, to institutional interdependence and to business-society relationships in particular.

b. The absence of focus produces an eclectic, and utterly *random targeting on public issues.* The environments that students are exposed to in their so called public affairs courses are seldom those which the public affairs professional has to face. Instead, course or issues content is merely the reflection of the professor's subjective and often single discipline-based fancy. *Issues come and go on the students' academic platter, not on the basis of a cohesive institutional public affairs philosophy, but as the by-products of changing professorial appointments.*

c. The *interdisciplinary grounding* promised by these schools is far too often *symbolic rather than substantive.* Correctly identifying the need for interdisciplinary education, many programmes nevertheless persist in applying these principles in a curious way. Far too often, students still must take their courses in political science, history or economics from discipline-based units (i.e. in the traditional academic departments). Thus they emerge from their learning experience not with a melting pot view of the social sciences but with an image of unrelated mosaics.

d. An even more frequent shortcoming is that the various *courses* which students take in their programme *are not driven, let alone affected, by institutional public affairs considerations.* The relevant political science, economics, sociology or history courses in most public affairs programmes are not taught to students in terms of their relationship to public affairs management. Thus students are left in the dark about the linkages between the various disciplines, and especially about how institutional public affairs and the disciplines relate to each other.

e. *Faculty development in public affairs competence* (or lack of it) is a serious challenge. The vestiges of discipline-based education run deep. Faculty members in the interdisciplinary school may be brilliant historians, economists or sociologists, and may even be found under one academic roof. Yet they are seldom able to speak to their students or to each other in the commonly shared language of institutional public affairs.

f. As in the case of business schools, *more emphasis should be placed on public affairs management skills development.* A broadly-based liberal arts education, while an extremely important component of the curriculum, is not sufficient to prepare students for active public affairs careers, research or graduate work. Surveys show that such one-sided liberal arts humanities-based programmes have produced only about 7 percent of the professionals currently employed in public affairs (see Table 7.5). In short, it is important to expose both business and non-business school students to a wide range of case study materials in public affairs management, and to various skill areas (communications, planning, prioritizing, environmental analysis, sur-

**Table 7.5 Sources of Qualified People for
Public Issues Management**

Source	Percent
Within the company	73.8
Government	52.4
Business school	23.8
Trade associations	14.3
Other companies	11.9
Law schools	9.5
Journalism schools	9.5
Liberal arts/humanities	7.1
Other	7.1

Source: R. Buchholz, *ibid.,* p. 17.

vey research, etc.) in order to equip them with the tools needed to function in this domain.[21]

g. A final and again frequent constraint on the development of interdisciplinary public affairs education is part of a larger, university-wide malaise. Very often, *the academic programmes of interdisciplinary public affairs schools are the prisoners of university obligations* (to various disciplines, degree requirements, bureaucracies, administrative units or administrators, etc.). By the time all of these external obligations are met, and academic politics has had its play, the schools are left with a public affairs core that is scarcely more than a token gesture towards the field.

In a period of financial austerity and falling enrollments, the established disciplinary programmes perceive new interdisciplinary academic units as threats to their existence. The "new kid on the block" is frequently the target of considerable *university-wide pressures that limit freedom and capacity to innovate.* The subsequent concessions that may be made to overcome this internal university-wide resistance to change frequently seriously dilute the substantive content of the new interdisciplinary public affairs programmes. The range of issues presented to students, the opportunities for field trips, exchanges, internships, guest lectures and animated learning opportunities can be increased in efforts to compensate for all this, and may provide a livelier and more enjoyable learning environment for students. But students in such institutions learn only upon graduation that they are very far indeed from possessing either the understanding or the skills that are essential to this new field. This study, based on the performance of a number of interdisciplinary schools, concludes that *success is largely a function of institutional autonomy. If the interdisciplinary school cannot have its own faculty and programme, then its overall performance is doomed to be second rate.* If the front line programme rationale of these schools is simply to provide another route towards a disciplinary major (say in political science, history, economics, sociology, etc.), it is inevitable that the public affairs component will play a backseat role to the demands of those other academic programmes and disciplines. Schools that are based on such an approach serve neither the best interests of their students nor those of society.

Eclecticism and detachment, the one-sided quest for theorizing and a disdain for practicality are some of the more serious distortions of many of the unfocused "liberal arts" or so called "generalist" educational approaches to this field. As Leon Botstein argued in another context, these unfocused and detached approaches have served to "prevent the more serious social and cultural issues from being addressed by the university. . . . A sanitized version of history, the humanities, arts and science has emerged, based on the notion that the liberal arts are essentially disinterested, free of ideology, merely a technique of thinking rather than the substance of thought or the carrier of values. In the new curricula, there is no vision of the good society, the good life, the ideal citizen. . . . It skirts the social and cultural issues that might inspire students. . . . There happens to be a real cultural crisis out there, one that threatens to cheat young people out of a chance to learn and develop as private individuals and citizens."[22] Botstein goes on to argue with considerable conviction that this crisis in higher learning is also reflected in "the profound alienation among young people, which lurks beneath their apparent conservatism and docility. . . . The problem is not that students, like their predecessors of ten years ago, crave relevance; the problem is that they are no longer able to recognize relevance."[23]

The above lists of shortcomings of social science-based interdisciplinary public affairs schools could be expanded by adding some of the constraints listed under the business school heading. Though these constraints add up to a considerable liability, they are by no means insurmountable. If interdisciplinary schools can overcome these initial hurdles, they can play an important and legitimate role in institutional public affairs education. The current domination of this educational field by other facilitators (e.g. business schools, or more often, by off-campus conference centres) is largely the consequence of the interdisciplinary schools' inability or unwillingness to put their houses in order. Removing the above listed constraints is an essential prerequisite for reform and programme development.

The Off-Campus Approach

In the United States, the leading off-campus education and research vehicles for institutional public affairs are the following:

a. The Conference Board
b. SRI International
c. The Public Affairs Council
d. The American Enterprise Institute for Public Policy
e. The Aspen Institute for Humanistic Studies
f. The Institute for the Future
g. The Brookings Institution
h. The National Chamber of Commerce
i. The National Association of Manufacturers
j. The New York Public Issues Group
k. The Issues Management Association
l. The Committee for Economic Development

These centres focus primarily on critical public policy issues confronting business, government and labour in North America, and also devote considerable attention to educating various levels of executives about the public policy process as it relates to corporations. (Among all these programmes, the one that most closely meets the developmental needs of public affairs practitioners is that offered by the Public Affairs Council.) These programmes run in length anywhere from one day to a week, and are offered on a number of occasions during the year.

In Canada, the leading off-campus professional education and research organizations for public affairs are:

a. The Niagara Institute
b. The Conference Board of Canada
c. The Institute for Political Involvement
d. The Institute for Research on Public Policy

The Niagara Institute is widely recognized as the leading "off-campus" public affairs training institute in Canada. The focus of the Institute for Political Involvement, of IRPP and most others in this realm is on various public policy issues and on the workings of federal or provincial governments.

Practicality and relevance to real world challenges are the obvious drawing cards of the off-campus approach to public affairs education. The programmes are run by professionals for professionals. In most cases, efforts are made to include leading academicians in seminars, either as resource persons or as participants. While quality can fluctuate from session to session, and while some programmes are more useful than others, the off-campus approach is attractive in that it enables practitioners to exchange views, experiences and information about specific aspects of their profession.

The weakness of most of these approaches stems largely from their structure and duration. They often cannot reach a high level of analytical rigour or substantive depth. The one or two day intensive seminar does not allow much time for reflection, reading or intellectual growth.

THE DIRECTIONS FOR INNOVATION: THE CHANGING CONTENT OF INSTITUTIONAL PUBLIC AFFAIRS EDUCATION

Opportunities for all three of the above outlined educational sectors as well as for individual disciplines (e.g. political science) abound in the area of institutional public affairs. All three sectors can play a legitimate role both in the academic and professional development of this management function.

In designing programmes for each of these sectors, the first important principle to bear in mind is that content should be individually tailored to fit specific levels of students. The topics, course content, focus and requirements should vary according to whether the users are pre-career undergraduate or graduate students, generalist or specialized mid-career executives. Obviously, what may work well for one segment of students will be inadequate or inappropriate for another.[24] It is critical for educational institutions to first determine their target clientele, to establish the needs of that clientele, and then to develop the appropriate programme response.

At the *pre-career undergraduate* level it is not advisable to utilize a strictly "professional" or "vocational" approach. First of all, there are few professional public affairs management opportunities for undergraduates. Entry level positions in corporate public affairs *management* are extremely limited. While public affairs positions have opened up in substantial numbers during the past few years (see Table 7.6), the overwhelming trend is to staff these positions internally or from other professions, rather than directly from the university. Buchholz's survey of 42 companies in the United States showed that only two had entry level positions that could be filled by people coming directly out of universities.[25] Therefore, public affairs programmes in Canada or the United States that promise their pre-career students entry level management positions into this field upon graduation are generating false expectations. This point is especially true in the case of the non-business school, or interdisciplinary public affairs programme, and primarily in that of its undergraduate variant. The figures in Table 7.5 clearly identify the recruitment patterns for professional public affairs jobs. Academia must take great care to note these figures during its curriculum planning and in its counselling for pre-career students, *especially at the undergraduate level.*

**Table 7.6 Number of Full Time People Involved in Functions:
Increase from 1977 to 1980 in Percentages**

Function	Numbers Up By
Public affairs	41.9
Environmental forecasting	86.7
Policy or issues analysis	36.0
Corporate strategic planning	57.5
Business-government relations	43.0

Source: R. Buchholz, "Education for Public Issues Management," Typescript, p. 15.

Again, strict professionalization at the undergraduate level is not advisable for a host of reasons, only one of which is the shortage of entry level management opportunities. This condition should not, however, lead one to conclude that no *focus* is needed at this level, or that the practical skills, problem solving approaches, and analytical tools that are germane to *institutional* public affairs can be ignored by undergraduates. A broadly based, non-professional programme focusing on government, business, labour and other sectors *can* be organized around the institutional definition of public affairs given in this study. A generalist approach need not be eclectic and indeed should have both a purpose and a focus. It should concern itself with the development of cooperative organizational-environmental relations, with relevance and societal problem solving, the laws of institutional interdependence, changing values and ethics, and the skills required in these domains.

The research that validates this book, as well as the surveys of others, suggest that a consensus of some kind is emerging about the types of *knowledge* and *skills* that are appropriate to this field as far as undergraduate and graduate education are concerned. Clearly, the foundation has to be interdisciplinary, linking elements of the social sciences, the humanities and courses from administration and policy into a *focused* programme of studies. Table 7.7 contains the most frequently recurring capabilities that Canadian public affairs executives see as essential to their profession.

Analysis of the survey responses and interview data enables us to produce a coherent programme design that reflects the educational needs of modern institutions, private or public, as far as the management of interdependence is concerned. The *knowledge components* of this new curriculum should provide students with an understanding of:

1. The changing economic, social, political, economic and technological environments of organizations, both *private and public.* (Note: It follows that courses should not simply generalize in economics, political science, history, etc., but should *relate* those fields to organizational behaviour);

Table 7.7 The Perceptions of Surveyed Canadian Public Affairs Executives About the Knowledge-Skill Components that University Public Affairs Programmes Should Emphasize

Knowledge Components	Skills Components
Government affairs	Judgement
Political sensitivity	Problem analysis and research
Public policy process	analytical skills
Sociology	Behavioural flexibility
Sensitivity to socio-economic trends	Public speaking
The environment of organizations	Art of negotiating
Understanding of community affairs	Interpersonal relationships,
and community development	understanding people
Economics and economic analysis	Writing/communications
Psychology	Report and brief writing/layout
Finance	How to read a balance sheet
Marketing	Budget and financial analysis
Public relations	Management skills
Business law	Corporate planning
Human relations	Decision-making
Management sciences	Issues tracking and analysis
Corporate social responsibility	Case study analysis
How media operates	Media relations
How pressure groups behave	Survey research
Organizational behaviour	How to manage change

2. How organizations function (private or public sector) in such areas as strategy development, acquiring resources, motivating employees, producing products and services, pursuing profits, efficiency or equality, etc.;

3. How organizations and their environments interpenetrate each other, how organizations interact with their community, the social responsibilities of corporations, etc.; and

4. The changing ethical or normative values, ideologies and cultures governing the relationships between organizations and their various environments.

The *skill components* should consist of the following:

1. *Analytical and problem solving skills* (survey techniques, environmental scanning and forecasting approaches, statistics, cost-benefit analysis, scenarios, multidimensional scaling, systems analysis, model building, etc.) designed to explore and understand the dynamics of changing organizational and environmental relationships;

2. *Planning skills* to develop effective programmes in response to or in anticipation of changing organizational-environmental relationships;

3. *Communication skills* (oral and written), of various kinds: How to communicate effectively with employees, with the media, with superiors, with subordinates, with adversary groups, how to write and argue clearly, how to listen, how to use newly emerging communications tools;

4. *Management skills* to make policy decisions and to operate action programmes that have clearly identifiable objectives and budgets;

5. *Interpersonal skills* for working with people in small or large group settings; leadership, motivation skills, group animation, etc.;

6. A final component, which is increasingly useful, is an *internship,* whereby students are placed for a certain period of time *during* their studies, into a working environment relevant to their field.

Pre-career undergraduate students going through a programme such as the above will derive substantial benefits from this *focused* blending of vocational and theoretical approaches. These students certainly would not be considered, by any stretch of the imagination, as being narrowly, or "technocratically" educated. *The above structure could be applied to all kinds of sectors and not simply to business.* Graduates of such programmes would possess a good introductory feel for the diverse environmental forces that are shaping society and its diverse institutions. And unlike most undergraduates, they would also have some capacity to participate creatively in organizational-environmental processes that they have spent three to four years investigating. While professional public affairs jobs may not be immediately open for their taking, these undergraduate students would most certainly be well equipped for lower level entry or to begin preparing for a higher level professional degree. While their entry level employment opportunities as public affairs professionals would be limited, they could compete successfully with other undergraduates for a wide range of jobs, some which indeed, could serve as convenient *routes* into practical and rewarding careers in public affairs management.

Specialization at the graduate level must build upon the conceptual framework outlined above, first by sharpening the focus and increasing the depth of the above listed *knowledge* areas. Secondly, public affairs training at graduate levels should assign a substantially greater and more rigorous weight to skills components than the undergraduate programme can achieve. The mix of knowledge and skills demanded of professional public affairs specialists is also clearly reflected in the surveys of Buchholz and others and should be instructive to curriculum planners (see Tables 7.8 and 7.9).

An important and growing source of demand for new institutional public affairs programmes is from the professional client sectors of the university—such as specialized public affairs training for operational managers, for public affairs practitioners or public affairs education for senior executives, division managers, planners, etc. in business, government and labour.

Table 7.8 Important Skills for Public Issues Management
Key: 1 = very important; 2 = important; 3 = neutral; 4 = not very important
5 = not important at all

Skill	Score
Communication	1.2
Analytical	1.6
Interpersonal	2.0
Planning	2.1
Negotiating	2.5
Quantitative	2.8

Source: R. Buchholz, "Education for Public Issue Management," *op. cit.,* p. 20.

Table 7.9 Important Knowledge for Public Issues Management
(Same 5 point scale used as in Table 7.8)

Field of Knowledge	Score
Economics	1.9
Political Science	1.9
History	2.5
Sociology	2.5
Law	2.5
Humanities	2.6
Finance	2.7
Marketing	2.8
Statistics	2.9
Production	3.2
Philosophy	3.2
Accounting	3.4
Mathematics	3.5

Source: R. Buchholz, *ibid.,* p. 21.

These groups together have the potential of becoming an extremely important and rapidly expanding clientele for universities. Yet with a few exceptions, they are virtually ignored by academic planners.

This is no place to engage in a lengthy analysis of the changing educational demands facing universities. Suffice it to say that for a host of reasons, among which rapid technological change is the leading one, more and more people will find themselves coming back to the university once, possibly twice, in their lifetimes, to retool for new careers, new opportunities and new horizons. In the area of institutional public affairs, an increasing number of employed professionals want the university to provide them with the knowledge and skills needed in this field. However, in an overwhelming number of cases, universities are complacent about responding to this new demand, as Richard Armstrong and Michael Jones (and others) have shown:

> Nowhere is there a forum for experienced public affairs officers, experts in their own field, and experienced people in other disciplines, to rigorously examine their positions, strategy, and management of public affairs, and the external issues crucial to this field.[26]

In short, the need for new university programmes in institutional public affairs is tremendous. A broader comprehension of its clientele would permit the university to provide educational services to a rapidly emerging population of mid-career students, and enable it to make a significant contribution to the advancement of the new managerial revolution.

In the United States, academic responses to the demands for mid-career education have tended to be quicker off the mark than in Canada. Most of the new programmes are housed in management schools, such as the following:

1. Boston University's "Public Affairs Management Course," offered by the School of Management, runs for eight consecutive Friday afternoons, and is an innovative attempt at overcoming some of the problems listed under the "off-campus" approach to this field.

2. The Hubert Humphrey Institute of Public Affairs at the University of Minnesota offers a number of courses, workshops and colloquia for mid-career professionals in public and community service.

3. Harvard University's Graduate School of Business and the John F. Kennedy School of Government offer jointly and separately a variety of programmes for professionals (e.g. three-week summer programmes for "Senior Managers in Government," "Business, Government and the International Economy," etc.).

4. The University of Maryland's Center for Business and Public Policy, under the directorship of Lee Preston, is another lively place for professional and mid-career public affairs development.

5. The Washington Campus Program, formed as a consortium by nine universities in 1979, runs a range of new programmes for both pre-career and mid-career executives on various aspects of public affairs (particularly business-government relations).

Indiana University's "Managing External Forces" programme, the University of South Carolina's "Institute on Corporate Public Affairs and the Political Process," the University of Virginia's "Changing Environment of United States Business" and Berkeley's "Managing Business Public Affairs in the 1980s" all deserve attention and emulation.

In Canada, the only serious academic effort directed towards *mid-career* public affairs clientele is at the recently founded Max Bell Business-

Table 7.10 Public Affairs Programme Emphasis for Professional Target Clientele

Programme Characteristics	Early Career General Managers	Division Presidents and General Managers	Top Corporate Executives	Early Career Public Affairs Staff	Senior Public Affairs Executive
1. The nature of the public policy process	X			X	
2. The nature of the policy process at local, state, federal and even international levels		X			
3. The public policy process, particularly in those committees or agencies which handle issues of great importance to the company			X		
4. The current state of public policy demands on business in personnel, production, product quality and safety, occupational safety, etc.		X			
5. Aspects of corporate performance that are of concern to the public policy makers	X			X	
6. The nature of regulation and other government interventions in business affairs	X			X	
7. How public policy can affect corporate operations and corporate profitability	X			X	
8. How corporations can respond to public policy through compliance and advocacy	X			X	
9. Issue monitoring and how to anticipate corporate impact of public policy issues		X			
10. Personal relationships with legislators, administrators and interest group leaders who have concerns about the corporation			X		

11. Emerging trends in state, local or federal government which may affect business

12. Macro-economic issues, corporate governance issues, and others which have the broadest impact on the large American corporation

13. Emerging issues which may have a long term impact on business as an institution

14. New issues of importance to a specific corporation

15. How corporations organize to manage public affairs concerns

16. Techniques of public affairs and their effectiveness

17. The public affairs planning process: monitoring the environment, selecting objectives, relating objectives to corporate strategy, implementing public affairs plans, monitoring success

18. Public affairs skills needed to represent company before the media, government committees, public speaking, testimony giving

19. How corporate strategy and public affairs strategy are interrelated

Source: K. Hanson and R. Lind, "Executive Education" in J.S. Nagelschmidt (ed.), *The Public Affairs Handbook* (AMACOM, The American Management Associations, 1982), pp. 275-77.

Government Studies Program, which is housed in the Faculty of Administrative Studies at York University, Toronto.

Educational needs at the mid-career level can vary substantially. Executive programmes should carefully target or differentiate their materials to meet these divergent needs. Probably the best guide currently available in this realm is that which Kirk Hanson and Robert Lind have recently worked out, and which requires no further elaboration (see Table 7.10 for a schematic representation).[27]

To conclude then, the growing number of studies of public affairs education all point towards one direction. They all suggest that the innovative blending of knowledge and skill components into mid-career specialized, or more generalist (but focused) pre-career educational programmes is both possible and highly desirable.

The forces of social change demand a shift in the managerial agenda. We have developed evidence to demonstrate that social change and corporate strategy are closely interlinked. Whether academia chooses to abdicate or to provide guidance for this managerial revolution remains to be seen.

The fox is in among the chickens!

Notes

1. *Paris Conference on the Environment of Management in the 21st Century,* 1980, "Conclusions and Recommendations," p. 17.

2. "The Future of Management Education and Role of the American Assembly of Collegiate Schools of Business: A Report of the AACSB Education Innovation Committee," December 5, 1975.

3. F.W. Steckmest, "Career Development for the Public Policy Dimension of Executive Performance," *Public Affairs Review,* Vol. II, 1981, p. 80. For additional review of curriculum development, the following are particularly useful: R. Buchholz,*Business Environment/Public Policy: A Study of Teaching and Research in Schools of Business and Management* (Center for the Study of American Business and the American Assembly of Collegiate Schools of Business, 1979); J. Dunlop, "The Educational Opportunity" in J. Dunlop (ed.), *Business and Public Policy* (Harvard University Press, 1980); G. Steiner, "Future Curricula in Schools of Management" in G. Steiner (ed.), *Business and Its Environment* (Graduate School of Management, UCLA, 1977).

4. J. Post, "Public Affairs and Management Policy in the 1980s," *Public Affairs Review,* Vol. I., 1980, p. 3.

5. This is not to suggest that all these business professors are products of management education. As Buchholz has shown, a significant number of them are trained in economics, law or political science, *op. cit.,* p. 59.

6. Quoted in F.W. Steckmest, *op. cit.,* p. 78. Buchholz also refers to a meeting of business school Deans in the United States under the auspices of the AACSB which reached the same conclusions, *op. cit.,* p. 4. For a similar view, see S.F. Divita, "The Business School Graduate—Does the Product Fit the Need?" in L. Preston (ed.), *Business Environment/Public Policy, op. cit.,* pp. 167-178.

7. See R.T. Mactaggart, D. Kelly, P. Broadmore and L. Preston, *Corporate Social Performance in Canada,* Study No. 21, Royal Commission on Corporate Concentration, Minister of Supply and Services Canada, 1977, also L. Preston, M. Dierkes, and F. Rey, "Comparing Corporate Social Performance: An Analysis of Recent Studies in Germany, France and Canada, and Comparisons with U.S. Experience," *California Management Review,* Summer, 1978.

8. R. Buchholz, *op. cit.,* pp. 16-17.

9. *Ibid.,* pp. 26-27.

10. *Ibid.,* pp. 26-27.

11. R.A. Armstrong and M.R. Jones, "Education for Public Affairs," *Public Affairs Review,* Vol. 1, 1980, p. 39.

12. R. Buchholz, *op. cit.,* p. 114.

13. *Ibid.,* p. 112.

14. On this point, see L. Preston, "The Business School" in J.S. Nagelschmidt (ed.), *The Public Affairs Handbook* (AMACOM, American Management Associations, 1982).

15. D.K. Banner's *Business and Society: Canadian Issues* (McGraw-Hill Ryerson Ltd., 1979) while useful as an omnibus volume of current events, does not discuss actual management cases in this area. Apart from Banner's text, other works are extremely sketchy and hard to come by.

16. See H. Uyterhoeven, "Educational Challenges in Teaching Business-Government Relations" in J. Dunlop (ed.), *op. cit.,* p. 99.

17. R.A. Armstrong and M.R. Jones, *op. cit.,* p. 49; F.W. Steckmest, *op. cit.,* p. 81; and R. Buchholz, *op. cit.,* pp. 125-26 and 129.

18. S.F. Divita, *op. cit.,* p. 173.

19. *Ibid.,* p. 176. James O'Toole's comments perhaps are appropriate in this footnote (O'Toole teaches at USC's Graduate School of Business Administration). "In private (and after a few drinks) most of us who teach MBAs will admit that the letters should stand for Master of Business Arrogance. Compared with more broad-based European and Asian managers, American MBAs often don't know how to listen, don't know how to ask questions, don't feel the need to read, and don't feel that there is anything they can learn from other disciplines or other countries. In fact, a paradoxical characteristic of the successful corporate innovator is the willingness to imitate the good ideas of others—that is why the 'imitative' Japanese are also so innovative. But American MBAs have had the curiosity and open-

mindedness necessary for innovation trained out of them—and they are often too egotistical to be successfully imitative." *Declining Innovation, op. cit.,* p. 10.

20. For a useful review of the contribution that political science can make to public affairs, see A. Altschuler, "Public Affairs Education: The Political Scientist" in J.S. Nagelschmidt (ed.), *op. cit.,* pp. 267-273.

21. L. Preston, "Public Affairs Education," *op. cit.*

22. L. Botstein, *CAUT Bulletin,* December, 1979.

23. *Ibid.*

24. These points are particulary well taken by K.O. Hanson, and R.C. Lind, "Executive Education for Public Affairs" in J.S. Nagelschmidt (ed.), *op. cit.,* pp. 273-281.

25. R. Buchholz, "Education for Public Issues Management," Typescript, p. 16.

26. R.A. Armstrong and M.R. Jones, *op. cit.,* p. 48.

27. Another useful approach is that devised by F. Steckmest, *op. cit.,* pp. 84-87.

APPENDIX
List of Interviewees

1. Mr. Perry Anglin
   Assistant Secretary to the Cabinet
   Government of Canada
   Ottawa, Ontario

2. Mr. William Archbold
   President (retired)
   Business Council on National
   Issues
   Toronto, Ontario

3. Mr. Tom Atkinson
   Senior Project Director, Research
   for Management
   Hay Associates, Canada
   Toronto, Ontario

4. Mr. Peter Bartha
   Manager, Strategic Studies and
   Corporate Planning
   External Affairs Department
   Imperial Oil, Ltd.
   Toronto, Ontario

5. Mr. William Barton
   President
   International Business-Government
   Counsellors, Inc.
   Washington, D.C.

6. Mr. Dan Bon
   Analyst
   The Conference Board of Canada
   Ottawa, Ontario

7. Mr. Wayne Boucher
   Research Director
   Center for Futures Research
   University of Southern California
   Los Angeles, California

8. Mr. William R. Bradt
   Executive Assistant
   The Business Roundtable
   New York, New York

9. Mr. Peter Broadmore
   Manager, External Programs
   I.B.M. Canada, Ltd.
   Toronto, Ontario

10. Mr. Peter M. Brophey
    Vice President, Corporate Affairs
    Xerox of Canada, Ltd.
    Toronto, Ontario

11. Mr. James E. Brown
    Director, Management Planning
    and Systems Research
    The Conference Board
    New York, New York

12. Mr. Tom Chumura
    Deputy Project Director
    Public/Private Partnerships Project
    Stanford Research Institute
    Washington, D.C.

13. Mr. Ken Colby
    Vice President, Corporate Affairs
    Norcen Energy Resources, Ltd.
    Toronto, Ontario

14. Ms. Lilly Correwynn
    Manager, Public Relations
    ITT Canada, Ltd.
    Toronto, Ontario

15. Mr. Roy Cottier
    Vice President, Corporate Relations
    Northern Telecom, Ltd.
    Mississauga, Ontario

16. Mr. Sheldon Ehrenworth
    Special Adviser to the Deputy
    Minister
    Labour Canada, Government of
    Canada
    Ottawa, Ontario

17. Dr. Edwin M. Epstein
    Professor and Chairman
    Business and Public Policy Group
    University of California
    Berkeley, California

18. Mr. Robert Fenner
    Vice President, Public Affairs
    Gulf Canada, Ltd.
    Toronto, Ontario

19. Mr. Scott Fossler
    Vice President
    Committee for Economic
       Development
    Washington, D.C.

20. Mr. Michel Fournier
    Vice President, Public Affairs
    Air Canada
    Montreal, Quebec

21. Dr. James Frank
    Vice President
    The Conference Board of Canada
    Ottawa, Ontario

22. Mr. Doug Fyfe
    Director, Information Directorate
    Department of Industry, Trade and
       Commerce, Government of
       Canada
    Ottawa, Ontario

23. Mr. Patrick Garner
    Vice President
    Southern California Gas Company
    Los Angeles, California

24. Mr. James Gillies
    Director
    Max Bell Program in Business-
       Government Studies
    York University, Toronto

25. Mr. Alan B. Goddard
    Director, Communications & Public
       Affairs
    Dofasco, Inc.
    Hamilton, Ontario

26. Mr. Larry Gordon
    Director of Public Affairs,
       Environment Canada
    Government of Canada
    Ottawa, Ontario

27. Mr. David Grier
    Vice President and Chief Advisor,
       Public Affairs Planning
    The Royal Bank of Canada
    Montreal, Quebec

28. Dr. Hector Guenther
    Assistant Director
    The Committee for Economic
       Development
    New York, New York

29. Mr. Walter Hamilton (deceased)
    Vice President, Public Affairs
       Research
    The Conference Board
    New York, New York

30. Dr. Kirk Hanson
    Professor, Business and Public
       Policy
    Stanford University
    Palo Alto, California

31. Mr. Charles A. Harris
    Chairman
    Harris Heal, Ltd.
    Toronto, Ontario

32. Dr. Kenneth Hart
    Director, Public Affairs Research
    The Conference Board of Canada
    Ottawa, Ontario

33. Ms. Cynthia von Maerestetten
    Director, Corporate Affairs
    Benson & Hedges, Canada
    Montreal, Quebec

34. Mr. Ray Hoewing
    Vice President
    Public Affairs Council
    Washington, D.C.

35. Mr. Donald M. Jarvis
    Vice President, Public Affairs
    Canada Safeway, Ltd.
    Toronto, Ontario

36. Mr. Cedric Jennings
    Director General, Public Affairs
    Employment and Immigration
    Government of Canada
    Ottawa, Ontario

37. Mr. Archibald F. Johnson
    Vice President, Public Affairs and
        Government Relations
    Canadian General Electric
        Company, Ltd.
    Toronto, Ontario

38. Dr. Jon Johnson
    Senior Manager, Information and
        Analysis
    Bank of Montreal
    Montreal, Quebec

39. Mr. Alex Jupp
    Vice President, Public Affairs
    Molson's Brewery
    Toronto, Ontario

40. Mr. John Kochever
    Manager, Public Affairs
    U.S. Chamber of Commerce
    Washington, D.C.

41. Mr. Robert Landry
    Vice President
    Imperial Oil, Ltd.
    Ottawa, Ontario

42. Mr. Peter Liebel
    Director of Communications
    Ministry of State for Economic
        Development
    Government of Canada
    Ottawa, Ontario

43. Mr. Leonard Lund
    Manager, Urban Research
        Department
    Business-Government Program
    The Conference Board
    New York, New York

44. Mr. Seymour Lusterman
    Senior Research Associate, Public
        Affairs
    The Conference Board
    New York, New York

45. Ms. Maureen I. Mahoney
    Vice President, Public Affairs
    Employers' Council of British
        Columbia
    Vancouver, British Columbia

46. Mr. Stephen Markey
    Vice President
    Executive Consultants
    Ottawa, Ontario

47. Mr. Duncan McDowall
    Analyst
    The Conference Board of Canada
    Ottawa, Ontario

48. Mr. Joseph F. Michenfelder
    Vice President
    Public Affairs Analysts, Inc.
    New York, New York

49. Mr. Dennis Mills
    Senior Policy Advisor,
        Communications
    Prime Minister's Office
    Ottawa, Ontario

50. Mr. Grant Murray
    Vice President, General Counsel
        and Secretary
    I.B.M. Canada, Ltd.
    Toronto, Ontario

51. Dr. Arthur J. Naperstek
    Director
    Washington Public Affairs Center
    University of Southern California
    Los Angeles, California

52. Mr. Antoine Normand
    Chairman
    Council of Federal Information
        Directorate
    Government of Canada
    Ottawa, Ontario

53. Mr. Richard B. Norment
    Managing Director, Public Affairs
    National Association of
        Manufacturers
    Washington, D.C.

54. Mr. Patrick O'Hara
    Eastern Region Manager, Public
        Affairs
    I.B.M. Canada, Ltd.
    Montreal, Quebec

55. Mr. Dan G. Ozenne
    Public Affairs Planning Manager
    Southern California Gas Company
    Los Angeles, California

56. Ms. Susan Peterson
    Special Advisor, Privy Council
        Office
    Government of Canada
    Ottawa, Ontario

57. Dr. James Post
    Professor and Director
    Public Affairs Research Group
    Boston University
    Boston, Massachusetts

58. Dr. Lee Preston
    Professor and Director
    Center for Business and Public
        Policy
    University of Maryland at College
        Park
    College Park, Maryland

59. Mr. Joe Robertson
    Executive Director
    National Association of Schools of
        Public Affairs and Administration
    Washington, D.C.

60. Mr. Michael Robinson
    President
    Public Affairs International, Ltd.
    Ottawa, Ontario

61. Mr. Bruce Rozenhart
    Manager of Public Affairs
    Aluminum Company of Canada
    Vancouver, British Columbia

62. Ms. Helen Seni
    Coordinator, Public Affairs
    Alcan Smelters and Chemicals, Ltd.
    Montreal, Quebec

63. Ms. Hillary Sills
    Analyst
    Government Research Corporation
    Washington, D.C.

64. Mr. Fred Tobachnik
    Director of Public Affairs
    Canadian Union of Public
        Employees
    Ottawa, Ontario

65. Mr. David Vogel
    Professor, Business-Government
        Relations
    University of California
    Berkeley, California

66. Dr. Max von Zur-Muehlen
    Statistics Canada, Education Branch
    Government of Canada
    Ottawa, Ontario

67. Mr. David Votaw
    Professor, Business and Public
        Policy
    University of California
    Berkeley, California

68. Mr. Donald Webster
    Vice President
    American Enterprise Institute
    Washington, D.C.

69. Mr. Ian Wilson
    Senior Management Consultant
    Stanford Research Institute
    Stanford, California

70. Mr. John W. Wouters
    Director, Corporate Relations &
        Advertising
    I.T.&T. Canada, Ltd.
    Toronto, Ontario

71. Mr. Marc Zwelling
    Consulting Associate, Labour
        Programmes
    The Niagara Institute
    Niagara-on-the-Lake, Ontario

Selected Bibliography

Business and Society: General Concepts and Issues

Aram, J.D. *Business and Public Policy.* Marshfield, MA: Pitman, 1983.

Banner, D. *Business and Society: Canadian Issues.* Toronto: McGraw-Hill Ryerson, 1980.

Buchholz, R. *Business Environment and Public Policy.* Englewood Cliffs, NJ: Prentice-Hall, 1982.

Carroll, A. B. *Business and Society: Managing Corporate Social Performance.* Boston: Little, Brown & Co., 1981.

Epstein, E. and Votaw, D. (eds.). *Rationality, Legitimacy, Responsibility: The Search for New Directions in Business and Society.* Santa Monica, CA: Goodyear, 1978.

Hay, R., Gray, E. and Gates, J. *Business and Society: Cases and Text.* Cincinnati, OH: South Western, 1976.

Krasny, M. (ed.). *Executive Seminar Readings on the Corporation and Society.* New York: Aspen Institute for Humanistic Studies, 1979.

Post, J. "The Corporation and Society: Research on Patterns of Response to Change" in Preston, L. (ed.). *Research in Corporate Social Performance and Policy.* Greenwich, CT: JAI Press, 1978.

Preston, L. "Corporation and Society: The Search for a Paradigm." *Journal of Economic Literature,* Vol. 13, No. 2, June, 1975.

Starling, G. *The Changing Environment of Business: A Managerial Approach.* Boston: Kent Publishing Co., 1980.

Steade, R. *Business and Society in Transition: Issues and Concepts.* San Francisco: Canfield, 1975.

Steiner, G. A. and Steiner, J. F. *Business, Government and Society,* 4th ed. New York: Random House, 1983.

Sturdivant, F. *Business and Society: A Managerial Approach.* Homewood, IL: Richard D. Irwin, 1977.

General Works on the History, Challenges to and Future of Capitalism

Baran, P. and Sweezy, P. *Monopoly Capital.* New York: Monthly Review Press, 1968.

Bell, D. *The Coming of Post Industrial Society: A Venture in Social Forecasting.* New York: Basic Books, 1973.

Bell, D. and Kristol, I. (eds.). *Capitalism Today.* New York: Basic Books, 1971.

Drucker, P. *The Age of Discontinuity: Guidelines to our Changing Society.* New York: Harper and Row, 1969.

Friedman, M. *Capitalism and Freedom.* Chicago: University of Chicago Press, 1962.

Galbraith, J. *The New Industrial State.* Boston: Houghton Mifflin, 1967.

Gilder, G. *Wealth and Poverty.* New York: Basic Books, 1981.

Heilbroner, R. L. *Between Capitalism and Socialism: Essays in Political Economics.* New York: Random House, 1970.

Kristol, I. *Two Cheers for Capitalism.* New York: Basic Books, 1978.

Miliband, R. *The State in Capitalist Society.* London: Weidenfeld and Nicolson, 1969.

Schumpeter, J. *Capitalism, Socialism and Democracy,* 3rd ed. New York: Harper and Row, 1950.

Shonfield, A. *Modern Capitalism: The Changing Balance of Public and Private Power.* New York: Oxford University Press, 1966.

Steiner, G. "The Redefinition of Capitalism and Its Impact on Management Practice and Theory." Academy of Management Proceedings, Thirty-second Annual Meeting, Minneapolis, Minnesota, August 13-16, 1972.

Theobald, R. *An Alternative Future for America's Third Century,* Chicago: Swallow Press, 1976.

Management and its Changing Environment: The Issues and Challenges of the Future

Amara, R. *The Future of Management: Ten Shapers of Management in the '80s.* Menlo Park, CA: Institute for the Future, February, 1980.

Bright, J. "Opportunity and Threat in Technological Change." *Harvard Business Review,* Vol. 41, November-December, 1963.

Callahan, R. "Management Dilemma Revisited: Must Business Choose Between Stability and Adaptability?" *Sloan Management Review,* Vol. 21, Fall, 1979.

Chamberlain, N. *Enterprise and Environment.* New York: McGraw-Hill, 1968.

Hacker, A. (ed.). *The Corporation Take-Over.* New York: Harper and Row, 1964.

Jacoby, N. "Six Challenges to Business Management." *Business Horizons,* August, 1976.

McCallum, J. "Business Beware: Here Come the Post-Keynesians."*Business Quarterly,* Spring, 1981.

Monsen, R. *Business and the Changing Environment.* New York: McGraw-Hill, 1973.

Morris, S. (ed.). *Perspectives for the '70s and '80s.* New York: National Industrial Conference Board, 1970.

Paluszek, J. *Will the Corporation Survive?* Reston, VA: Reston, 1977.

Panabaker, J. "Basic Social Questions Facing Management of the Future." *Financial Post,* Vol. 72, October 7, 1978.

Pitfield, M. "The Shape of Government in the 1980s: Techniques and Instruments for Policy Formulation at the Federal Level." *Canadian Public Administration,* Vol. 19, Spring, 1976.

Roeber, R. *The Organization in a Changing Environment.* Reading, MA: Addison-Wesley, 1973.

Schon, D. *Beyond the Stable State.* New York: W. W. Norton, 1971.

Sethi, P. *Up Against the Corporate Wall: Modern Corporations and Social Issues of the Seventies,* 3rd ed. Englewood Cliffs, NJ: Prentice-Hall, 1977.

Steiner, G. A. *The New CEO.* New York: The Free Press, 1983.

This, L. "Critical Issues Confronting Managers in the 1980s." *Training and Development Journal,* Vol. 34, January, 1980.

U. S. Department of Commerce, Task Force on Corporate Social Performance. *Business and Society: Strategies for the '80s.* Washington: U. S. Department of Commerce, December, 1980.

Walton, S. *American Business and Its Environment.* New York: Macmillan, 1966.

White, A. and Hochstein, M. "The Climate for Business in the 1980s: New Challenges, New Opportunities" in U. S. Department of Commerce, Task Force on Corporate Social Performance. Washington: U. S. Department of Commerce, December, 1980.

Yankelovich, D. *New Rules: Searching for Self-Fulfillment in a World Turned Upside Down.* New York: Random House, 1981.

Changing Social Values

Bell, D. *The Cultural Contradictions of Capitalism.* New York: Basic Books, 1976.

Bell, D. "The Revolution of Rising Entitlements." *Fortune,* April, 1975.

Business Week. "Egalitarianism: Threat to a Free Market." *Business Week,* December 1, 1975.

Cavanagh, G. *American Business Values in Transition.* Englewood Cliffs, NJ: Prentice-Hall, 1976.

Chamberlain, N. *Remaking American Values: Challenge to a Business Society.* New York: Basic Books, 1977.

Hofstadter, R. *Social Darwinism in American Thought.* Boston: Beacon, 1955.

Kristol, I. "About Equality." *Commentary,* Vol. 54, November, 1972.

Lodge, G. C. "Top Priority: Renovating Our Ideology." *Harvard Business Review,* Vol. 48, September-October, 1970.

Lowi, T. J. *The End of Liberalism: Ideology, Policy and the Crisis of Public Authority,* 1st ed. New York: W. W. Norton, 1969.

Madden, C. *Clash of Culture: Management in an Age of Changing Values.* Washington: National Planning Association, 1972.

Novak, M. *The American Vision: An Essay on the Future of Democratic Capitalism.* Washington: American Enterprise Institute for Public Policy Research, 1978.

Rawls, J. *A Theory of Justice.* Cambridge: Harvard University Press, 1971.

Reich, C. *The Greening of America.* New York: Random House, 1970.

The Challenge of Declining Corporate Credibility

Coulson, R. "Corporate Credibility: What It's All About." *Business Quarterly,* Vol. 45, Spring, 1980.

Finlay, J. "De-Coding the Corporate Credibility Dilemma." *Business Quarterly,* Vol. 44, Summer, 1979.

Hamilton, W. "On the Credibility of Institutions." *The Conference Board Record,* March, 1973.

Lipset, S. M. and Schneider, W. *The Confidence Gap: How Americans View Their Institutions.* New York: Free Press, 1981.

Corporate Social Responsibility, Profits and Efficiency: General Concepts and Management Strategies

Ackerman, R. and Bauer, R. *Corporate Social Responsiveness: The Modern Dilemma.* Reston, VA: Reston, 1976.

Arrow, K. "Limitations of the Profit Motive." *Challenge,* Vol. 22, September, 1979.

Baumol, W., Likert, R., Wallish, H. and McGowan, J. *A New Rationale for Corporate Social Policy.* New York: Committee for Economic Development, 1970.

Beesley, M. and Evans, T. *Corporate Social Responsibility: A Reassessment.* London: Croom Helm, 1978.

Bleeker, S. "Building the Public's Trust and the Bottom Line Together." *Public Relations Quarterly,* Vol. 25, Winter, 1980.

Bowen, H. *Social Responsibilities of the Businessman.* New York: Harper, 1953.

Brooks, L. J. "Canadian Corporate Social Responsibility: Questionnaire, Findings and Analysis." Toronto: University of Toronto, April, 1982.

Brown, C. *Beyond the Bottom Line.* New York: MacMillan, 1979.

Burck, G. "The Hazards of Corporate Responsibility." *Fortune,* Vol. 87, No. 6, June, 1973.

Chamberlain, N. *The Limits of Corporate Responsibility.* New York: Basic Books, 1973.

Committee for Economic Development. *A New Rationale for Corporate Social Policy,* Supplementary paper #31. New York: Committee for Economic Development, 1970.

Committee for Economic Development. *Social Responsibilities of Business Corporations.* New York: Committee for Economic Development, 1971.

Edmunds, S. "Unifying Concepts in Social Responsibility." *Academy of Management Review,* Vol. 2, January, 1977.

Engel, D. "An Approach to Corporate Social Responsibility." *Stanford Law Review,* Vol. 32, No. 1, November 1979.

Epstein, E. "Societal, Managerial, and Legal Perspectives on Corporate Social Responsibility."*Hastings Law Journal,* Hastings College of the Law, University of California, May, 1979.

Fisher, J. "Profit: What Responsibility Does Business Have Beyond the Bottom Line?" *Marketing,* Vol. 84, December 17, 1979.

Friedman, M. "The Social Responsibility of Business is to Increase Its Profits." *The New York Times Magazine,* September 13, 1970.

Henning, J. "Corporate Social Responsibility: Shell Game for the Seventies" in Nader, R. and Green, M. (eds.). *Corporate Power in America.* New York: Grossman, 1973.

Human Resources Network. *Profiles of Involvement.* Philadelphia, PA: Human Resources Network Corporation, 1972.

Humble, J. "Practical Approach to Social Responsibility." *Management Review,* Vol. 67, May, 1978.

Jones, T. "Corporate Social Responsibility Revisited, Redefined." *California Management Review,* Vol. 22, Spring, 1980.

Levitt, T. "The Dangers of Social Responsibility." *Harvard Business Review,* Vol. 36, September-October, 1958.

Mactaggart, R., Kelly, D., Broadmore, P. and Preston, L. *Corporate Social Performance in Canada.* Background study prepared for the Royal Commission on Corporate Concentration. Ottawa: Minister of Supply and Services, Canada, 1977.

Preston, L. and Post, J. *Private Management and Public Policy: The Principle of Public Responsibility.* Englewood Cliffs, NJ: Prentice-Hall, 1975.

Schroeder, H. *Corporate Social Performance in Canada: A Survey.* Alberta: University of Lethbridge, 1983.

Szepan, S. "Corporate Social Responsibility—An Update." *Journal of Accountancy,* Vol. 150, July, 1980.

Votaw, D. and Sethi, P. *The Corporate Dilemma.* Englewood Cliffs, NJ: Prentice-Hall, 1973.

Business Ethics

Baumhart, R. *An Honest Profit: What Businessmen Say About Ethics in Business.* New York: Holt, Rinehart and Winston, 1968.

Center for Business Ethics. *A Bibliography of Business Ethics Articles.* Waltham, MA: Center for Business Ethics, 1978.

Cohn, J. *The Conscience of the Corporations.* Baltimore: The Johns Hopkins Press, 1971.

DeGeorge, R. and Pichler, J. (eds.). *Ethics, Free Enterprise and Public Policy.* New York: Oxford University Press, 1978.

Johnson, H. "Ethics and the Executive." *Business Horizons,* Vol. 24, May/June, 1981.

Linowes, D. *The Corporate Conscience.* New York: Hawthorne Books, 1974.

Petit, T. *The Moral Crisis in Management.* New York: McGraw-Hill, 1967.

Silva, M. "Business Ethics: What's Right? What's Wrong ?" *Management World,* Vol. 9, August, 1980.

Silk, L. and Vogel, D. *Ethics and Profits: The Crisis of Confidence in American Business.* New York: Simon and Schuster, 1978.

Stearns, M. "What Are Business Ethics?" *Data Management,* Vol. 19, May, 1981.

The Evolution and Future of Corporate Public Affairs

Armstrong, R. "What is Public Affairs?" in Nagelschmidt, J. S. (ed.). *The Public Affairs Handbook.* New York: AMACOM, American Management Associations, 1982.

Caldwell, G. "The Public Affairs Function: Management Response." *Canadian Business Review,* Winter, 1976.

Cheesman, N. *Public Affairs in Canadian Corporate Management.* Manuscript, December, 1979.

Finlay, J. "Toward a Neoenterprise Spirit: The Task and Responsibility of the Public Affairs Function." *Business Quarterly,* Summer, 1978.

Greyser, S. "Changing Roles for Public Relations: Their Significance and Management Implications." *Public Relations Journal,* Vol. 37, January, 1981.

Gruber, W. and Hoewing, R. "The New Management in Corporate Public Affairs." *Public Affairs Review,* Vol. 1, 1980.

Lusterman, S. *Managerial Competence: The Public Affairs Aspects.* New York: The Conference Board, 1981.

McGrath, P. *Managing Corporate External Relations: Changing Perspectives and Responses.* New York: The Conference Board, 1976.

Moore, R. "The Evolution of Public Affairs" in Nagelschmidt, J. S. (ed.). *The Public Affairs Handbook.* New York: AMACOM, American Management Associations, 1982.

Morris, S. "Managing Corporate External Affairs." *Management Review,* Vol. 69, March, 1980.

Nagelschmidt, J. S. (ed.). *The Public Affairs Handbook.* New York: AMACOM, American Management Associations, 1982.

Post, J. "Public Affairs and Management Policy." *Public Affairs Review,* Vol. 1, 1980.

Votaw, D. and Sethi, P. "Do We Need a New Corporate Response to a Changing Social Environment?" *California Management Review,* Vol. XII, No. 1, 1969.

White, F. "Four Steps to Developing a Public Affairs Program." *Public Relations Journal,* Vol. 35, March, 1979.

The Management of Business Government Relations: New Techniques in Corporate Political Involvement

Alexander, H. "Political Action Committees and Their Corporate Sponsors in the 1980s." *Public Affairs Review,* Vol. 2, 1981.

Bauer, R., De Sola Pool, I. and Dexter, L. *American Business and Public Policy.* New York: Atherton Press, 1963.

Epstein, E. *The Corporation in American Politics.* Englewood Cliffs, NJ: Prentice-Hall, 1969.

Epstein, E. "The Emergence of Political Action Committees" in Herbert E. Alexander (ed.). *Political Finance.* Beverly Hills, CA: Sage Publications, 1979.

Faulkner, J. "Business-Government Relationships in Canada." *Optimum,* Vol. 7, No. 1, 1976.

Fleming, J. "Possible Future of Government-Corporate Relations." *Business Horizons,* Vol. 22, December, 1979.

Grefe, E. *Fighting to Win: Business Political Power.* New York: Harcourt, Brace, Jovanovich, 1981.

Gillies, J. *Where Business Fails: Business/Government Relations at the Federal Level in Canada.* Montreal: Institute for Research on Public Policy, 1981.

Institute for Political Involvement. *A Report on the Prospects for Increased Involvement of Business People in the Canadian Political System.* Toronto: Institute for Political Involvement, April, 1978.

Jacoby, N. (ed.). *The Business-Government Relationship: A Reassessment.* Pacific Palisades, CA: Goodyear, 1975.

Keim, G. "Foundations of a Political Strategy for Business." *California Management Review,* Vol. 23, Spring, 1981.

Lisowski, B. "Corporate Influence in Government Decision-Making." *Business Quarterly,* Vol. 43, No. 3, Autumn, 1978.

Litvak, I. "Ottawa Syndrome: Improving Business/Government Relations." *Business Quarterly,* Vol. 44, No. 2, Summer, 1979.

Litvak, I. "Government Intervention and Corporate-Government Relations. *Business Quarterly,* Vol. 46, No. 3, Autumn, 1981.

McGrath, P. *Developing Employee Political Awareness,* Information Bulletin No. 80. New York: The Conference Board, 1980.

McQuaid, K. "Big Business and Public Policy in Contemporary United States." *Quarterly Review of Economics and Business,* Vol. 20, Summer, 1980.

Moore, D. *Politics and the Corporate Chief Executive,* Research Report No. 777. New York: The Conference Board, 1980.

Nader, R. and Green, M. (eds.). *Corporate Power in America.* New York: Grossman, 1973.

O'Toole, J. *The Immobilized State: An Assay on the Future of Government/Corporate Relations.* Los Angeles: Center for Futures Research, Graduate School of Business Administration, University of Southern California, July, 1978.

Pare, P. "Political Involvement: From a Necessary Evil to a Management Skill." *Canadian Banker and ICB Review,* Vol. 85, October, 1978.

Sethi, P. "Grassroots Lobbying and the Corporation." *Business and Society Review,* No. 29, Spring, 1979.

Sethi, P. "Serving the Public Interest: Corporate Political Action Strategies for the 1980s." *Management Review,* Vol. 70, March, 1981.

Sneath, W. "Note of Caution about Business in Politics." *Dun's Review,* Vol. 113, April, 1979.

Thain, D. and Baetz, M. "Increasing Trouble Ahead for Business-Government Relations in Canada?" *Business Quarterly,* Vol. 44, No. 2, Summer, 1979.

Thain, D. "Mistakes of Business in Dealing with Government and Politics." *Business Quarterly,* Vol. 44, No. 3, Autumn, 1979.

Thain, D. "Improving Competence to Deal with Politics and Government: The Management Challenge of the 1980s." *Business Quarterly,* Vol. 45, No. 1, Spring, 1980.

Van Dam, A. "Government and Business: Bringing the Two Together." *Canadian Business,* Vol. 49, October, 1976.

New Directions in the Management of Community Relations

Amara, R. *The Future of Voluntarism: Meeting Societal Needs.* Menlo Park, CA: Institute for the Future, November, 1978.

Kugel, O. *A Preliminary Evaluation of Major Trends in Corporate Involvement in Urban Problem Solving.* U. S. Chamber of Commerce, 1971.

Committee for Economic Development. *Public-Private Partnership: An Opportunity for Urban Communities.* New York: Committee for Economic Development, 1982.

Lippin, P. "When Business and the Community Cooperate." *Administrative Management,* Vol. 42, February, 1981.

Lund, L. and Weber, N. *Corporations in the Community: How Six Major Firms Conduct Community Participation Programs.* New York: The Conference Board, 1981.

McGuire, E. and Weber, N. *Business Voluntarism: Prospects for 1982,* Research Bulletin, No. 111. New York: The Conference Board, 1982.

Reeder, J. "Corporate Social Involvement at the Local Level" in Jeffrey C. Susbauer, (ed.). *Academy of Management Proceedings '78.* San Francisco, CA, August 9-13, 1978.

Stanford Research Institute (SRI) International. *Redefining Partnership: Developing Public-Private Approaches to Community Problem Solving.* Menlo Park, CA: SRI International, January, 1982. (Draft)

Wintner, L. *Business and the Cities: Programs and Practices,* Information Bulletin No. 87. New York: The Conference Board, 1981.

Coping With Special Interest Groups

Cameron, J. "Nader's Invaders Are Inside the Gates." *Fortune,* Vol. 96, No. 4, October, 1977.

Crew, B. "How U. S. Companies Tackle the Pressure Group Challenge." *Industrial Management,* December, 1978/January, 1979.

Johnson, M. (ed.). *The Attack on Corporate America: The Corporate Issues Sourcebook.* New York: McGraw-Hill, 1978.

Ladd, E. "How to Tame the Special-Interest Groups." *Fortune,* Vol. 102, October 20, 1980.

Loescher, S. "Public Interest Movements and Private Interest Systems: A Healthy Schizophrenia." *Journal of Economic Issues,* Vol. 15, No. 2.

Nader, R., Green, M. and Seligman, J. *Taming the Giant Corporation.* New York: W. W. Norton, 1976.

Place, J. "Special Interests: Democracy or Disaster?" *Journal of Commercial Bank Lending,* Vol. 62, July, 1980.

Seligman, D. "Politics and Economics of Public Interest Lobbying." *Fortune,* Vol. 100, November 5, 1979.

Vogel, D. *Lobbying the Corporation: Citizen Challenges to Business Authority.* New York: Basic Books, 1978.

Vogel, D. "The Public Interest Movement and the American Reform Tradition." *Political Science Quarterly,* Vol. 93, Winter, 1980-81.

The Management of Corporate Donations and Charity

Brown, J. "All About Planned Giving." *Trusts and Estates,* Vol. 117, No. 12, December, 1978.

Fremont-Smith, M. *Philanthropy and the Business Corporation.* New York: Russell Sage Foundation, 1972.

Shortt, C. "Sponsorships and Donations: Where to Draw the Line." *Food Service Marketing,* Vol. 41, August, 1979.

Stafford, J. "Corporate Charity: How Much to Give?" *Savings and Loan News,* Vol. 99, December, 1978.

Troy, K. *Managing Corporate Contributions,* Research Report No. 792. New York: The Conference Board, 1980.

Witten, M. "Corporate Welfare Guidebook." *Canadian Business Magazine,* Vol. 52, September, 1979.

Labour Participation and Affirmative Action

Committee for Economic Development. *Jobs for the Hard-to-Employ: New Directions for a Public-Private Partnership.* New York: Committee for Economic Development, 1978.

Gordon, F. and Strober, M. (eds.). *Bringing Women into Management.* New York: McGraw-Hill, 1975.

Josefowitz, N. "Management Men and Women: Closed vs. Open Doors." *Harvard Business Review,* Vol. 58, No. 5, September/October, 1980.

Kemp, D. "Employee Participation in Organizational Development." *The Canadian Personnel and Industrial Relations Journal,* Vol. 25, May, 1978.

Lear, F. "EEO Compliance: Behind the Corporate Mask." *Harvard Business Review,* Vol. 53, No. 4, July-August, 1975.

U. S. Equal Employment Opportunity Commission. *Affirmative Action and Equal Employment: A Guidebook for Employers,* Vols. I and II. Washington: U. S. Government Printing Office, 1974.

How to Improve Media Relations

Detwiler, R. "Managing the News." *Across the Board,* November, 1977.

Finn, D. "Why Business Has Trouble with the Media and Vice Versa." *Across the Board,* February, 1978.

The Nation's Business. "Business and the Media: How to Get Along." *The Nation's Business,* Vol. 66, April, 1978.

Savings and Loan News. "How to Deal with the Press When Times are Troubled." *Savings and Loan News,* Vol. 102, August, 1981.

Security Management. "Stress from the Press—and How to Meet It." *Security Management,* Vol. 24, February, 1980.

Standing, J. "Business and the Press: How to Improve Relations." *Business Quarterly,* Vol. 34, Summer, 1980.

Building the International Public Affairs Function

Blake, D. "How to Get Operating Managers to Manage Public Affairs in Foreign Subsidiaries." *Journal of World Business,* Vol. 16, Spring, 1981.

Drobnick, R. *The Twenty Year Forecast Project: Eighth Year—Political Risk Analysis of Foreign Business Opportunities.* Los Angeles: Center for Futures Research, Graduate School of Business Administration, University of Southern California, July, 1981.

Dunn, S. W., Cahill, M. and Boddewyn, J. *How Fifteen Transnational Corporations Manage Public Affairs.* Chicago: Crain Books, 1979.

Mason, R. "Major Issues in the Multinational Firm's Business and Society Relationships" in Steiner, G. (ed.). *Business and Its Changing Environment.* Graduate School of Management, UCLA, April, 1978.

Sharp, D. *Managing Political Risks: Strategies and Techniques.* Washington: Georgetown University, 1983.

Van Dam, A. "Corporate Role in the North/South Dialogue." *Managerial Planning,* Vol. 28, July, 1979.

Wallender, H. and Lentz, A. "Building the International Public Affairs Function." *Public Affairs Review,* Vol. 2, 1981.

The Uses of Survey Research

Bachman, W. "How Public Opinion is Formed." *Oil and Gas Journal,* Vol. 78, March 31, 1980.

Bates, D. "Using Polls." *Public Relations Journal,* Vol. 37, March, 1981.

Gallup, G. "Public Opinion and Social Crisis in the '80s." *Public Relations Journal,* Vol. 35, January, 1979.

Grunig, J. "New Measure of Public Opinions on Corporate Social Responsibility." *Academy of Management Journal,* Vol. 22, December, 1979.

Molitor, G. "The Hatching of Public Opinion" in Allio, R.J. and Pennington, M.W. (eds.). *Corporate Planning Technique and Applications.* New York: American Management Associations, 1979.

Tortorello, N. "The Uses of Polling" in Nagelschmidt, J. S. (ed.). *The Public Affairs Handbook.* New York: AMACOM, American Management Associations, 1982.

Zentner, R. "Survey Research" in Nagelschmidt, J. S. (ed.). *The Public Affairs Handbook.* New York: AMACOM, American Management Associations, 1982.

Linking Public Affairs to Strategic Planning, Environmental Scanning, Forecasting and Issues Management

Aldag, R. and Jackson, D. "Planning for Corporate Social Actions." *Managerial Planning,* Vol. 29, September/October, 1980.

Andersen, A. *Practice Guidelines for Social Impact Planning and Reporting.* Chicago: Arthur Andersen and Co., 1975.

Brown, A. "When the Planner Speaks, Does Management Really Listen?" *Management Review,* Vol. 67, November, 1978.

Brown, J. *This Business of Issues: Coping with the Company's Environment,* Research Report No. 758. New York: The Conference Board, 1979.

Brown, J. *Guidelines for Managing Corporate Issues Programs,* Research Report No. 795. New York: The Conference Board, 1981.

Carroll, A. and Newgren, K. "Social Forecasting in U. S. Corporations—A Survey." *Long Range Planning,* Vol. 12, August, 1979.

Chase, W. H. "Issues Management" in Nagelschmidt, J. S. (ed.). *The Public Affairs Handbook.* New York: AMACOM, American Management Associations, 1982.

Dalal, J. "Managing Change." *Journal of Systems Management,* Vol. 31, April, 1980.

Duncan, O. "Social Forecasting—The State of the Art." *The Public Interest,* No. 17, Fall, 1969.

Enzer, S. *Interax: An Interactive Model for Studying Future Business Environment.* Los Angeles: Center for Futures Research, Graduate School of Business Administration, University of Southern California, December, 1979.

Ewing, R. "Uses of Futurist Techniques in Issue Management." *Public Relations Quarterly,* Vol. 24, Winter, 1979.

Ewing, R. "Issues Management." *Public Relations Journal,* Vol. 36, June, 1980.

Fahey, L. and King, W. "Environmental Scanning for Corporate Planning." *Business Horizons,* Vol. 20, No. 4, August, 1977.

Fahey, L., King, W. and Narayanan, V. "Environmental Scanning and Forecasting in Strategic Planning—The State of the Art." *Long Range Planning,* Vol. 14, February, 1981.

Fleming, J. "Linking Public Affairs with Corporate Planning." *California Management Review,* Vol. 23, Winter, 1980.

Hanson, K. "Strategic Planning and Social Performance" in U. S. Department of Commerce, Task Force on Corporate Social Performance. Washington: U. S. Department of Commerce, December, 1980.

Higgins, J. and Romano, D. "Social Forecasting: An Integral Part of Corporate Planning?" *Long Range Planning,* Vol. 13, April, 1980.

Higgins, J. and Romano, D. "Socio-Political Forecasting and Management Information Systems." *Omega,* Vol. 8, 1980.

Holcomb, J. "Anticipating Public Policy: An Interest Group Approach." *Public Affairs Review,* Vol. 1, 1980.

Kast, F. "Scanning the Future Environment: Social Indicators." *California Management Review,* Vol. 23, Fall, 1980.

Kastens, M. "Why and How of Planning." *Managerial Planning,* Vol. 28, July, 1979.

Kellaway, A. and Richardson, C. "Social Forecasting for Corporate Priorities." *Personnel Management,* Vol. 12, September, 1980.

Klein, H. and Newman, W. "How to Integrate New Environmental Forces into Strategic Planning." *Management Review,* Vol. 69, July, 1980.

Moore, R. "Planning for Emerging Issues." *Public Relations Journal,* Vol. 35, November, 1979.

Nanus, B. *QUEST: Quick Environmental Scanning Technique.* Los Angeles: Center for Futures Research, Graduate School of Business Administration, University of Southern California, August, 1979.

Newgrew, K. "Social Forecasting: An Overview of Current Practices" in Carroll, A. (ed.). *Managing Corporate Social Responsibility.* Boston: Little, Brown and Co., 1977.

Preble, J. "Corporate Use of Environmental Scanning." *Michigan Business Review,* Vol. 13, June, 1980.

Smith, J. "Futures Research and Corporate Planning." Address before the Chicago Chapter of the Planning Executives' Institute, March 2, 1978.

Taylor, B. "Strategic Planning for Social and Political Change" in Purdie, W. and Taylor, B. (eds.). *Business Strategies for Survival.* London: Heinemann, 1976.

Thomas, P. "Environmental Scanning—The State of the Art." *Long Range Planning,* Vol. 13, February, 1980.

Thompson, D. "Issue Management: New Key to Corporate Survival." *Industry Week,* Vol. 36, February 23, 1981.

Wilson, I. "Environmental Analysis" in Albert, K. (ed.). *The Strategic Management Handbook.* New York: McGraw-Hill, 1982.

Techniques of Effective Communications: Advocacy Advertising, External and Internal Communications

Canadian Training Methods. "Public Communications for Senior Executives." *Canadian Training Methods,* Vol. 11, No. 3, October, 1978.

CGA Magazine. "Communicating Change to Employees." *CGA Magazine,* Vol. 12, No. 9, November, 1978.

Change, K. "Mind Your Business: When Did You Last Communicate With Your Employees?" *American Druggist,* Vol. 182, August, 1980.

The Director. "Internal Communication Challenge of the 1980s." *The Director,* Vol. 33, May, 1981.

Ehrbar, A. "Backlash Against Business Advocacy." *Fortune,* Vol. 98, August 28, 1978.

Fegley, R. "When Your Chief Executive Goes Public." *Public Relations Quarterly,* Vol. 24, Summer, 1979.

Foltz, R. "Internal Communications: What's Ahead?" *Public Relations Journal,* Vol. 35, December, 1979.

Halperin, F. and Schlachtmeyer, A. "Criteria Based Planning for Employee Communication." *Personnel Administration,* Vol. 24, August, 1979.

Hilgert, R. "Management through Communications." *Real Estate Today,* Vol. 13, June, 1980.

Huseman, R. "Planning for Organizational Change: The Role of Communication." *Managerial Planning,* Vol. 28, May/June, 1980.

Hussey, R. "Company Reports for Employees: Some Do's and Don'ts." *Personnel Management,* Vol. 12, June, 1980.

Lesly, P. "Mastering the Techniques of Two-Way Communication." *Supervisory Management,* Vol. 24, November, 1979.

Lewis, C. "How to Make Internal Communications Work." *Public Relations Journal,* Vol. 36, February, 1980.

Olsen, F. "Corporations Who Succeed through Communication—Three Case Studies." *Personnel Journal,* Vol. 58, December, 1979.

Personnel Administration. "Corporate Communications." *Personnel Administration,* Vol. 24, July, 1979.

Samaras, J. "Two-Way Communication Practices for Managers." *Personnel Journal,* Vol. 59, August, 1980.

Sethi, P. "Advocacy Advertising as a Strategy of Corporate Response to Societal Pressures: The American Experience" in Steiner, G. A. (ed.). *Business and its Changing Environment,* Graduate School of Management, UCLA, April, 1978.

Tavernier, G. "Using Employee Communications to Support Corporate Objectives." *Management Review,* Vol. 69, November, 1980.

Tisdall, C. "Communicating in the Doubting '80s." *Business Quarterly,* Vol. 45, No. 3, Autumn, 1980.

The Corporate Social Audit, and the Measurement of Public Affairs Effectiveness

Abt, C. *The Social Audit for Management.* New York: AMACOM, American Management Associations, 1977.

American Institute of Certified Public Accountants. *Measurement of Corporate Social Performance.* New York: AICPA, 1977.

Anderson, R. "Social Responsibility Accounting—How to Get Started."*CA Magazine,* Vol. 111, September, 1978.

Bauer, R. and Fenn, D. "What is a Corporate Social Audit?" *Harvard Business Review,* Vol. 51, January/February, 1973.

Blake, D., Frederick, W. and Myers, M. *Social Auditing: Evaluating the Impact of Corporate Programs.* New York: Praeger, 1976.

Blake, D. "The Measurement of Public Affairs" in Nagelschmidt, J. S. (ed.). *The Public Affairs Handbook.* New York: AMACOM, American Management Associations, 1982.

Corson, J. and Steiner, G. *Measuring Business and Social Performance: The Corporate Social Audit.* New York: Committee for Economic Development, 1974.

Jacobson, H. "Guidelines for Evaluating Public Relations Programs." *Public Relations Quarterly,* Vol. 25, Summer, 1980.

Preston, L. "Analyzing Corporate Social Performance: Methods and Results." *Journal of Contemporary Business,* Vol. 17, Winter, 1978.

Robinson, C. "Benefits of Social Auditing." *Financial Post,* Vol. 74, April 12, 1980.

Scott-Atkinson, D. "Case for P. R. Audits." *Marketing,* Vol. 84, July 2, 1979.

Strenski, J. "Measuring Public Relations Results." *Public Relations Quarterly,* Vol. 25, Summer, 1980.

Public Relations: New Challenges and Changing Roles

Amernic, J. "Public Relations Status Report." *Business Journal,* July/August, 1979.

Burson, H. "The Public Relations Function in the Socially Responsible Corporation" in Anshen, M. (ed.). *Managing the Socially Responsible Corporation.* New York: MacMillan, 1974.

Fetherling, D. "New Image of Public Relations." *Canadian Business Magazine,* Vol. 52, December, 1979.

Finlay, J. "P. R. Failure: Despite Big-Buck Spending Corporate P. R. Functions are Dismal Failures on all Fronts." *Marketing,* Vol. 84, April 16, 1979.

Ibarra, K. and Stagnitto, L. "Public Relations Role in Management." *Public Relations Journal,* Vol. 36, October, 1980.

Morisey, J. "Will the Real Public Relations Professional Please Stand Up." *Public Relations Journal,* Vol. 34, December, 1978.

Newman, L. "Public Relations Phase II: Adviser Becomes Decision-Maker." *Public Relations Journal,* Vol. 36, October, 1980.

Strenski, J. "Top 12 P. R. Challenges for 1980." *Public Relations Journal,* Vol. 36, February, 1980.

Education for Public Affairs

Armstrong, R. and Jones, M. "Education for Public Affairs." *Public Affairs Review,* Vol. 1, 1980.

Buchholz, R. *Business Environment/Public Policy: A Study of Teaching and Research in Schools of Business and Management,* Working Paper No. 41. St. Louis: Washington University Center for the Study of American Business, 1979.

Buchholz, R. *Business Environment/Public Policy: Corporate Executive Viewpoints and Educational Implications,* Working Paper No. 55. St. Louis: Washington University Center for the Study of American Business, 1980.

Buchholz, R. *Education for Public Issues Management.* Manuscript, 1981.

Fatehi, K. "Educating for Social Responsibility in Business." *Management World,* Vol. 8, October, 1979.

Fredericks, W. "Business and Society Curriculum: Suggested Guidelines for Accreditation."*AACSB Bulletin,* Spring, 1977.

Hanson, K. and Lind, R. "Executive Education in Public Affairs" in Nagelschmidt, J.S. (ed.). *The Public Affairs Handbook.* New York: AMACOM, American Management Association, 1982.

Hoover, J. "Task Force Reports on Curriculum Development and Teaching" in Preston, L.E. (ed.). *Business Environment/Public Policy: 1979 Conference Papers.* St. Louis: American Assembly of Collegiate Schools of Business, 1980.

Preston, L. "Public Affairs Education: The Business School" in Nagelschmidt, J. S. (ed.). *The Public Affairs Handbook.* New York: AMACOM, American Management Associations, 1982.

Steckmest, F. "Career Development for the Public Policy Dimension of Executive Performance." *Public Affairs Review,* Vol. 2, 1981.

Uyterhoeven, H. "Educational Challenges in Teaching Business-Government Relations" in Dunlop, J. (ed.). *Business and Public Policy.* Boston: Harvard University Press, 1980.

Index